Jewish Prayer

The Origins of the Christian Liturgy

by
Carmine Di Sante

Translated
by
Matthew J. O'Connell

PAULIST PRESS
New York/Mahwah, N.J.

Library of Congress Cataloging-in-Publication Data

Di Sante, Carmine, 1941–
    [Preghiera di Israele, English]
    Jewish prayer: the origins of the Christian liturgy/by Carmine di Sante; translated by Matthew J. O'Connell.
        p.   cm.
    Translation of: La Preghiera di Israele.
    Includes index.
    ISBN 0-8091-3207-9
    1. Judaism—Liturgy.   2. Prayer—Judaism.   3. Liturgies, Early Christian.   I. Title.
    BM660.D5213   1991
    297.4—dc20   90–22369
                                                                          CIP

Published by Paulist Press
997 Macarthur Boulevard
Mahwah, New Jersey 07430

Printed and bound in the
United States of America

Contents

Preface

"The doors of prayer are never closed," says Deuteronomy Rabba 11, 12. These simple words show human beings the way to direct dialogue with God.

In his study of the Jewish liturgy Carmine Di Sante gives us a clear picture of how this way has been conceived and lived by Judaism, in its beginnings, down the centuries, and in our own day.

This is probably the first Catholic attempt, at least here in Italy, to enter into the spirit of Jewish prayer as embodied in its daily and festal structures. The author's purpose is to stimulate the attention of Christians and get them thinking about common liturgical origins, although he does not actually compare the Jewish and Christian liturgies.

As the author himself says, the aim of his study is to present the Jewish liturgy in its "original freshness," so that all, both Jews and Christians, may realize "how greatly Jesus and the original Christian community were indebted" to it. This aim is all the more relevant today in light of the recently published Vatican document, "Notes on the Proper Way to Present the Jewish Faith" (1985), which says without qualification: "Jesus was and always remained a Jew. . . . Jesus is fully a man of His time and of His environment—the Jewish Palestinian one of the first century, the anxieties and hopes of which he shared."[1]

An effort at reevaluating the liturgical Jewishness of Jesus was made a few years back by Robert Aron in his book *The Jewish Jesus*. Di Sante is, in a sense, taking over Aron's discovery and turning it into a Christian discovery by presenting, in a theological and hermeneutical (rather than historical and critical) form, the salient existential contents of the vast range of prayers and celebrations that, beginning with Exodus 13, have given the Jewish religious outlook its vital characteristics.

For a Jewish reader, the Introduction and Chapter 1 will perhaps be the most important parts of the book since their purpose is to make clear the original relationship between the contents of the Jewish liturgical universe and those of the Christian, as seen in the persons of Jesus and the apostles. In the process, the author seeks,

from the very beginning of his book, to show in the Jewish liturgy the
interior spirit of loving communion with God, which Christians for
centuries refused to admit it possessed.

In my opinion, the real merit of the book is to have rediscovered
and shown, in the wording of Jewish prayers, the sincerity and feeling, or what the Hasidim calls the *hitlahavaut* (fervor), that have
always characterized the relationship of Jews with God. It was with
this in mind that the rabbis of the time of Jesus said: "When thou
prayest make not thy prayer a fixed form, but [a plea for] mercies and
supplications";[2] and again: "He that makes his prayer a fixed task,
his prayer is no supplication."[3] It was precisely to keep prayers from
becoming "fixed forms" that they were for many centuries not written down: "He who puts a prayer into writing commits the same sin
as if he has burned the Torah" (Tosefta Shabbat 14, 4).

Perhaps because he is concentrating on grasping and bringing
out the inner meaning of prayers, the author fails to emphasize the
fact that in the end the prayers were in fact written down and thus
became a "religious institution." It must be added, however, that
Jewish interpretation of these set prayers has been no less rich, down
the centuries, than interpretation of free prayer had been. In this
context, J. Leibovich, a contemporary scholar and defender of fixed
prayers, has this to say: "The greatness and power of prayer, of the
obligatory set prayers of the *halakah*, consists in the rejection, by
human beings conscious of their position before God, of all selfish
interests and personal motives that would demand concrete fulfillment in various forms and ways . . . a denial of the human will when
faced with the duty of serving God."[4]

Without going into the merits of the author's careful study of the
several parts of the liturgy (that is a critique which a rabbi who is
expert in the liturgy could do more satisfactorily than I can), I shall
simply call attention to the existential and anthropological interpretation which the author gives of the interior meaning of the individual prayers (the *berakot* [benedictions], the *shema'* ["Hear, O
Israel"], the *tefillah* ["prayer"], the *qeri'at Torah* ["reading of the
Torah"]).

When the author suggests that the *berakah* has the power to
"make us see the world as replete with a spiritual radiance" or that it
"transforms the profane into the sacred," or when he writes that
"benedictions prevent us from claiming the rights of ownership over
things," so that we attribute ownership to God and hold ourselves in
readiness for the gifts he gives us—in all these instances he pene-
trates to the essence of the Jewish benediction, which by its nature

defines the relationship between human beings and God and, conversely, between God and human beings in the way described in the prayer known as the *ne'ilah:* "Thou hast from the beginning set man apart, and made him worthy to stand before thee." A.J. Heschel has said that in prayer human beings "entrust themselves to him to whom their being and existence belong; they take a definitive position, spring up to make a claim before God, make a declaration, confess, pledge their souls, take possession, and enter into a covenant."

Di Sante finds this mutual relationship between God and human beings expressed once again in the intrinsic meaning of the three scripture passages that follow upon the *shema'* and in the benedictions that accompany it. In discussing the latter, he emphasizes the difference between the morning benedictions, which are filled with praise and love of the day that is beginning, and the evening benedictions, which seek rest, peace, and salvation from the shadows of the night.

There is perhaps only one aspect of the complex Jewish liturgical world that has escaped the author's attention: the idea of the prayer of God, that is, of God who prays. This notion does not lead to setting limitations on God, but rather to making the mutual relationship with human beings even closer and more effective. In the Babylonian Talmud, *Ber.* 7a, we read: "(Thus the Holy One prays:) May it be my will that my mercy overcome my anger and that my mercy take precedence over the norms of my justice, so that I may deal with my children according to my mercy and receive indulgence from them in turn." Such is the answer which Jews expect when in their prayer on the Day of Atonement they twice ask: "Answer us, O Lord, answer us."

This is but a detail in the concept Jews have of their relationship with God, a relationship in which one may think that at times human beings are more necessary to God than God is to them (see A.J. Heschel's title, *God in Search of Man*). Its omission does not impoverish the analysis presented to us by Di Sante, even if the analysis evidently reflects a Christian approach to liturgy. On the contrary, in my opinion the panoramic view given of the Jewish liturgy not only introduces readers to its most characteristic aspects but can induce many Christian readers to reflect on their own indifference and, in many instances, narrow judgments regarding certain themes of Judaism. It can inspire them to ask themselves how it is that in their daily recitation of the biblical psalms—written by Jews for Jews, who still recite them with the same emotions that marked their composition—they have not realized and still do not realize the interior religious spirit and the communion with God that are peculiar to Judaism.

My hope, therefore, is that this book with its various aspects and details will represent a new and important advance in Christian understanding of Judaism. In its daily synagogue services and in its formulas for domestic and private prayer, Judaism has been and continues to be faithful to that faith and trust which spring from a real past and are the expression of a hope for a peaceful future that will someday dawn at last if human beings commit themselves to its coming "with all their heart, and with all their soul, and with all their strength."

June 26, 1985   Lea Sestieri

Introduction

The Rediscovery of Judaism

The Second Ecumenical Council of the Vatican (1962–1965) is undoubtedly the most important ecclesial event of our century. Its Constitutions, Decrees, and Declarations mark the end of an age and the point of departure for a new self-understanding of the Church, both within (the Church looked at in itself, in its basic theological makeup) and without (the Church looked at in its relation to the world in the broad sense of this term).

The process of renewed self-understanding was made possible chiefly by the biblical, liturgical, and theological movements, the results of which were accepted by the council and found a place in the three major conciliar constitutions: on the liturgy, on the Church, and on revelation.

But no renewal can come about except through a rediscovery of roots and of the historical, spiritual, and cultural soil in which these roots pushed their way to the light, following the logic of differentiation and individualization. This principle holds even for the Church: it was born of Judaism and lived its life within Judaism for several decades (even if the relationship was dialectical and sometimes one of conflict), and only in the light of Judaism can it perceive and recover its vital identity. It is from the acknowledgment of this that *Nostra aetate* 4 draws a power and freshness that are becoming increasingly clear twenty years after the council.

An Important Turning Point

It is not a mere rhetorical flourish to say that *Nostra aetate* 4 represented an important turning point. The phrase was used by an authoritative source, Cardinal Willebrands, President of the Committee for Religious Relations with the Jews, in an official document which he signed in 1974: *Guidelines for Catholic-Jewish Relations* (on the Application of *Nostra aetate* 4).[1]

"Historical turning point" applies indeed at the ideological level, inasmuch as *Nostra aetate* 4 compels historical Christianity to reexamine and change its own philosophical outlook, in which contempt

1

and hatred for Jews had unfortunately acquired a solidly established place. But it also applies at the theological level, for it compels, and cannot help but compel, a rethinking of the whole of theology.

But "rethinking theology" can mean only one thing: the rediscovery of the Hebrew and Jewish categories within which Christian experience first appeared and which this experience used in order to thematize and communicate itself. We are hearing more and more today such statements as this one of L. Swidler:

> Jesus was a 'Rabbi' and not a 'Father,' a 'teacher' and not a 'reverend'; he was a Jew and not a Christian; he attended the synagogue and not a church; he celebrated the sabbath and not Sunday; he prayed in Aramaic and not in Greek or Latin; he read the Old Testament and not the New; he recited the psalms and not the rosary; he celebrated *pesah* (the Jewish Passover), *shavu'ot* (the Jewish Pentecost), and *sukkot* (huts) and not Christmas or Lent. . . .[2]

But do we have the theological courage to draw the proper theological conclusions from such statements? For, unless we are willing to settle for rhetorical gestures, assertion of the Jewishness of Jesus must mean an assertion of the inescapable centrality of Jewish categories and an acceptance of the need of returning to them and measuring ourselves by them in every effort we make to understand the Christian mystery.

But why should we return to Jewish categories? Why go back in heart and mind to distant, mythological ways of thinking that are so alien to the modern scientific and technological mentality? Moreover, how can the expressive and interpretative paradigms of the biblical and Hebraic tradition be of any help to us when we have seen R. Bultmann vigorously undertaking the demythologization without which religious language would be silent and meaningless to people today?

But despite the Bultmannian challenge—which in fact is concerned not so much to eliminate myth as correctly to decode and interpret it by bringing to light its deeper symbolism and its revelatory power, long blocked by reductive or false forms of rationalism[3] —and even because of the Bultmannian challenge, the rediscovery of the native Hebrew and Jewish categories becomes an urgently important duty for theologians. Those distant symbolic and mythological categories conceal words and expressions of meaning that if received and heard have power to enrich and give joy to human life by inspiring and revitalizing the models it uses for its own expression and interpretation. We need to rediscover Hebrew and Jewish categories so that we may once again hear in its original purity the *logos* of light and meaning that took flesh in them for the first time.

The Voice of Our Origins

This is the deeper reason for the theological challenge issued by *Nostra aetate:* we must rethink theology and rethink it with the aid of Hebrew and Jewish categories, because in these the pure and purifying voice of our origins is still to be heard. Pure: not infected by later compromises and mediations; purifying: capable of serving as critic ("critic" from Greek *krinein:* to sift/to judge) of all the other "voices" and suggestions for reinterpretation. But when we reaffirm the importance of origins we do not deny the present and become nostalgic *laudatores temporis acti* (people who praise the past and mourn for it). If that were what love of one's origins meant it would be simply a form of flight and not a theological effort at purification and renewal.

Love for our origins is in fact love for the present, a present marked by its high quality. From this point of view an "origin" is not something purely temporal but is more properly ontological and structural. A thing's origins are not simply events that took place in a distant time; rather they are as it were the foundations that support the present. The rediscovery of origins does not mean a distancing from the present but a recovery of the roots that sustain the present.

What are the "origins" from which our ecclesial "today" spring and on which this "today" is built and erected?

Nostra aetate 4 tells us in the following paragraph:

> The Church of Christ acknowledges that in God's plan of salvation the *beginning* of her *faith* and *election* is to be found in the patriarchs, Moses and the prophets. She professes that all Christ's faithful, who as men of faith are sons of Abraham (cf. Gal. 3:7), are included in the same patriarch's *call* and that the salvation of the Church is mysteriously prefigured in the *exodus* of God's *chosen people* from the *land of bondage*. On this account the Church cannot forget that she received the *revelation of the Old Testament* by way of that people with whom God in his inexpressible mercy established the *ancient covenant*. Nor can she forget that she draws nourishment from that good olive tree onto [the *root* of] which the wild olive branches of the Gentiles

have been grafted (cf. Rom. 11:17–24). The Church believes
that Christ who is our *peace* has through his cross *reconciled Jews and Gentiles* and made them one in himself (cf.
Eph. 2:14–16).[4]

The original categories in which Christianity is grounded and by
which it is sustained are the Hebrew and Jewish categories of faith,
election, call, exodus, people, bondage, Old Testament, covenant,
root, peace, and reconciliation. These categories are like so many
fountains located in the middle of the villages of Christian history,
where they slake the inhabitants' thirst and give them joy. If we
move away from these categories we risk dying of thirst.

The Liturgical Universe

Talk of "categories" has this drawback: that one is tempted to
understand them at the purely logical and rational level. Now the
term "category" certainly is in fact the product of rational activity,
but the content to which it refers in both the Jewish tradition and the
authentic Christian tradition is characteristically existential. In this
context, then, "categories" express and transmit vital realities and
not concepts. When we speak of faith or election, call or exodus, and
so on, we are not developing concepts or comparing ideas but summing up and condensing, in the bare essence captured by a word or
phrase, the deepest experience of life: the experience of encounter
with mystery, with God. The religious language of Judaism sprang
not from the demands of speculative reason but from the passionate
pressure of vital experience that was sealed by the presence and
word of God. For this reason Judaism does not have a theology in the
strict sense, that is, a systematically organized reflection on God; for
the same reason, it gives priority to practical action and parabolic
language, to *halakah* and *haggadah*.

This explains the primal, indeed foundational importance of the
liturgy, the latter being understood as the place of symbolic but direct encounter with God, the place where human beings do not
speak of God but *speak to God,* where they do not *think about God*
but *think in the presence of God,* and where God is not *an object of
thought* but a *subject who calls and challenges.* This space, made up
of gestures, words, music, movements, listening, story telling, silences, myths, and rites, is the privileged *historical space* wherein
Israel experienced encounter with God and learned to understand

itself and him, with the aid of such categories as election, covenant, call, reconciliation, and so on.

For the Church, then, a return to its origins must mean a return to this space in which Israel reflectively experienced itself as the people of God. It must mean entering into this universe of ritual that is also ours as Christians. *Nostra aetate* 4 begins, in fact, with this explicit statement: "Sounding the depths of the mystery which is the Church, this sacred Council remembers the spiritual ties which link the people of the New Covenant with the stock of Abraham."

This short sentence speaks of *ties* between the Church and Israel, a *something* that unites the two. The bond meant is not accidental but imperishable and essential, because it is not peripheral to the mystery of the Church but inherent in it; the Church discovers these "ties," this *unifying structure*, by "sounding the depths" of its own mystery. The participle "sounding" (*perscrutans*) can here simply describe what happens (while studying its own mystery, the Church discovers its ties with Judaism) or it can express an end result (in order to study its own reality the Church discovers that it cannot do without its ties to Judaism).

But even apart from these two interpretations, which complement one another, one thing emerges clearly: the Church's identity is structurally connected with a theological *space* which it shares with Israel. This space finds objective expression above all in the *liturgical universe* in which Israel lived its faith, formed its image of itself, and developed its categories. The liturgical universe is the place par excellence wherein the *ties* "which link the people of the New Covenant with the stock of Abraham" are expressed and transmitted.

Christian scholars have never taken seriously the fact that Christian experience and, above all, the Christian liturgy are bound up with Jewish cultic structures. If we look, for example, into the most important liturgical handbooks of recent decades,[5] the pattern for dealing with the problem of the origins of the Christian liturgy seems to be the following: Jesus Christ is presented as the originator of the Christian liturgy, for some an absolute originator in regard to both content and forms, for others an originator in regard to content but not to forms, which were borrowed from the Jewish tradition. The second of these two positions is the one adopted by the majority of Christian scholars.

Nowadays no informed scholar thinks of looking outside the biblical and Jewish tradition for the origin of the Christian sacraments.[6] That tradition is rightly regarded as the "context"[7] or "place of origin" of the Christian liturgy.[8] But in reading these scholars one has a sense that this "context" and "place of origin" are looked upon as a provisional and unimportant background, to which in addition the Christian tradition stands in a polemical relationship, rather than as the positive, vital, and substantial soil from which the Christian liturgy sprang. This interpretation is confirmed by two facts that can hardly be denied.

The first is the paucity of information given by these authors on Jewish worship in the intertestamental period, although Jesus was nourished by that worship and its spirituality. The authors to whom I am referring are usually satisfied to give a few references required by New Testament terms (in the time of Jesus Jews worshiped in the synagogue, celebrated Passover, kept the sabbath, and so on), but show no concern to tell their readers about the wealth of content in the formulas of which they speak. As a result, readers are confronted by skeletal remains, as it were, or by antiquated and meaningless structures.[9]

The second fact is the radically negative judgment passed on Jewish worship.[10] On reflection, this is of course a perfectly logical step, since once Jewish worship has been reduced to a lifeless skeleton, what is left but to decide that it is useless and a thing of the past?

Jesus and the Jewish Liturgy

I am certainly not denying the originality and specificity of Jesus in relation to contemporary Judaism and to the liturgy on whose riches he fed. Like every other great personality, Jesus is not reducible to the spiritual components found in the religion and culture of his time. Something in him sets him apart from his contemporaries and constitutes his moral grandeur. But at this point a remark of fundamental importance is in place: we need not declare contemporary Judaism beneath our notice, much less caricature it, in order to assert the true stature of Jesus. Such an uncalled for approach does injustice not only to Judaism but to Jesus himself, since, to use the image proposed by Louis Bouyer, it turns him into a "meteorite that fell to earth in Palestine."[11]

Our need is to reverse the procedure of the scholars I have been describing and accustom ourselves to asserting the greatness and originality of Jesus not *outside of* Judaism or *in opposition to* it, but *along with* it and *within* it. Judaism is not the negative that makes the positive in Jesus and Christianity stand out more clearly; rather it is the "divine melody" whose music is a standard for measuring the greatness and originality of Jesus and Christianity.

If we are to succeed in really reversing the usual approach we must accustom ourselves to seeing Judaism and its many manifestations as autonomous realities and not simply in relation to Christ and Christianity. We can do this by disinterested listening and by cultivating knowledge that is respectful of its object.

The liturgy is the privileged place for this knowledge and this listening, for here, more than in any other expression of the Jewish tradition, the inexhaustible treasures of the Bible and spirituality that have inspired and nourished that tradition from its beginnings down to the present day are summed up and brought together. Jesus himself, the Virgin Mary, the apostles, the early communities, and the first Christians were all nourished by that liturgy with its symbols and rites, its echoes and silences.

In the following pages we shall be listening again to some of the more important of those musical notes. The purpose is not to compare the Jewish liturgy with the Christian, but rather to let those notes sound again in their original freshness. If each reader truly listens to those ancient notes, he or she will understand how greatly Jesus and the original Christian community were indebted to them and, above all, how much a part they are of the "ties" between the stock of Abraham and the New Testament Church, ties that *Nostra aetate* locates in the depths of the mystery which is the Church.

Chapter I

The Sources of the Jewish Liturgy

The New Testament, that is, the collection of Christian writings that came into existence in the second half of the first century, bears abundant witness to the existence of the Jewish liturgy. The witness is, however, straightforwardly indicative rather than descriptive, that is, it tells us that in the time of Jesus certain cultic forms existed, but it does not tell us in what they consisted or how they were practiced.

Readers of the New Testament are in the same situation here as Muslims or Hindus who might read in a church newspaper that the Pope had celebrated Mass, administered baptism, and taken part in Matins. These unfortunate readers would now know of the existence of things called Mass and baptism and Matins, but would know nothing of their content, structure, and symbolic and ritual dynamics. If they wanted to learn what the realities were behind the terms they had read or heard, they would have only one course open to them: to draw on experience and a variety of sources, either by participating directly in the liturgy they had read about or by gathering and reading the liturgical texts and rites actually used. The situation would be different, of course, for Christians reading the same newspaper. In their case, such words as Mass, baptism, and Matins would be linked to personal experiences and to realities that are an immediate part of their everyday cultural world. No explanation would be required for these readers.

The apostles and the first readers of the Christian scriptures were in a privileged hermeneutical position: when they read of synagogue and sabbath and Passover, they were brought in contact with realities they knew and were familiar with. They had a sense of the beauty and complexity of these things but also of their contradictions and ambiguities, of their symbolic and spiritual riches but also of the ways in which they could be manipulated or reduced to lifeless functions.

This may explain why the New Testament writers take a polemical attitude toward the rites of the Jewish liturgy. Their hostility is harsh, sometimes even violent, but at least it is always the hostility of persons who know the liturgy of their fathers "from inside" and who, precisely because they know and love it, can also be critical of it. And the purpose of their criticism is the same as the purpose of the prophets: not to reject the liturgy but to rediscover it in all its purity and authenticity.

Present-day readers (and those of centuries past) of the Christian scriptures find themselves in the opposite hermeneutical situation: a situation of uneasiness and danger. Uneasiness, because they keep encountering terms now outside their cultural horizon; danger, because they are easily tempted to fill the Jewish words with a content alien to them, a content that is the fruit rather of polemics than of honest study. It is probably the working of this mechanism that explains the following strange phenomenon: that it is Christian readers rather than Jewish readers who find the New Testament writings to be anti-Jewish. I offer as an example Robert Aron's book, *The Jewish Jesus*.[1] Whereas the majority of Christian exegetes dealing with the New Testament sources prefer to emphasize the polemical attitude of Jesus toward Jewish worship and its replacement by Christian worship, Aron, a Jewish scholar, finds in these writings a rich and deep, fresh and joyous spirituality without which it is impossible to understand either Jesus himself or the experience of his followers.

This example is not unimportant, for it shows clearly that the New Testament writings can be approached with different sensibilities which may be in harmony or out of harmony with those of Judaism. If they are in harmony, the writings reveal, to our surprise, new hidden yet luminous meanings; if they are out of harmony, the writings are reduced to lifeless words that are used for polemical purposes instead of being listened to with respect.

If, then, we are to avoid interpreting reductively the liturgical information provided in the New Testament literature, we must have recourse to other sources that are more directly and explicitly Jewish. This statement explains the plan of the present chapter. I shall first cite some of the many New Testament passages that attest the existence of certain forms of Jewish liturgy. I shall then call attention to the principal sources with which we can fill out and compare the references made in the Christian scriptures.

I. INFORMATION IN THE NEW TESTAMENT

I. The Temple and the Synagogue

The New Testament writings refer to the temple about seventy times. Here are some examples. Mt 21:12: "Jesus entered the temple"; Lk 22:53: "I was with you day after day in the temple"; Jn 7:14: "Jesus went up into the temple and taught"; Acts 3:1: "Peter and John were going up to the temple"; Mk 14:58: "We heard him say, 'I will destroy this temple that is made with hands, and in three days I will build another, not made with hands' "; 1 Cor 3:16: "Do you not know that you are God's temple?"

The New Testament also makes about seventy references to the synagogue, almost all of them simply factual. Mt 4:23: "He went about all Galilee, teaching in their synagogues"; Mt 12:35: "He . . . entered their synagogue"; Mt 13:54: "He taught them in their synagogues"; Mk 1:21: "On the sabbath he entered the synagogue and taught"; Mk 6:2: "On the sabbath he began to teach in the synagogue"; Jn 6:59: "This he said in the synagogue, as he taught at Capernaum"; Acts 9:20: "In the synagogues immediately he [Paul] proclaimed Jesus"; Acts 13:5: "They [Paul and Barnabas] proclaimed the word of God (logon tou Theou) in the synagogues of the Jews." But the richest New Testament testimony regarding the synagogue is in Lk 4:15–22:

> And he came to Nazareth, where he had been brought up; and he went to the synagogue, as his custom was, on the sabbath day. And he stood up to read; and there was given to him the book of the prophet Isaiah. He opened the book and found the place where it was written,
>
> > The Spirit of the Lord is upon me,
> > because he has anointed me to preach good news to
> > > the poor.
> > He has sent me to proclaim release to the captives
> > and recovering of sight to the blind,
> > to set at liberty those who are oppressed,
> > to proclaim the acceptable year of the Lord.
>
> And he closed the book, and gave it back to the attendant, and sat down; and the eyes of all in the synagogue were fixed on him. And he began to say to them, "Today this scripture has been fulfilled in your hearing." And all spoke well of him, and wondered at the gracious words which proceeded out of his mouth; and they said, "Is this not Joseph's son?"

This passage is especially valuable because it is the earliest source we have that provides information about the functioning of the Jewish synagogue. In particular, it tells us of:

—the existence of a synagogue at Nazareth;

—the day (Saturday, the sabbath) on which the people assembled in the synagogue;

—the "right" of each male present to read the Torah (v. 16: "he stood up to read");

—the actual passage from the prophets (the *haftarah*) that was read on that sabbath (Is 61:1–2);

—the practice of using and keeping the Torah on parchment rolls which, depending on their size, were opened and closed with the help of aides;

—the custom of having a homiletic commentary after the reading: "Today this scripture has been fulfilled in your hearing" (v. 21);

—the positive reaction of those present, who wonder at the words of Jesus.

The various passages cited exemplify the two ways of using the term "synagogue" in the Christian scriptures: at times factually (as in "He entered their synagogue"), at times descriptively. When descriptions, in the sense of further information, are given, they emphasize one aspect in particular: the synagogue as a place for study and teaching. This explains why Jesus is so often said to go to the synagogue "to teach," *didaskein* (see Mt 4:23; 13:54; Mk 1:21; 6:2; Jn 6:59; etc.). As well as being a place of assembly and prayer, the synagogue is a place for teaching, a place where people learn to read the scriptures and interpret the divine will in the light of Jesus.

2. The Sabbath

Another lengthy series of passages (about seventy) has to do with the sabbath, the feast day par excellence of the Jewish liturgy. The term "sabbath" almost always occurs in the context of the synagogue and, instead of simply recording an objective fact, usually has polemical overtones. Here are some examples. Mt 12:1–2: "At that time Jesus went through the grain fields on the sabbath; his disciples were hungry, and they began to pluck ears of grain and to eat. But when the Pharisees saw it, they said to him, 'Look, your disciples are doing what is not lawful to do on the sabbath' "; Mk 1:21: "On the sabbath he entered the synagogue and taught"; Mk 3:4–5: "He said to them, 'Is it lawful on the sabbath to do good or to do harm, to save life or to kill?' But they were silent. And he looked around at them with anger, grieved at their hardness of heart, and said to the man, 'Stretch out your hand.' He stretched it out and his hand was restored"; Mk 2:27–28: "He said to them, 'The sabbath was made for man, not man for the sabbath; so the Son of man is lord even of the sabbath.' "

As I pointed out, these texts (which are only a few of many) show that references to the sabbath are primarily polemical. But the polemical element must not be exaggerated. Even more importantly, we must not think that it implies a complete rejection of the institution of the sabbath. Like everything in the realm of ritual, the sabbath was in danger of losing its spiritual inspiration and being seen only as something external and as a formality. It is against this mystification and not against the sabbath as such that the attacks of Jesus and the early Christian tradition were directed. Careful examination shows that these attacks continued the prophetic denunciations so cherished by the main pre- and post-exilic biblical experience; their purpose was not to do away with ritual but on the contrary to restore its authenticity. If this be the case, and it is, the attacks of Jesus on the sabbath are a sign not of anti-Jewish sentiment but of fidelity to the authentic meaning of the sabbath.

3. Passover and Pentecost

The New Testament sources refer to Passover about thirty times and almost always in a factual way. Here are some examples. Mt 26:2: "You know that after two days the Passover is coming, and the Son of man will be delivered up to be crucified"; Mt 26:17: "Now on the first day of Unleavened Bread the disciples came to Jesus, saying, 'Where will you have us prepare for you to eat the Passover?' "; 1 Cor 5:7–8: "Christ, our paschal lamb, has been sacrificed. Let us, therefore, celebrate the festival, not with the old leaven, the leaven of malice and evil, but with the unleavened bread of sincerity and truth." Other references occur in Lk 22:1, 22:14–18; Jn 2:13; etc.

These passages provide little information about the actual course of the feast. We are told only the two names of the feast (Passover or Unleavened Bread), what time was allowed for preparation, and some sketchy details about the ritual actions (taking bread, offering the blessing, breaking the bread, and distributing it; see Lk 22:14–18). The sparse information shows nonetheless how important Passover was to Jesus and the Christian communities.

There were at least two reasons for this. The first is that according to a unanimous New Testament tradition it was in the context of Passover that Jesus "instituted" the Eucharist: "And as they were eating, he took bread . . . and gave it to them, and said: 'Take; this is my body' " (Mk 14:22–25 par.).

Despite the simplicity of the words, exegetes and liturgical scholars know how difficult it is to get back to their real meaning. What actually happened during this final meal of Jesus? At what point did Jesus introduce his command about commemoration? What did he really intend to say? And what did the disciples gathered around him understand him to be saying? Adequate answers to these questions cannot be derived from the New Testament sources alone. A great deal of light can however be derived from other sources that tell us of the structure and course of the Passover meal. Recourse to these is necessary, not because we disregard or deny the originality of Jesus' statements, but rather because we desire to understand them better and bring out their full meaning.

The second reason for the great importance of Passover to the Christian communities was its metaphorical applications: Christ is the new paschal lamb; Christians are the real "unleavened bread" (maṣṣot; see 1 Cor 5:7), in which the "leaven" of sin is no longer at work but only transparent truth. The Jewish Passover—to which the New Testament texts simply allude, since they suppose that the reader is familiar with it—is the most important topos of all for an understanding of the Christian experience. It supplies both the context and the text of Christian origins.

Regarding Pentecost (literally, "the fiftieth [day]," because the feast was celebrated fifty days after Passover), the New Testament has very little to say: Acts 20:16: "Paul had decided to sail past Ephesus, so that he might not have to spend time in Asia; for he was hastening to be in Jerusalem, if possible, on the day of Pentecost"; 1 Cor 16:8: "But I will stay in Ephesus until Pentecost." But despite the paucity of references to it, the feast of Pentecost became especially important to the early Church because it had been the day of the outpouring of the Spirit, as we see in the great picture painted by Luke in the Acts of the Apostles (2:1–13).

The New Testament provides no detailed information about Pentecost, any more than it does for the other feasts. It simply records its existence and makes known how important it became to the early community as the feast par excellence of the Holy Spirit. But why did this Jewish feast, which was the least popular of the pilgrimage feasts, become so central in Christianity that the act constitutive of the Christian community was associated with it? How did it become the privileged "locus" of the Spirit? In what sense was the Church born that day as a community of love, a community that reached out beyond the varied national and cultural frontiers?

Once again, the answer to these questions does not come from the New Testament sources. We must turn to other documents which enable us to reconstruct the course of this feast in the time of Jesus. Only by so doing will we be in a position to understand the reinterpretation of the feast by the Christian community and its transformation into the occasion of the gift of the Holy Spirit.

4. Huts or Tabernacles

John speaks of this feast under the Greek name *Skēnopēgia* (from *skēnē*, tent, and *pēgeō*, pitch, put up: "Pitching of Tents"). This is the feast known variously in English as Huts, Booths, Tents, and Tabernacles. For the occasion every Jew erected a hut on the bare ground in order to commemorate the time when his ancestors were wanderers in the wilderness.

The fourth evangelist has two references to the feast. The first is in Jn 7:2: "Now the Jews' feast of Tabernacles was at hand . . ."; the second is in Jn 7:37–39: "On the last day of the feast, the great day (*tē megalē tēs eortēs*), Jesus stood up and proclaimed, 'If any one thirst, let him come to me and drink. He who believes in me, as the scripture has said, "Out of his heart shall flow rivers of living water." ' Now this he said about the Spirit, which those who believed in him were to receive; for as yet the Spirit had not been given, because Jesus was not yet glorified."

These Johannine testimonies supply the following information:
—the two names of the feast: "Tabernacles" (Huts, etc.) and "the feast par excellence." According to the rabbis and the Mishnah the feast of Tabernacles was and is the most imaginative, popular, and joyous.

—the reinterpretation by Jesus of an element of the feast (the drawing of water; the pouring of it in lustrations) so that it now refers to the outpouring of the Holy Spirit: "Now this he said about the Spirit, which those who believed in him were to receive."

—the probable gradual identification of the feast of Tabernacles with the feast of Pentecost. Since the latter is the great feast of the Spirit it ended up absorbing the feast of Tabernacles. This would explain why of the three great feasts of the Jewish liturgy—Passover, Pentecost, and Tabernacles—the last-named has almost disappeared from the Christian tradition.

5. The Feasts of Dedication (Hanukkah) and Atonement (Yom Kippur)

The New Testament bears witness to the existence of another Jewish feast: "It was the feast of the Dedication at Jerusalem; it was winter, and Jesus was walking in the temple in the portico of Solomon" (Jn 10:22–23). The Greek word for "dedication" is *Egkainia*, which the Latin Bible simply transliterates as *Encaenia*. The Greek word is from the verb *egkainizo*, which means "to renew," "to make new all over again." On this feast the Jews commemorated the day when the Jerusalem temple was purified and rededicated in 164 B.C. after its unprecedented desecration by Antiochus Epiphanes who had offered sacrifice to Zeus there in 167 B.C.

Once again, the New Testament tells us nothing about the content of this feast. We must have recourse to other sources.

Finally, the New Testament also tells us of the existence of a feast which, oddly enough, is almost always passed over in silence and whose great importance is not even suggested. I refer to the feast of the Atonement, Yom Kippur, which is also called "the Day of Fasting" or "the Day of Days." The Book of Acts has an explicit reference to this feast: "As much time had been lost, and the voyage was already dangerous because the fast had already gone by, Paul advised them . . ." (Acts 27:9).

Even though the Christian scriptures say no more than this about the feast of Atonement (if we except Hebrews 9:1–28, which gives a christological interpretation of the content of the feast), its theological meaning seems to have left a profound mark on the preaching of Jesus. Mark (and the Synoptics generally) gives the following summary of the evangelizing activity of Jesus: "Jesus came into Galilee, preaching the gospel of God, and saying, 'The time is fulfilled, and the kingdom of God is at hand; repent, and believe in the gospel' " (Mk 1:14–15). A key element in the preaching of Jesus was repentance/*metanoia* (*metanoeite*).

The English word "repentance" and the Greek *metanoia* translate the Hebrew *shuv/teshuvah*, which mean "return" and supply the focus and refrain of the feast of Yom Kippur. On that day the Jewish people recall their infidelities to God's plan and determine to turn back (*teshuvah*) from the path of sin. It is impossible to understand the call of Jesus for *metanoia* if we are not familiar with the texts of the Jewish liturgy for the feast of Yom Kippur. Jesus himself fed on these texts and drew inspiration from them on his missionary journey from village to village of Galilee and Judea.

6. The Prayer of Benediction (Berakah)

The *berakah* (translated in the Christian scriptures as *eucharistia* [thanksgiving] or *eulogia* [blessing] and in the Latin Bible as benedictio [blessing] or gratiarum actio [thanksgiving]) was and is the chief form of prayer in Jewish liturgy and spirituality. "The chief form of prayer": because it determines the meaning and context of all prayer, as well as the dynamic movement and horizon of all liturgy and all the feasts. The berakah consists in an attitude-and-formula of wonder, praise, thanksgiving, and acknowledgment of the unmerited divine benevolence that provides for God's children and gladdens them with the fruits of the earth and every kind of blessing. In the course of time the mark of the berakah came to be the set, standardized words with which every prayer began and ended: "Blessed be you, Lord, our God." At times, the passive form ("Blessed be you . . .") might be replaced by the active form: "I bless you . . ."

The New Testament tells us of many berakot, some explicit, others—the majority—implicit. Among the best known is the one in which Jesus thanks the Father for having chosen "babes" as the recipients of his revelation:

> I thank thee, Father, Lord of heaven and earth, that thou hast hidden these things from the wise and understanding and revealed them to babes; yea, Father, for such was thy gracious will. All things have been delivered to me by my Father; and no one knows the Son except the Father, and no one knows the Father except the Son and any one to whom the Son chooses to reveal him (Mt 11:25–27; see Lk 10:21–22).

The most famous of the implicit berakot is the one to which all the Synoptic evangelists refer in the account of "the institution of the Eucharist": "And as they were eating, he took bread, and blessed, and broke it, and gave it to them, and said, 'Take; this is my body.' And he took a cup, and when he had given thanks he gave it to them, and they all drank of it. And he said to them, 'This is my blood of the covenant, which is poured out for many' " (Mk 14:22–24).

This passage shows that there were two berakot, one over the bread and one over the chalice, but it does not tell us what form they actually took. Here, as elsewhere, the New Testament sources do not adequately inform us.

Another testimony to Jesus' use of the berakah form is in Mk 6:41, where the influence of the Eucharist is undeniable: "And taking the five loaves and the two fish he looked up to heaven, and blessed, and broke the loaves . . ." (a very similar passage occurs again in Mk 8:6–7). Other references to blessings are to be seen in Mk

10:16, where Jesus takes the children in his arms and "blesses them," that is, says a berakah over them, and in Jn 11:41, where Jesus utters a berakah to the Father for the raising of Lazarus: "Jesus lifted up his eyes and said, 'Father, I thank thee that thou hast heard me. I knew that thou hearest me always. . . .'"

If we turn from the gospels to the other New Testament writings, we find many other pieces of evidence. Col 3:17 can serve as an example: "And whatever (pan) you do, in word or deed, do everything (panta) in the name of the Lord Jesus, giving thanks to God the Father through him." According to the rabbinical tradition the devout Jew ought to recite over a hundred berakot daily. We cannot fail to see the same sensibility at work in Paul's exhortation to "do everything" to the accompaniment of thanksgiving. In all things (panta), nothing excluded, Christians, like Jews, should utter a berakah. The only difference is that Christians are to do this "in the name of the Lord Jesus" or "through him," that is, with the same intention and the same fullness of commitment as he had.

No less meaningful is Eph 5:18–20: "Be filled with the Spirit, addressing one another in psalms and hymns and spiritual songs, singing and making melody to the Lord with all your hearts, always and for everything giving thanks (eucharistountes pantote hyper pantōn) in the name of our Lord Jesus Christ to God the Father." Christians should offer berakot at all times (pantote) and for everything (hyper pantōn).

The Pauline letters not only show the importance of the berakah; they also tell us the motives that give rise to it. These can be summed up under two headings: the existence of the new Christian communities and, above all, the event that is Jesus, now acknowledged and proclaimed as Messiah and Son of God. If Christians ought to utter a berakah in every situation and every event, then certainly this response is called for in face of the two main events of early Christianity: the multiplication of communities by the hundreds and the experience of the dead and risen Jesus. See, by way of example, 1 Cor 1:4–9; Col 1:3–5; and especially the well known passage, Eph 1:3–14.

7. The Prayer "Hear, O Israel" (Shema' Yiśra'el) and the Eighteen Benedictions (Tefillah)

The Shema' Yiśra'el, which is the Jewish people's most important profession of faith, is made up of three benedictions and some verses of the Bible. Among the latter is Deut 6:4–9, the passage which

Jesus cites in reply to the scribe who asked him: "Which commandment is the first of all?" (Mk 12:28 par.). "Jesus answered, 'The first is,
"Hear, O Israel: The Lord our God, the Lord is one; and you shall love
the Lord your God with all your heart, and with all your soul, and
with all your mind, and with all your strength" ' " (Mk 12:29–30).

The New Testament bears witness not only to the *Shema'*
Yiśra'el but also, quite probably, to the *tefillah*, the chief prayer of the
synagogal liturgy, which is also known by two other names: *she-
moneh 'eśreh* and *'amidah*. It consists of a series of benedictions, the
oldest of which go back to the second century B.C. and which were
already being recited in all synagogues by the time of Christ. We find
traces in the gospels of some of these benedictions that made up and
still make up the *tefillah*.

The first of the benedictions reads as follows: "Blessed art thou,
O Lord our God and God of our Fathers, God of Abraham, God of
Isaac, and God of Jacob, the great, mighty and revered God . . ."
(131).[2] The second reads: "Thou, O Lord, art mighty for ever, thou
revivest the dead, thou art mighty to save. . . . Thou . . . revivest the
dead with great mercy. . . . Who resembleth thee, O King, who orderest death and restorest life. . . . Yea, faithful art thou to revive the
dead. Blessed art thou, O lord, who revivest the dead" (133).

Jesus uses the theology of these two blessings to answer the Sadducees when they come and challenge him regarding the resurrection of the dead: "And as for the dead being raised, have you not read
in the book of Moses, in the passage about the bush, how God said to
him, 'I am the God of Abraham and the God of Isaac, and the God of
Jacob'? He is not God of the dead, but of the living" (Mk 12:26–27; see
Lk 20:27–40; Mt 22:23–33).

8. The Our Father

The Our Father, of which we have two versions (Lk 11:2–4 and
Mt 6:9–13), also reflects to an important degree the liturgy of the
synagogue. Contrary to the claims of apologetes who like to emphasize the radical originality of the Our Father, a careful analysis shows
that this prayer has deep roots in Judaism.

This statement applies first of all to the very structure of the Our
Father. This reflects the ideal structure of Jewish prayer, as seen, for
example, in biblical prayers such as that of David (1 Chron 29:10–20):
an opening *berakah*, petitions, and a final, summarizing *berakah*. For
this reason it is improbable that the Our Father ended with the
words: "but deliver us from evil." The ending given in some codices

of Matthew's gospel would seem closer to the original: "For thine is the kingdom and the power and the glory for ever. Amen."

When we turn from the structure to an analysis of the several parts of the Our Father, the connections with Jewish prayer become even clearer:

—"Our Father": the description of God as a "father" is a recurring trait of Jewish prayer. The practice is attested first in the Bible itself. In Deut 32:6 and Is 63:16, for example, God is called the father of Israel and Israelites are called his children. The name is attested above all, however, in the Jewish liturgy.

In the 'amidah, or Eighteen Benedictions, for example, the title occurs twice: "Cause us to return, O our Father, unto thy Torah; draw us near, O our King, unto thy service . . ." (fifth benediction [139]); "Forgive us, O our Father, for we have sinned; pardon us, O our King, for we have transgressed" (sixth benediction [139]). We also find it in the second benediction before the shema': "O our Father, our King, for our fathers' sake, who trusted in thee, and whom thou didst teach the statutes of life, be also gracious unto us and teach us. O our Father, ever compassionate, have mercy on us" (115).

The name "Father" is also widely used in the liturgy of the New Year and of Yom Kippur (Day of Atonement), where the phrases "Father of mercy" and "O our Father" occur with some frequency. The name "Father" emphasizes the trust of the people in the mercy of God, while the plural "our" underscores the solidarity of the community that is gathered for prayer.

If these similarities are taken seriously, then the opposition which theologians and exegetes like to see between the Jewish conception of God and that of Jesus becomes at least questionable. Ever since J. Jeremias argued the thesis that the invocation 'abba' is exclusively characteristic of Jesus,[3] this opposition has been stressed even more.

Here, for example, is a statement by an exegete: "In the Aramaic spoken by Jesus the word 'father' must have been 'abba', 'papa,' which a Jew would have thought scandalous and almost blasphemous as applied to God."[4] And a religion textbook reads as follows: "The Jews still had an incomplete and imperfect knowledge of God: God was for them the Almighty, the Awesome, the one who condemns and punishes. It was Jesus who taught us to call God 'father' or, more accurately, 'abba'."[5]

But, even if we prescind from the fact that the Jewish tradition is familiar with the title 'abba' as applied to God (see b. Ta'an. 23b), the difference between 'ab (father) and 'abba' (papa) should not be exaggerated. It may be true that the use of 'abba' is predominantly Christian, but it should not be contrasted with the use of 'ab; 'abba' represents at most a nuance of feeling.

—"Who art in heaven": this expression is likewise frequent in the Jewish liturgy. It occurs in the morning service: "Thou art the Lord our God in heaven and on earth" (31). In the treatise 'Abot, the oldest and most important in the Mishnah, there is a passage that reads: "Be courageous and do the will of your Father who is in heaven" ('Abot 5, 23). The words are obviously meant as metaphorical, not geographical. They express God's transcendence, his "otherness" in relation to human beings. If the word "Father" expresses God's closeness to humanity, the expression "who is in heaven" reminds us of the irreducible difference between him and us.

—"Hallowed be thy name": The expression immediately reminds us of the qaddish, one of the oldest of Jewish prayers, used at the end of the reading and study of the Torah and, later on, in the synagogue service: "Magnified and sanctified be his great Name in the world which he hath created according to his will" (423). The expression also occurs in the qedushah, the third benediction of the Tefillah: "We will sanctify thy Name in the world even as they sanctify it in the highest heaven" (135).

The parallel between these texts of the Jewish liturgy and the Our Father becomes even more startling when we realize the meaning of the words "sanctify the name of God." The teachers ask: "How can human beings sanctify the name of God?" They answer: by their words but above all by their lives. Those who are faithful to God's will and prefer it to their own "sanctify his Name." The true "sanctification of the Name" (qiddush ha-shem) consists in the gift of one's life; it consists in martyrdom.

We can now understand better what Jesus is referring to when he says "hallowed be Thy name": the words express his conception of God but above all they express the gift of his life, which is "sacrificed" for all (see Mt 26:24; Lk 22:19). By his "death on the cross" in obedience to the Father's will Jesus "sanctified the Name." The same thread runs through history from Jesus dying on the cross to the thousands of Jews who called upon God and glorified him as they entered the gas chambers: they as well as Jesus "sanctified the Name."

—"Thy kingdom come": these words are likewise to be found in the qaddish: "May he establish his kingdom during your life and during your days and during the life of all the house of Israel" (213).

This is clearly a kingdom to be established not in some metahistorical realm but in our present history. The kingdom of God is to become a reality in this world and not just in the next. When Jesus calls for the coming of the kingdom of God he is thinking of a humanized world in which human beings can live in a fruitful peace as brothers and sisters.

—"Thy will be done": these words occur in 1 Mac 3:59–60: "It is better for us to die in battle than to see the misfortunes of our nation and of the sanctuary. But as his will in heaven may be, so he will do." The same attitude of abandonment to God's will finds expression in the prayer which Jews utter as they feel death drawing near: "May it be thy will to send me a perfect healing. Yet if my death be fully determined by thee, I will in love to accept it at thy hand" (1065).

—"Give us this day our daily bread": the preceding invocations had God as their object; this and the following ones have human needs as their object. The petition for "bread" is part of the ninth benediction of the tefillah: "Bless this year unto us, O Lord our God, together with every kind of the produce thereof, for our welfare; give a blessing upon the face of the earth. Oh satisfy us with thy goodness, and bless our year like other good years. Blessed art thou, O Lord, who blessest the years."

Some commentators liked to see in this Jewish blessing an allusion to the manna in the wilderness. Not without reason, some Fathers of the Church liked to see in the "daily bread" of the Our Father an allusion to the Eucharist. Thus the Our Father is linked to the Jewish liturgy not only textually but even hermeneutically. The allusion to the manna may also shed light on the difficult Greek adjective epiousion: just as the Israelites were to gather the manna, "each as much as he could eat" (Ex 16:21) because any surplus gathered "bred worms and became foul" (Ex 16:20), so the bread which we ask of God is bread that is enough for each day and frees us of any worry about the future and any hoarding. The same thought is expressed in Prov 30:8: "Give me neither poverty nor riches; feed me with the food that is needful for me."

—"Forgive us our debts as we forgive our debtors": the idea of forgiveness finds expression in the sixth benediction of the tefillah: "Forgive us, O our Father, for we have sinned; pardon us, O our King, for we have transgressed; for thou dost pardon and forgive. Blessed art thou, O Lord, who art gracious, and dost abundantly forgive" (139). Even the thought in "as we forgive our debtors" has its origin in the synagogue and the Old Testament. We find it in the Yom Kippur liturgy and in Sir 28:2: "Forgive your neighbor the wrong he has done, and then your sins will be pardoned when you pray." The same doctrine is found in the majority of the rabbis, who teach that "if you forgive your neighbor, the One will forgive you; but if you do not forgive your neighbor, no one will have mercy on you."[6]

—"Lead us not into temptation but deliver us from evil": this idea of deliverance (redemption) is found in the seventh benediction of the tefillah: "Look upon our affliction and plead our cause, and redeem us speedily for thy Name's sake; for thou art a mighty Redeemer. Blessed art thou, O Lord, the Redeemer of Israel" (141). There is an even closer resemblance in the Talmud, b. Ber. 60b: "Do not abandon me to the power of sin or to the power of guilt or to the power of temptation or to the power of shame." It is true, of course, that the Talmud was composed many centuries after Christ, but many of its materials go back to a far distant period, even prior to the time of Christ.

I have dwelt at length on the Jewish roots of the Our Father, not in order to belittle the value and riches of this prayer but rather to help us better appreciate and delight in it. Jesus called on the same God as did his Jewish brothers and sisters and used the same turns of phrase as they did. His originality consisted in bringing to fulfillment what the biblical and liturgical texts proclaimed and expressed (see Mt 5:17: "Think not that I have come to abolish the law and the prophets; I have come not to abolish them but to fulfill them"). The prayer which Jesus gives us is not opposed to the prayers of the Jews but brings them to fulfillment.

II. Sources in the Mishnah

The New Testament offers us many testimonies to the Jewish liturgy. But, as we have also seen, these are testimonies to the existence of that liturgy and not descriptions of it.

The New Testament presupposes the existence of Jewish worship, and for that reason its references to it are mostly implicit, allusive, and scanty. Since this is the case, we must, if we wish to understand these New Testament references, have recourse to other sources that will directly and explicitly help us to reconstruct the world of Jewish worship in the time of Jesus and the early Christian community.

Among all these sources, the first and most important is still the Mishnah, a compilation of Jewish laws and regulations that goes back to 200 A.D., but whose materials are very ancient and antedate even the time of Christ. "Though produced two generations later than NT times, the Mishna contains fairly reliable accounts of Jewish practices that prevailed during NT times. The authorities quoted in the Mishna were mostly persons who lived during the first 130 years of the Christian era."[7]

I. The Liturgical Tractates of the Mishnah

One of the most important areas of Jewish practice on which the Mishnah informs us quite fully is the area of liturgy and worship. Of the six "Orders" that make up the book two are devoted explicitly and exclusively to this kind of practice. They are therefore a necessary liturgical source if we are to become familiar with the concrete way in which the Jewish people prayed and celebrated, especially during the intertestamental period and at the time of Jesus.

More concretely, the Mishnah tells us about:

—*the sacrificial worship* conducted in the Jerusalem temple. The entire fifth Order, *Qodashim* ("Holy things"), is dedicated to this subject and deals with sacrifices, offerings of grain and beverages, the slaughter of animals, the daily ritual of the temple, and the architecture of the temple. The eleven tractates of this Order are meant as answers to the following practical questions: What are the various kinds of sacrifices (grains, doves, etc.; offerings as fines)? With what intention are such sacrifices to be offered? How are the animals destined for sacrifice to be slaughtered? And how should the temple be built in which these sacrifices are to be offered to the divinity?

These treatises, however, are not very important for an understanding of the New Testament liturgy, since, as everyone knows, the latter drew its inspiration from the liturgy of the synagogue rather than that of the temple. The former of these two was practiced by the many and was popular; the latter was quite specialized and elitist (it was the work of the Levitical and priestly class and only indirectly of the people).

—*the various feasts and anniversaries of the Jewish people.* The entire second Order, *Mo'ed* ("feasts," "important dates"), is devoted to this subject. It deals with *shabbat* (the sabbath), *pesaḥ* (Passover), *yom kippur* (the day of atonement), *sukkot* (tabernacles, huts), *rosh ha-shanah* (New Year's), and *purim* (from the Akkadian *pur* = "lot," "fate"; the feast recalls that 14th of Adar [February–March] on which Aman, who had "drawn lots" for the death of the Hebrews, saw his plan fail and, instead of slaying, was himself slain).

Unlike the Order on sacrificial worship, this Order is especially important for a knowledge of the New Testament liturgy. The reason is that it tells us about the entire synagogal liturgy and its principal forms and institutions (the sabbath; pilgrimage feasts; lesser feasts). As I said above, although these tractates were not composed until two centuries after Jesus and the first Christian communities, they refer to liturgical and rubrical practices that in all probability were current in the intertestamental period.

—the berakah (benediction), which was the inspiration and expression of Jewish liturgy and prayer, its inner power, and its inexhaustible treasure. The Mishnah devotes the entire first tractate of the first Order to this subject. The tractate is entitled Berakot and its nine chapters are distributed as follows: the first three develop the theme of the shema' Yiśra'el; the fourth and fifth speak of prayer in general; the sixth, seventh, and eighth deal with the birkat ha-mazon (the benediction after a meal, which is the benediction par excellence since it is of biblical origin, as attested by Deut 8:10); the ninth and final chapter deals with other benedictions.

The tractate Berakot is important not simply for its contents but also by reason of its position, for it begins not only the first Order of the Mishnah but the Mishnah in its entirety and therefore the remaining five Orders. Is it an accident that the benedictions are the first subject discussed in the Mishnah, or can we see some deeper inspiration at work? Many have asked why the tractate on benedictions was not made part of the second Order, which deals with the feasts, rather than of the first, which is concerned with "seeds" (Zera'im) or agriculture. Was this due simply to an illogical choice, or does the seeming illogicality conceal a higher logic?

Those who have grasped the dynamism at work in the berakah and understood its importance for the entire biblical and Jewish spiritual universe will have no doubts: the berakah stands at the beginning of the Mishnah (and of its commentary in the Talmud) not by chance but for theological reasons. These are principally two: one justifying its position as the beginning of the entire Mishnah, and another justifying its position as the beginning of the Order devoted to "seeds."

The berakah is the "beginning" of the entire Mishnah in the sense that it is not simply a part or stage of it but rather its root and foundation: it generates and establishes the Mishnah, it explains and justifies it. In other words, this tractate is a logical and theological starting point, and not simply a historicochronological beginning. The entire Torah derives its meaning from the berakah: it is the expression of berakah and calls urgently for it, it evokes and suggests it.

Berakah is also the beginning of the Order dealing with "seeds," that is, with the fruits of human labor and the soil. For berakah involves more than a generic thanking of God; it also means using the "fruits of the earth" in accordance with God's will. To be capable of berakah means being able to live by the logic of gift and sharing, of gratuitousness and participation. For this reason the tractate Berakot is followed by the tractates Pe'ah ("Corner"), Demai ("Doubt"), Kil'aim ("Mixtures"), and Shevi'it ("Seventh Year"), the first two and the last of which deal with the rights of the poor. This is because where berakah exists there can be no injustice and poverty but only equality and brotherhood-sisterhood.

2. The Talmud

Once composed, the Mishnah became the object of study and discussion not only in Palestine, where it originated, but also in Babylon, where there were sizable and flourishing academies (Nehardea, Sura, Pumbedita, Mahoza, etc.). The procedure and study method in these schools was to read an article of the Mishnah and then endeavor to plumb its meaning more fully through discussion and comparison. The Talmud (from the Hebrew root, lmd, to study) can be regarded as the vast collection of these discussions.

If the Mishnah was the textbook of the academies, the Talmud was an extensive critical commentary on it. For this reason the Talmud (the name is an abbreviation of Talmud Torah, "study of the Law") is made up of two parts: the first reproduces the text of the Mishnah, the second is an analysis and further discussion in which internal contradictions are resolved and the whole is brought into harmony with the haggadic tradition. This second part is called the Gemara, an Aramaic word meaning "interpretation" or, more accurately, "completion": it "completes" the Mishnah by shedding light on difficulties and applying its meaning, especially with the aid of midrashic stories.

Talmud Torah, "the study of the Law," was conducted in the great schools and academies. These institutions drew their inspiration, for practical purposes, from one or other of the two great centers of Judaism at that time: Babylon and Jerusalem (the latter was replaced after its destruction by other nearby centers: Jamnia, Caesarea, Sepphoris, Lydda, and Tiberias). Consequently, when the need was felt of putting into writing the discussions of the Mishnaic text, it was natural that there should be two redactions. The result was two Talmuds, one called (not quite accurately) the Jerusalem Talmud, which was compiled probably in the fifth century, and the other the Babylonian Talmud, which was also compiled in the fifth century at the academy in Sura when Rabbi Ashi (d. 427) was its president.

The two Talmuds display many similarities but also important differences. The Palestinian Talmud (as the Jerusalem Talmud is often called) is written in Jewish-Aramaic, with many words and phrases being borrowed from the Greek spoken in Syria and Palestine. It uses a text of the Mishnah that is different (and perhaps older) from that used in the Babylonian Talmud. It comments on only thirty-nine tractates, takes a free approach to the text, and its style is sober by comparison with that of its counterpart.

The Babylonian Talmud is written in Eastern Jewish-Aramaic but with large sections in Hebrew. It omits any commentary on many tractates of the Mishnah (those especially that have to do with the temple and with Levitical practices no longer relevant to Jewish life after the destruction of the temple). It is extremely rigid in its respect for the text and must therefore have recourse at times to very subtle techniques in order to interpret it without additions or alterations. Most notably, it gives greater room to the haggadic tradition.

Both Talmuds begin with a commentary on tractate *Berakot* (this is the only tractate of the first Order that is received and commented on in the Babylonian Talmud). The commentaries are an inexhaustible source for understanding the soul of the Jewish liturgy. The Babylonian commentary is especially rich.

III. THE *SIDDUR* OR PRAYER BOOK

Even the Mishnah is an inadequate source of access to the Jewish liturgy, since it is a primarily halakic or juridical work and does not cite the complete texts of the prayers and rites used in the synagogues or in homes. For this reason, we must go a step further and turn to the prayer books of the Jewish liturgy in which all the official euchological texts are set down. Familiarity with these books is indispensable for a knowledge of the Jewish liturgy not only as it is today but also as it was in the time of Jesus and the early Church.

Let me explain what I mean. The prayer books were not compiled until many centuries after the New Testament writings. Furthermore, many of the prayers in these books, like the order in which they are to be recited, are of uncertain origin and difficult to date. But what was said above of the Mishnah holds also for the prayer books: that the materials are from times far earlier than the period of compilation. The prayer book as we have it today goes back to about the tenth century of the Christian era. But, as J. Petuchowski says, "many of the prayers went back to the first century and beyond."[8] The same author says, with no less validity, that "in spite of all the variety [that is, differences between the Babylonian and Palestinian liturgies] the basic rubrics of the synagogue service have remained constant from at least the first century, if not before."[9] These statements explain why in a chapter on the New Testament liturgy I have referred to texts that are so far removed in time from the period when the Christian Church came into existence.

Let me repeat: The prayer book is the principal book used by the praying Jew. In its turns of phrase and even in many of its prayers we can find echoes of Jesus himself and the early communities. For this reason, it must be regarded, along with the Mishnah, as an irreplaceable source for understanding the prayer of Jesus and the sparse information that can be gotten from the New Testament.

I. The First Official Prayer Books

While tradition attributes the first "Prayer Book" to Moses (b. Ros. Has. 17b says that God showed Moses the "Seder Tefillah"), the first historically attested authentic compilation of official Jewish prayers was the work of Rav Amram Gaon in 785 A.D. It was known as a Seder (a Hebrew word meaning "order," "orderly sequence") or Siddur ("ordering," "putting in order") or, more rarely, Mahzor. These words presuppose a following tefillot ("prayers"), so that the complete title would be Seder tefillot, "Order of Prayers." From the ninth century on this was the official title which most Jews gave to their prayer book. An exception was the German Jews and the Sephardic Jews, who called it simply Tefillah, "Prayer."

Amram was Gaon (President; the literal meaning of Gaon is "great or illustrious one") of the academy at Sura in Babylonia and, as such, was at that time spiritual head of all Jews throughout the world. He was asked to organize into a single document all the prayers used by the various dispersed Jewish communities. The immediate source of the request was Spanish Jewish scholars, who thought that the existence of a single prayer book would better ensure the unity of Judaism and agreement on its spiritual values.

In response to this request Amram made a compilation which,

because of its editor's prestige, captured the attention of the entire Jewish world. It was publicized by countless copies, many of which (admittedly revised and expanded) survived until 1865, the year in which the book was printed for the first time in Warsaw.

But because Amram's *Siddur* was a response to a group of Jewish scholars, it met their needs rather than the needs of the people. For this reason it was followed almost immediately by another, that of Rav Saadia Gaon (882–942), the greatest of the teachers in the Babylonian academy at Sura and one of the greatest geniuses of the Jewish Middle Ages. As the author explains in his preface, his collection was inspired by the concrete needs of Jewish communities (and not by the needs of the rabbis, as was that of Rav Amram). He was worried by the liturgical anarchy which threatened the Jewish communities, and he therefore collected and arranged an "order of prayers [which he wanted to see] used everywhere and by everyone."[10]

In his work he followed certain criteria:

—texts to be selected on the basis of their authority, which in turn derived from their unchallenged and documented use;

—restoration of the original and uncontaminated form of the texts, whether these dated from the pre-exilic or the post-exilic period;

—elimination of additions subsequently made by individuals, groups, or schools in order to meet the specific needs of communities, centers, or trends;

—addition of some poetic texts (his own among them) that expand the traditional repertory;

—arrangement of the texts within an explanatory theological framework, and their further division according to a daily (daily prayers and offices) and yearly (liturgies for the feasts) rhythm.

I have dwelt at length on these two *Suddurim*, not only because they still supply the basic structure of the Jewish prayer book, which is "essentially . . . one from China to Peru,"[11] but also and above all because they are a necessary step in the effort to understand the liturgical universe that has sustained the Jewish world from the beginning, including the time of Jesus.

2. Before the Siddurim of Rav Amram Gaon and Rav Saadia Gaon

We must not think that before Amram Gaon and Saadia Gaon there were no prayer books (passed on either orally or in the form of notes). The *Siddurim* of these two men were in fact compilations of already existing and even ancient materials and not a creation out of nothing. This is why Jewish scholar Evelyn Garfiel could write: "It is reasonably certain that by the early days of the Second Temple, about 400 B.C.E., some form of group prayer service existed among the Jews. That service included recitation of Psalms, the *Shema*, possibly some other prayers, and readings from the Torah."[12]

Those *Siddurim*, which were compiled, learned, and transmitted orally, came into being and reached completion in connection with the "synagogues," the weekly gatherings that probably originated during the Babylonian exile, when the Jews, far removed from their homeland, assembled to read the Torah and listen to the prophets.

There are divergent views among scholars as to the origin of the synagogue, but this much is certain: from the post-exilic period on, another form of worship came into existence alongside the worship in the temple. Worship in the temple was administered by the priestly class and was far from meeting the needs of the people. The new form of worship, on the other hand, was non-priestly and democratic; it was based not on sacrifice but on prayer and Torah.

This new form of worship would subsequently become known as "synagogal" and would develop during the centuries between the rebuilding of the Second Temple, 520–515 B.C., and its destruction in 70 A.D. It would finally prevail and become the most authentic expression of the Jewish liturgy. It can be said to have achieved its adequate structure by the first century of the Christian era: "By the generation after the destruction of the Temple in 70 C.E., the synagogue service was fairly well established, though there was as yet no written *Prayer Book* recording in one place all the prayers then already in use, nor any single written record of the order of the various services."[13]

It is this liturgy, already "organized" and to some extent structured, that flowed into the *Siddurim* of Amram and Saadia and through them reaches us.

3. *Recent* Siddurim

Down the centuries the prayer books of Amram Gaon and Saadia Gaon were gradually enriched with new texts and rites, especially after the invention of printing. The additions and new compositions (usually known as *piyyuṭim*, "poems," the word itself derived from Greek) became so numerous that the *Siddurim* had sometimes to be printed in more than one volume, as we see from the apology which one publisher prefixed to a *Siddur* of 1600: "Observing that the material in this book is constantly increasing . . . and has become too cumbersome to be carried to the synagogue, the present publisher, with a pure heart, decided to print the *Siddur* in two volumes."[14]

This overabundant, sometimes muddled and mediocre output led in the last century to a call for revision and simplification of the *Siddurim*. The result was, among others, *The Authorized Daily Prayer Book of the United Hebrew Congregation of the British Commonwealth*, which was published, with an English translation, in 1890 and recently revised in 1962. Other prayer books were published in other countries and to meet the needs of new currents of Jewish thought (Reformed, Orthodox, and Conservative Judaism).

In the pages that follow I shall refer chiefly to the prayer book of Joseph H. Hertz,[15] which was originally published in 1948 and was revised in 1975.

Those not at home in this field may well find that, despite its Hebrew name, *Siddur* ("Order"), the prayer book is an "inextricable confusion."[16] I shall therefore describe its usual structure.

It is divided into three parts: the daily liturgy, the liturgy of the sabbath and feasts, and the liturgy for special occasions, including sickness and death.

Daily prayers are in turn organized around the three principal times of the day (morning, afternoon, and evening) and always include, in addition to a set of opening and closing texts, the *Shema' Yisra'el* (the supreme act of faith) and the *tefillah* (which is the basic prayer).

The second part of the prayer book contains the prayers for the sabbath and feasts. The most important ritual moments óf the sabbath are: the lighting of lamps, the "welcome" of the sabbath, the synagogal service for Friday and Saturday, the service of readings, the conclusion of the sabbath, and the *havdalah* (the farewell to the sabbath). The feasts are presented in the following order: *pesah* (Passover), *shavu'ot* (Pentecost), *sukkot* (Tabernacles), *rosh ha-shanah* (New Year's), *yom kippur* (Day of Atonement), *hannukah* (feast of Lights), and *purim* (feast of Lots).

The third part of the prayer book contains the prayers connected with the most important events of life: meals (including the *birkat ha-mazon*, the thanksgiving prayer par excellence of the Jewish liturgy), marriage, sickness, death, funerals, and so on.

Chapter 2

The Structure of the Jewish Liturgy

G.E. Biddle, looking at the prayer book from the viewpoint of a "stranger," speaks, not unfairly, of a bewildering confusion:

> There appears to be no design in the composition, little sense of order, no central culminating point, scant feeling for proportion, no just estimation of values, no salient features—nothing, in short, by which [the stranger] may get a grip of the thing! an inextricable confusion; a prodigious tangle!
>
> But the confusion is not so badly confounded after all, presupposing that sympathy and respectful attention are exercised. The student will then gradually discern more and more of order *within* the chaos, and will find that, in common with all human productions, this noble volume is explainable and explicable without great difficulty in accordance with the genius of the people to whom it owes its origin. For the Jewish Prayer Book is what it is because its compilers and contributors were *what they were*. Its pages completely exhibit well marked features of Jewish character.[1]

At first sight, then, the Jewish liturgical universe may seem disorderly and full of overlaps. More careful observation, however, shows that it is in fact rigorously and thoroughly structured. In this context a distinction must be made between the generative nucleus or "foundation stone"[2] of the Jewish liturgy and its triple carrying structure. The generative nucleus is the *berakah* and its carrying structure consists of the *shema' Yiśra'el*, the *tefillah*, and the *miqrat Torah* ("reading of the Torah").

This logically ordered whole can be visualized as made up ideally of three concentric circles. The center is the *berakah*, the generative nucleus; the first circle is the *shema' Yiśra'el*, the second is the *tefillah*, and the third is the *miqrat Torah*. The relation between the

33

nucleus and the circles is not static but dynamic, and the relation of
the circles to each other is one not of juxtaposition but of recapitula-
tion, enrichment, and amplification. Just as in a musical composition
the same theme is repeated in ever new and original forms, so the
several structures (whether principal or secondary) of Jewish prayer
give varied expression to the ever new and inexhaustible meaning
contained in the berakah.

This "architecture of the service" remains unchanged at the
center of every liturgical action, whether individual or synagogal: in
morning, afternoon, and evening prayer; on weekdays and the sabbath; on the feasts and special anniversaries. From the time of Jesus
(and even before) down to our own time this has been and continues
to be the inner pattern of Jewish prayer, in all countries and in all
rites, and "neither minor variations nor the major additions for certain special occasions nor the prayers added by later generations can
blur that pattern for those who understand the essential structure of
the service."[3]

The pattern is always and inevitably present, even if with constantly new and original modalities, whether in the span of the week
(Monday, Thursday, and, above all, Saturday) or the span of the year
(pesah, shavu'ot, sukkot, and so on), whether in the context of the
family or the context of the synagogue.

Since Jewish prayer has the triple carrying structure which I
have mentioned, I must study each of its parts, but must begin with
the berakah, which is the hidden soul of it all. The present chapter
therefore has four parts: the first will speak of the berakah, the second of the shema' Yiśra'el, the third of the tefillah, and the fourth of
the reading of the Torah.

I. THE IMPORTANCE AND MEANING OF THE BERAKAH

Berakah (usually translated as "blessing" or "benediction," or at
times as "wonder-praise-gratitude") is one of those words in which
the entire richness and originality of Jewish thought is summed up. It
is arguably the word that best sums up Jewish anthropology, that is,
its way of situating human beings in relation to God and the world.

The berakah conveys a threefold relationship: with God, with
the world, and with our fellow human beings. But the relationship is
really not threefold: it is single, but may be described as triangular.
Not only does the berakah militate against any separation of God
from human beings (so that theology becomes speculative) and the

world (in a disincarnate theology), or human beings from God (an atheistic anthropology) and the world (a pseudo-spiritual anthropology), or the world from God (a secularized cosmology) and human beings (a cosmology geared to estheticism). On the contrary, it keeps these three points of reference united and inseparable and states clearly the conditions thanks to which they remain in a truthful relationship.

As far as human beings and the world are concerned, God is the "source" and the "norm": he places them in existence and determines the ways in which they are to achieve fruition and bear fruit. Human beings for their part are the interpreters of God and the world, but also the beneficiaries of these, for they are the objects of God's care and recipients of the fruits of the earth. The world, finally, in its relation to God and human beings is sacrament and gift: sign of God's good will and concrete gift to human beings.

In the prayer of blessing Jews acknowledge these three poles and the true nature of their relationship with each other. When they say "Blessed art thou, O Lord, for the fruits of the earth . . ." they are acknowledging God as origin and "owner" of all things; the world as a gift to be accepted and shared; human beings as their brothers and sisters with whom they are to share in the one banquet of life. The *berakah* thus sums up the real purpose of the world and thereby asserts itself as a condition for making the Kingdom of God a reality. Without it the world remains bleak and opaque, closed in upon itself, and given over to evil: "He who uses the good things of this world without reciting a blessing profanes what is holy."[4] Thanks to the *berakah*, the world recovers its original splendor, showing itself to be in all things the dwelling place of meaning, that is, of the sacred.

I. The Parable of the Alphabet

The centrality of the *berakah* in Jewish thought finds effective expression in the following parable, which has for its personages the twenty-two personified letters of the Hebrew alphabet.

The reader will see that no effort at thematic reflection, however exacting, has ever succeeded in capturing the axiological importance of the *berakah* as effectively as this parable with its poetic tale.

When God was about to create the world by His word, the twenty-two letters of the alphabet descended from the terrible and august crown of God whereon they were engraved with a pen of flaming fire. They stood round about God, and one after the other spake and entreated, "Create the world through me!" The first to step forward was the letter Taw. It said: "O Lord of the world! May it be Thy will to create Thy world through me, seeing that it is through me that Thou wilt give the Torah to Israel by the hand of Moses, as it is written, 'Moses commanded us the Torah.' " The Holy One, blessed be He, made reply, and said, "No!" Taw asked, "Why not?" and God answered: "Because in days to come I shall place thee as a sign of death on the foreheads of men."[5] As soon as Taw heard these words issue from the mouth of the Holy One, blessed be He, it retired from His presence disappointed.

The Shin then stepped forward, and pleaded: "O Lord of the world, create Thy world through me, seeing that Thine own name Shaddai begins with me." Unfortunately, it is also the first letter of Shaw, lie, and of Sheker, false-hood, and that incapacitated it.

Resh had no better luck. It was pointed out that it was the initial letter of Ra', wicked, and Rasha', evil, and after that the distinction it enjoys of being the first letter in the Name of God, Raḥum, the Merciful, counted for naught.

The Ḳof was rejected, because Ḳelalah, curse, outweighs the advantage of being the first in Ḳadosh, the Holy One.

In vain did Ẓadde call attention to Ẓaddik, the Righteous One; there was Ẓarot, the misfortunes of Israel, to testify against it.

Pe had Podeh, redeemer, to its credit, but Pesha', trans-gression, reflected dishonor upon it.

'Ain was declared unfit, because, though it begins 'An-awah, humility, it performs the same service for 'Erwah, immorality.

Samek said: "O Lord, may it be Thy will to begin the creation with me, for Thou art called Samek, after me, the Upholder of all that fall." But God said: "Thou art needed in the place in which thou art; thou must continue to uphold all that fall."

Nun introduces Ner, "the lamp of the Lord," which is "the spirit of men," but it also introduces Ner, "the lamp of the wicked," which will be put out by God.

Mem starts Melek, king, one of the titles of God. As it is

the first letter of Mehumah, confusion, as well, it had no chance of accomplishing its desire.

The claim of Lamed bore its refutation within itself. It advanced the argument that it was the first letter of Luḥot, the celestial tables for the Ten Commandments; it forgot that these tables were shivered in pieces by Moses.

Kaf was sure of victory. Kisseh, the throne of God, Kabod, His honor, and Keter, His crown, all begin with it. God had to remind it that He would smite together His hands, Kaf, in despair over the misfortunes of Israel.

Yod at first sight seemed the appropriate letter for the beginning of creation, on account of its association with Yah, God, if only Yeẓer ha-Ra', the evil inclination, had not happened to begin with it, too.

Ṭet is identified with Ṭob, the good. However, the truly good is not in this world; it belongs to the world to come.

Ḥet is the first letter of Ḥanun, the Gracious One; but this advantage is offset by its place in the word for sin, Ḥaṭṭat.

Zain suggests Zakkor, remembrance, but it is itself the word for weapon, the doer of mischief.

Waw and He compose the Ineffable Name of God; they are therefore too exalted to be pressed into the service of the mundane world.

If Dalet had stood only for Dabar, the Divine Word, it would have been used, but it also stands for Din, justice, and under the rule of law without love the world have fallen to ruin.

Finally, in spite of reminding one of Gadol, great, Gimel would not do, because Gemul, retribution, starts with it.

After the claims of all these letters had been disposed of, Bet stepped before the Holy One, blessed be He, and pleaded before Him: "O Lord of the world! May it be Thy will create Thy world through me, seeing that all the dwellers in the world give praise daily through me, as it is said, 'Blessed be the Lord forever. Amen, and Amen.' " The Holy One, blessed be He, at once granted the petition of Bet. He said, "Blessed be he that cometh in the name of the Lord." And He created His world though Bet, as it is said, "Bereshit God created the heaven and the earth."

The only letter that had refrained from urging its claims was the modest Alef, and God rewarded it later for its humility by giving it the first place in the Decalogue.[6]

2. A Benediction for Everything

The power of narrative language enables the parable of the alphabet to express in a striking way the central function of the *berakah* in Jewish prayer and spirituality. Of all the letters of the alphabet (which is a metaphor for the entire universe of values) it is the letter *bet* that created the world, and it did so because it is the first letter of the word *berakah*. One way of saying that the world is based on *berakah* is to say that it reveals its identity and discloses its meaning only to those who know how to say a *berakah*. For this reason, according to the Jewish tradition a *berakah* should be pronounced in every situation:

> One who sees a place where miracles have been worked in behalf of Israel should say: "Blessed is he who worked miracles for our fathers in this place." One who sees a place in which a foreign worship was rooted out should say: "Blessed is he who rooted foreign worship out of our land." Of comets, storms, thunder, wind, and lightning one should say: "Blessed is he whose strength and power fill the world." Of mountains, hills, rivers, and deserts one should say: "Blessed is he who accomplishes the work of creation." R. Jehudah says: "One who sees the ocean should say: 'Blessed is he who made the ocean,' each time he sees it." Of rains and good news one should say: "Blessed is he who is good and kind," and of bad news one should say: "Blessed is the truthful Judge."
>
> One who has built a new house and bought new furniture should say: "Blessed is he who has given us life, preserved us in being, and brought us to this moment." Human beings should bless (the Lord) for evil just as they do for good, and for good just as they bless him for evil. If one cries out to the Lord because of something that has happened, that prayer is vain.[7]

Of all the benedictions raised up to God, those connected with the fruits of the earth are especially important. Before eating bread a Jew says: "Blessed art thou, O Lord our God, King of the Universe, who bringest forth bread from the earth" (963). Before drinking a cup of wine he says: "Blessed art thou, O Lord our God, King of the universe, who createst the fruit of the vine" (985). When he sees grain: "Blessed art thou, O Lord, who createst the foods of the earth." When using a perfume: "Blessed art thou, O Lord, who createst perfumed herbs." And so on.

There is nothing, therefore, that is not an occasion for a blessing. Even negative things, such as injustice or sickness, should inspire not a withdrawal into the self or despair, but rather blessing and praise. Nor should anyone think that this readiness to bless is typical only of the naive or the simple. When S.Y. Agnon (1880–1970) received news of his Nobel Prize (1966), he immediately uttered a benediction: "Blessed art thou, O Lord, who art good and doest good." And when he went to Stockholm for the prize and saw the King of Sweden, he recited another benediction: "Blessed art thou, O Lord, who makest mortals sharers in thy glory."

These examples already make one thing clear: berakah is the expression of an unhindered mind that can see the whole of reality in a new light. It is the greatest of human activities because it has the power to "make all things new" (see Rev 21:5). It is continually urged upon Jews, not out of a taste for infantile casuistry, but because of insight into its revelatory aspect. As in the gospel parable, the berakah is the true "treasure" that makes everything else superfluous or secondary.

3. The Berakah for the Torah

Jews bless the Lord not only for the fruits of the earth but also for the gift of the Torah: "Blessed art thou, O Lord our God, King of the universe, who hast given us the Law of truth, and hast planted everlasting life in our midst. Blessed art thou, O Lord, Giver of the Torah" (487). God is blessed for the Torah because, no less than the fruits of the earth, it nourishes and delights the human heart. It even nourishes and delights more than do the fruits of the earth. The latter by themselves are not enough for human beings who live "by everything that proceeds out of the mouth of the Lord" (Deut 8:3; see Mt 4:4). The Torah is the "more" of which scripture speaks here: not a "more" added to the fruits of the earth, but a "more" that reveals the fullness of fruition and meaning. It reveals the intrinsic purpose of the good things of the earth, showing them to be mediations and gifts of the divine benevolence.

If the entire Torah is an occasion for berakah on the part of Jews, this is especially true of its fundamental contents: the covenant, the temple, and the messianic promise. Particularly important are the *berakot* connected with the promise, for they help us understand the apparently ambiguous rabbinic command that Jews "should bless the Lord for evil just as they bless him for good."[8] In face of painful or tragic situations Jews are called upon to bless, not because they enjoy suffering, but they preserve a firm and unshakable messianic hope. This hope alone makes it possible to bless God amid negation and in the face of negation. This act of faith redeems and overcomes all that is negative; the latter is victorious on the historical level but is declared the loser at the eschatological level. The offering of blessing to God "for evil" is not a gesture of submission to fate and inevitability but an act of rebellion against the seemingly victorious logic of destiny.

4. Berakah *and Miracle*

The prayer of benediction, inspired by the fruits of the earth and the gift of the Torah, presupposes and gives expression to a sense of admiration and wonder. According to a widespread view, the word "miracle" applies to everything that is contrary to natural laws and appears as "extra-ordinary." The rising of the sun is not seen as miraculous because it happens every day and is therefore considered to be normal; the same is true of a flower that emits its perfume, a flowing river, or a field of grain. But if people are present at an instantaneous cure which seems to suspend the operation of the natural order of things, they cry "miracle," because such things do not happen "regularly" and are "outside" the ordinary.

Such views belittle and betray the biblical conception of things, in which "miracles" are to be found not outside the ordinary but at the innermost, hidden heart of the ordinary. A miracle is not something exceptional; rather it is anything whatsoever (from the most quotidian and trite to the most rare and unimaginable) when understood in light of the ultimate purpose that gives it existence and sustains it in being.

The world and the things in it have two faces: one that is immediately apparent and one that is hidden and foundational. At the level of immediate perception bread is a means of sustenance, and the sun a source of light. At a deeper level, however, they are "signs" of God's benevolence and expressions of his creative love, for, in addition to sustaining and giving light, they refer human beings to a generous, magnanimous Thou. At the first level, things remain quotidian, ordinary, taken for granted; at the second, they take on new meanings and become "extra-ordinary."

The passage from the first to the second is effected by the act of blessing; a benediction rises above the sheer factuality of things and leads us into their inner core where they embody the intentionality that brought them into being. A benediction is a reflection of the light hidden within things. Where *berakah* is present, it creates miracles; where it is absent, opaqueness grows.

The author of the Book of Exodus tells how one evening during their wandering in the wilderness the Israelites saw quails come up and cover the camp. Then, "in the morning dew lay round about the camp. And when the dew had gone up, there was on the face of the wilderness a fine, flake-like thing, fine as hoarfrost on the ground. When the people of Israel saw it, they said to one another, 'What is it?' [Hebrew, *Man hu'*?]. For they did not know what it was. And Moses said, 'It is the bread which the Lord has given you to eat' " (Ex 16:14–15).

In the presence of all things we should ask, as the Israelites did at sight of the dew, "What is it?" and like Moses we should answer: "It is the bread which the Lord has given you to eat." For those capable of *berakah* everything is "manna," everything is miraculous. The Baal Shem said: "Replete is the world with a spiritual radiance, replete with sublime and marvelous secrets. But a small hand held against the eye hides it all."[9]

Blessings have the power to remove this "small hand" and make us see the world as "replete with a spiritual radiance."

5. Berakah *and Awe*

A *berakah* does not have for its purpose to give a thing certain powers or qualities which it did not have before, although this is the meaning which "bless" has acquired in the Christian tradition, where "to bless" means "to bless things" rather than "to bless God for the things he has given to us." The purpose of a *berakah* is to reveal the ultimate, deepest, and innermost identity of a thing, namely, that it exists in relation to its creator and is a tangible sign of his attentiveness and care. This perception of things is brought about by *berakah* and consists of connecting things with the purpose of God in creating them. It finds expression in the Bible in the word "awe," which A.J. Heschel analyzes as follows:

> Awe is an intuition of the creaturely dignity of all things and their preciousness to God; a realization that things not only

are what they are but also stand, however remotely, for
something absolute. Awe is a sense for the transcendence,
the reference everywhere to Him who is beyond all things.
It is an insight better conveyed in attitudes than in words.[10]

While awe gives the ability to understand things in their connection with God, it also, and at the same time, gives insight into new
meanings hidden in individual events.

The meaning of awe is to realize that life takes place under
wide horizons, horizons that range beyond the span of an
individual life or even the life of a nation, a generation, or an
era. Awe enables us to perceive in the world intimations of
the divine, to sense in small things the beginning of infinite
significance, to sense the ultimate in the common and the
simple, to feel in the rush of the passing the stillness of the
eternal.
        In analyzing or evaluating an object, we think and
judge from a particular point of view. The psychologist,
economist, and chemist pay attention to different aspects of
the same object. Such is the limitation of the mind that it
can never see three sides of a building at the same time. The
danger begins when, completely caught in one perspective,
we attempt to consider a part as the whole. In the twilight of
such perspectivism, even the sight of the part is distorted.
What we cannot comprehend by analysis, we become
aware of in awe. When we "stand still and consider," we
face and witness what is immune to analysis.[11]

Berakah is born of awe and produces awe because it links things
with God's love by situating them in his creative and provident presence. A berakah transforms the profane into the sacred, objects into
gifts, and things into words of love. Thanks to the berakah, the universe becomes an immense sanctuary into which we are to enter
with veneration and as contemplatives.

6. Berakah *and Gift*

If we try to give conceptual expression to the meaning of this
new perception which berakah brings, we may distinguish various
levels.
        First of all, "to bless God for bread" is to acknowledge to God the
fatherliness of it rather than to the strength and intelligence of hu-

man beings. Bread belongs not to human beings but to God; here, however, "belongs to" signifies meaning rather than possession. Benedictions prevent us from claiming the rights of ownership over things and cause us, instead, to attribute them to God; we renounce a relation to them based on possession or production and declare that the source of their intentionality and meaning is to be found outside of us men and women. A benediction thus sets in motion a real "epistemological break": it takes away from human beings power over things and puts it in the hands of God. This, then, is the first effect of a benediction: a shift from one's personal center to God.

If God is the real "owner" of things, then the only true relationship of human beings to things must be that of beneficiaries. This fact brings us to the second level of the restructuring effected by the berakah: a shift from possession to receptivity. The world does not belong to human beings, but they may make use of it; things do not belong to them, but they may use them; they have not made the house, but they may live in it.

But if we are to dispose ourselves for receptivity by renouncing the spirit of autonomy and possessiveness, we must be ready for gifts, that is, have the ability to understand things according to the logic of gratuitousness. Now we are at the third level of the restructuring effected by benedictions: the shift from object to gift. A benediction restores to the created order its character of gift, while the absence of benediction plunges things back into the thick gloom wherein they are simply instruments and wares.

This "transfiguring" power of benedictions, apart from which things are reified and given a purely monetary value, is given ironical expression in the midrash on a supposed dialogue between Abraham and his guests.

> Abraham received the travelers as guests, and when they had eaten and drunk, he said to them: "Offer a benediction." They asked: "How?" He answered: "Say: Blessed be the eternal God because we have eaten what is his." If the guests agreed and offered the benediction, they would have eaten and drunk and departed. If they did not agree to offer the benediction, he would say to them: "Pay what you owe."[12]

The deeper meaning of the midrash is clear: where there is benediction, there is gratuitousness; where benediction is absent, relations based on commodities and payment prevail ("pay what you owe").

There is a fourth and final operation set in motion by the prayer of benediction: the shift from manipulation to obedient listening. For if things are indeed gifts of God, they must be used with respect for the giver and docility toward him; his love must be acknowledged and there must be compliance with the intentionality of things. This means concretely that things must not be used in accord with the plans of self-centered individuals or nations but in accord with the plan of God himself, which is a plan of universal sharing.

The revelation that reality is a gift is at the heart of the biblical message. This fact is also attested by the Christian scriptures, which are focused on the experience of Jesus as dead and risen. Thus Peter says: "By his divine power, he has lavished on us all things we need for life and true devotion, through the knowledge of him who has called us by his own glory and goodness" (2 Pet 1:3, NJB). As himself the supreme gift of God's love to human beings, Jesus not only reveals that reality is a gift; he also sums it up in his person and his mystery.

7. Berakah *and Sharing*

The hermeneutic of gift, to which the berakah leads, is not applicable solely at the psychological and individualistic level. Rather, it commits one to a profoundly ethical outlook and is translated into specific social choices.

When the Israelites saw "on the face of the wilderness a fine, flake-like thing, fine as hoarfrost on the ground" (Ex 16:14), they asked one another: "*Man hu*'?—What is it?" Moses replied: "It is the bread which the Lord has given you to eat" (Ex 16:15). But to this explanatory answer he immediately added a command and condition: "This is what the Lord has commanded: 'Gather of it, every man of you, as much as he can eat; you shall take an omer apiece [a unit of measure equal to about four liters], according to the number of persons whom each of you has in his tent' " (Ex 16:16). What is given may not be hoarded but only accepted and enjoyed according to one's capacity. "And the people of Israel did so; they gathered, some more, some less. But when they measured it with an omer, he that gathered much had nothing left over, and he that gathered little had no lack; each gathered according to what he could eat" (Ex 16:17–18).

The command not to gather more than is required by one's personal need is followed by another that forbids hoarding for the morrow: "And Moses said to them: 'Let no man leave any of it till the morning' " (Ex 16:19). Not only should one not have "more," but one should also not be concerned for "the morrow," for both the "more" and "the morrow" contradict the logic of gift and hinder the joy of fruition.

When things are hoarded in obedience to the logic of "more" and "for the morrow," they lose their freshness, and enjoyment of them is no longer possible; they become signs of death. This is the lesson of the biblical story, which goes on to tell how the people disobeyed Moses' two commands and what the consequence was: "But they did not listen to Moses; some left part of it till the morning, and it bred worms and became foul; and Moses was angry with them" (Ex 16:20).

The logic of ownership is destructive in two ways: it disfigures the face of things ("it bred worms and became foul"), and it elicits prophetic anger ("Moses was angry with them"); it destroys reality and offends God. It destroys reality by depriving it of its God-given purpose, namely, to be for the enjoyment of all; it offends God because it denies the good will by which he cares for all his creatures and provides for them.

The manna shared (the manna being a symbol of all the fruits of the earth) is a bread of life ("it is the bread which the Lord has given you to eat"), while the manna hoarded (a symbol of all forms of undue and unjust hoarding) is a seed of destruction ("it bred worms and became foul").

The passage is an exceptionally effective parable that may be seen as summing up an entire treatise on social morality.

8. Berakah *and Joy*

In addition to expressing an understanding that reality is a gift to be received and shared, the prayer of benediction also expresses a sense of joy and well-being. The ability to "bless God" is indeed the ability to give thanks, but, prior to this, it is the ability to express a sense of plenitude: the plenitude of those making the divine intention their own and carrying it out in the world, having found and entered the house of being. A berakah is a sign of a heart at peace, a heart inhabited and filled by meaning. The joy which berakah bestows is twofold: the joy of knowing oneself to be the object of the divine good will, and the joy that comes from seeing the world as a parable of unity and harmony.

Everything that exists, from blade of grass to galaxy, is the expression of God's creative and ordering will that transforms chaos into cosmos and that can say of each part: "It is good" (see Gen 1:10).

According to a beautiful Jewish legend, God had created all things
"in mutual embrace," so much so that he found it difficult to separate the waters (Gen 1:6):

> The separation of the waters into upper and lower waters
> was the only act of the sort done by God in connection with
> the work of creation. All other acts were unifying. It there-
> fore caused some difficulties. When God commanded, "Let
> the waters be gathered together, unto one place, and let the
> dry land appear," certain parts refused to obey. They em-
> braced each other all the more closely. In His wrath at the
> waters, God determined to let the whole of creation resolve
> itself into chaos again. . . . Then began the singer of God's
> praises: "O Lord of the world, in days to come Thy creatures
> will sing praises without end to Thee, they will bless Thee
> boundlessly, and they will glorify Thee without measure.
> Thou wilt set Abraham apart from all mankind as Thine
> own; one of his sons Thou wilt call 'My first-born'; and his
> descendants will take the yoke of Thy kingdom upon them-
> selves. . . . And now I beseech Thee, have pity upon Thy
> world, destroy it not, for if Thou destroyest it, who will fulfil
> Thy will?" God was pacified; He withdrew the command
> ordaining the destruction of the world, but the waters He
> put under the mountains, to remain there forever. . . .
>   The second day of creation was an untoward day in
> more than the one respect that it introduced a breach where
> before there had been nothing but unity; for it was the day
> that also saw the creation of hell. Therefore God could not
> say of this day as of the others, that He "saw that it was
> good." A division may be necessary, but it cannot be
> called good.[13]

Joy springs from the cosmic, universal embrace, from consciousness of that "mutual embrace" of things that is bestowed by berakah.

9. The Connection Between Berakah and Petition

The Jewish liturgy (like the Christian) is structured around two
focal points: not only berakah but also appeal or petition. Jews at
prayer not only praise God for his wonderful deeds and gifts but also
beg him to supply their needs and forgive their infidelities. Praise

and appeal, admiration and petition, thanksgiving and entreaty: these are the two focal points of Jewish prayer, whether private or communal. These same two foci give the Book of Psalms its structure, for many of the psalms are hymns of praise, while others are prayers of petition, and still others combine praise and petition. But the two foci or poles are not equal in value or importance. The prayer of praise is logically prior to and more important than the prayer of petition.

The prayer of benediction is the perfect and complete form of prayer. It situates God and human beings in their ultimate, ontological reality: God as the one who creates and bestows good things, and human beings as those who receive and acknowledge these. But in their everyday life and in the course of their history human beings experience not only the good but its opposite: darkness, injustice, oppression, sin, death, and so on. It is in this context, where they come to realize the gap between God's plan and its execution, between Edenic creation and Adamic disobedience, that the prayer of petition arises. Prayer of petition is not opposed to the prayer of benediction but presupposes it and, at the same time, is ordered to it and finds its purpose in it.

The rabbis teach that when the Messiah comes, "all prayers will cease except the prayer of thanksgiving, and this will never cease."[14] The prayer of petition belongs to unredeemed time and meets a twofold need. First and foremost, it gives the believer strength in face of the gap between God's plan and the rejections of it in human history. At every point the Bible always promised peace and prosperity to human beings who are upright, docile, and obedient to the divine will. And yet, too, at all periods of history, the just are constantly vanquished, as is attested by the story of Job, who stands for all just human beings afflicted by hatred and injustice (not least the six million Jews burned in the Nazi crematoria). The prayer of petition sustains the "poor" in their ordeal: it helps them retain their trust in God and prevents them from succumbing in the face of rejection; it gives them assurance of the final victory of the divine goodness and prevents them from despairing in the face of defeat.

But this strength which the prayer of petition gives is always ordered to praise (and here we have the second demand made by this form of prayer). If the poor call upon God for help, they do so in order better to "praise and thank" him. "Turn, O Lord, save my life; deliver me for the sake of thy steadfast love. For in death there is no remembrance of thee; in Sheol who can give thee praise?" (Ps 6:4–5;

see Ps 30:10; 88:12–13; 115:17; Is 38:18). The ultimate purpose of every petition (whether for an individual healing or for the deliverance of Jerusalem) is to enable the petitioner to fulfill his or her vocation, which is to praise and thank.

10. The Berakah Formula

Maimonides divides the various formulas of benediction into three classes, each with its special structure: benedictions inspired by concrete objects ("good things"); benedictions inspired by joy springing from observance of the Torah; and benedictions not inspired by any particular occasion and expressing either petition or gratitude.

1) *Benedictions inspired by concrete "good things."* These are the simplest benedictions. They begin with the formula: "Blessed art thou, O Lord our God, King of the universe." They end with mention of the thing or experience that inspired them; for example, in the benediction before a meal: "who bringest forth bread out of the earth"; or before drinking a cup of wine: "who createst the fruit of the vine."

2) *Benedictions inspired by joy in the Torah.* These are the benedictions recited before carrying out a prescription; they begin with some such formula as this: "Blessed art thou, O Lord our God, King of the universe, who hast hallowed us by thy commandments, and commanded us. . . ." The formula goes on then to mention the particular prescription, for example, ". . . to kindle the Sabbath light."

3) *Benedictions not inspired by any particular occasion and expressing either petition or gratitude.* These are the most common blessings of the liturgy, whether public or private, and differ from the foregoing in content and form. In form, they begin and end with the same words: "Blessed art thou, O Lord." Their content consists of varied statements located between the opening and closing benedictions.

There is one more observation to be made regarding the literary formula of the *berakah*. A benediction usually uses two different forms of the verb: one which addresses God directly ("Blessed art thou, O Lord"), and one which speaks of him in the third person ("who has hallowed us by his commandments"). Why this linguistic inconsistency? The rabbis offer a provocative explanation. The directly personal part of the prayer ("Blessed art thou, O Lord") expresses the direct and dialogical relationship with God, the consciousness of his loving, paternal closeness to us. But, no matter how close he is to us, God always remains the Wholly Other and not subject to human logic and its requirements. The second, indirectly personal part of the prayer ("who has hallowed us") gives expression to this second awareness, which does not deny the first but presupposes and completes it.

A *berakah* thus expresses at one and the same time the nearness of God and his remoteness from us, his immanence and his transcendence. The believer confesses that God is at once present and absent: present even though absent, absent even though present. A God who was only "present" would become an "idol" for human beings; instead of serving him they would make use of him. A God who was only absent would become alien to human beings; instead of calling upon him they would ignore him. By confessing him to be simultaneously personal ("thou") and impersonal ("his"), the *berakah* maps out the space in which human beings discover the Mystery, receive it, and adore it.

II. THE FIRST STRUCTURAL UNIT: THE *SHEMA' YIŚRA'EL*

If the *berakah* is the soul of Jewish prayer, the *shema' Yiśra'el* is its first structural unit. I call it a "unit," because, though made up of several parts, it is liturgically a single prayer. I speak of it as "structural," because the parts making it up are not simply juxtaposed but obey a dynamic thrust toward harmony and coherence.

1. Composition and Origin

The *shema' Yiśra'el* is composed of three passages from the Bible and some benedictions that precede and follow the passages. It is not easy to determine how and when the passages were chosen and then framed by some prayers of benediction. It is certain, however, that the essential components of the unit go back to the pre-Christian period and were recited by Jesus himself and the early Church.[15] The first historical testimony regarding the structure of the composition is in the Mishnah:

> The officer said to them [the priests], "Recite ye a Benediction!" They recited a Benediction, and recited the Ten Commandments, the *Shema'* [Deut 6:4–9], and the *And it shall come to pass if ye hearken* [Deut 11:13–21], and the *And the Lord spoke unto Moses* [Num 15:37–41]. They pronounced

three Benedictions with the people: "True and sure," and
"Abadal" [a benediction thanking the Lord for the worship
he enables them to offer to him in the temple], and the
Priestly Blessing, and on the Sabbath they pronounced a
further Benediction for the outgoing Course of priests.[16]

This passage is important because it provides us with a great deal
of information about the use already made of the *shema'* in the liturgy of the temple: the reading of the ten commandments, the three
passages making up the *shema'* itself, the benediction after the
shema' ("True and firm"), and a further benediction before the
shema' (a benediction later identified with the *'ahavah rabbah*,
"With abounding love").[17] All these components made their way
over into the synagogue, except for the reading of the ten commandments, which was suppressed after the destruction of the Second
Temple (70 A.D.) in order to discourage the view of certain heretics
who thought that the recitation of the ten commandments in synagogal prayer dispensed them from observance of the other commandments of the Torah.

Of all these elements the one most extensively commented on in
the Mishnah and the Talmud (*Ber* 13b and *Suk* 42a) is the first verse
of the *shema'*: "Hear, O Israel: The Lord is our God, the Lord is one"
(Deut 6:4; Hertz 117). This verse is therefore rightly regarded as the
most ancient part and the generative nucleus of this first structural
unit of Jewish prayer. The principal phases in the development of the
shema' may, with a good degree of probability, be reconstructed as
follows:

—initially, Deut 6:4 was recited: "Hear, O Israel: the Lord is our
God, the Lord is one";

—verses 5–9 were then added to v. 4;

—in the third stage, two other passages of the Bible were added:
Deut 11:13–21 and Num 15:37–41, as were the two most important
berakot: 'emet wa-yaṣiv ("True and firm") and *'ahavah rabbah*
("With abounding love");

—in the final stage, the other *berakot* were added.

The Mishnaic and Talmudic tradition also supplies information
on the *times* and *manner* of recitation of the *shema'*. In *b. Ber* 4b we
read this saying of Rabbi Joshua ben Levi: "Even if the *shema'* has
been recited in the synagogue, it is meritorious to recite it again on
one's bed." This testimony shows clearly that the *shema'* was used in
two settings: in the synagogue and privately.

Still more explicit practical information is given in the Mishnah

(Ber 1), which reports the divergent opinions of the schools of Hillel and Shammai on the manner of reciting the prayer:

> The School of Shammai say: In the evening all should recline when they recite [the Shema'], but in the morning they should stand up, for it is written, *And when thou liest down and when thou risest up* [Deut 6:7]. But the School of Hillel say: They may recite it everyone in his own way, for it is written: *And when thou walkest by the way.*[18] Why then is it written: *And when thou liest down and when thou risest up?* [It means] the time when men usually lie down and the time when men usually rise up. R. Tarfon said: I was once on a journey and I reclined to recite [the Shema'] in accordance with the words of the School of Shammai, and so put myself in jeopardy by reason of robbers. They said to him: Thou hadst deserved aught that befell thee in that thou didst transgress the words of the School of Hillel (Ber 1, 3; Danby 2).

This text is important especially by reason of its date, which can be easily determined. Hillel and Shammai were two great teachers of pre-Christian Judaism, who lived during the reign of Herod the Great (37–4 B.C.). The former was an intelligent man with a critical mind, and favored interpretation and adaptation of the Torah; the latter was rigid and intransigent and defended a literal observance. This passage of the Mishnah thus supplies historical evidence for dating the liturgical use of the shema'; a century before Christ the duty of reciting it morning and evening was already regarded as traditional.[19]

The dispute between Hillel and Shammai was not *whether* the shema' ought to be recited morning and evening (this is taken for granted throughout the tractate Berakot, the first chapter of which is entitled: "From what time in the evening may the Shema' be recited?") but *how* it ought to be recited. How is Deut 6:7, which is part of the shema', to be understood when it orders Jews to repeat the Lord's commandments to their children "when thou sittest in thine house, and when thou walkest by the way, and when thou liest down, and when thou risest up"? Contrary to Shammai, Hillel proposed a flexible reading of the verse, in order to avoid ambiguities and untenable situations, such as are exemplified in the parabolic and somewhat humorous story of R. Tarfon. But despite the difference of interpretation between the two schools, one thing is beyond

doubt: that the central nucleus of the shema' dates back to long before the Christian era and that, day after day, morning and evening,
Jesus, the Virgin Mary, the apostles, and the first Christian communities all nourished their souls on this prayer.[20]

2. The Supreme Creed of Judaism

The first three chapters of Tractate Berakot in both the Mishnah
and the Talmud discuss the shema' Yiśra'el at length. Although the
entire tractate contains only nine chapters, a third of it is devoted to
problems of the shema'. To give the reader a more concrete idea of
what this means, I note that the Babylonian Talmud devotes almost
200 pages to these three chapters. This interest in the shema' shows
how central the prayer is to Jewish tradition and spirituality. It is,
in fact,

> the profession of faith that accompanies Jews from their ear-
> liest years to the grave. The shema' is with them when they
> are apart or isolated from their brothers and sisters, and
> makes them aware that they are Jews. The shema' is the
> foundation of the educational activity of parents toward
> their children, and in every Jewish home it is recited at
> retiring and at rising. The shema' is the first principle of
> thought and the guide for the will in family life and commu-
> nity life. The shema' was chosen from among the 4875
> verses of the Pentateuch to be the sign by which Israel is to
> be recognized at all times and in every place. It was with the
> shema' on their lips that the martyrs went to the stake and
> suffered for Israel and their God.[21]

a) Confession of the Oneness of God

"Hear, O Israel: The Lord our God is the only Lord." These
words, which are regarded as, without qualification, the most important words in all of Judaism, define the relationship of the Jewish
people with God, a relationship best expressed in the term berit,
"covenant." According to the logic of the covenant, God and human
beings are not to be identified with the world of nature but transcend
it and give it its meaning. By defining God as the Word that commands (see the call of Abraham in Gen 12:1) and the human person
as obedient response ("Hear, O Israel . . .": Deut 6:4), Judaism introduces into the world a revolutionary conception of reality.

According to this conception, reality is no longer abandoned and

subject to inevitable fate, nor is it self-sufficient by reason of its in-
nate powers; rather it is dynamized by the free, conscious will of God
who sustains it in benevolent love. In the Bible, unlike cosmobiol-
ogy,[22] God is not identified with the world (pantheism) nor does he
withdraw himself from it (mechanicism), but neither is he its creative and directive soul. The world is like a love letter or a gesture
inspired by love, and becomes intelligible only to those who grasp
the intention that brings it into existence, the plan that accounts for
its being.

From this view of things flows a command: "Hear, O Israel." The
command is so important, and summarizes all the others to such an
extent, that Israel and, later, Judaism would turn it into its privileged
act of faith. But what is it that is to be heard? What is the object of this
radically important "listening"? "The Lord our God is the only
Lord." The command (imperative) is followed by a statement (indicative): God is one ('ehad). Along with the word shema' ("hear"), 'ehad
("one") is perhaps the most cherished, venerated, and mystery-filled
word in Judaism: it watches over the secret of God, his most profound
and distinctive attribute. For this reason, the manner in which the
word is to be pronounced is explored in the Talmud, which speaks of
various ways of prolonging the sound and of the various benefits to
be derived therefrom:

> Thus was it taught: Symmachus said: "Those who lengthen
> the word "one" ('ehad) will have their days and years
> lengthened." R. Aha, son of Jaaqob, said: "Those who
> lengthen the [final] consonant in 'ehad will have their days
> and years lengthened." R. Ashi said: "Provided they do not
> fail to pronounce the letter ḥet."[23] Rabbi Jirmejah was
> seated before R. Hijja bar Abba, and the latter saw him no-
> ticeably prolonging the word "one" ('ehad). Then he said to
> him: "After you have declared God to be king on high and in
> the depths and in the four corners of the world, the precept
> of intensity no longer applies."[24]

But what does it mean to confess the "oneness" of God, and why
is this oneness regarded as so radically important in the biblical and
Jewish tradition? If we are to grasp the meaning of this "oneness," we
must set aside the philosophical approach that is so characteristic of
the Western mentality, and enter into the biblical outlook, which
focuses on the experience of salvation. Judaism discovers God to be
one, not by way of rational argument, but with an immediacy based

on personal and communal history. God reveals his oneness first to the heart of Israel and only secondly to its understanding, first to its existential reality and only secondly to its mental activity.

It is here, in its real history (in which indeed the exercise of reason is an important but not foundational phase of reflection), that Judaism discovers God and his oneness. This oneness, moreover, is valid not for Judaism alone but for all the peoples of the world. In fact, when the rabbinical commentaries explain the words: "The Lord our God is the only Lord," they point out that the text says: "The Lord our God is the only Lord," and not: "Our God, the Lord, is the only Lord," lest other peoples conclude that their God, too, is one as the God of Israel is one. By saying: "The Lord . . . is the only Lord," the text shows that he is Lord of all peoples and not merely the Lord of Israel.[25]

The assertion of the oneness of God has to do, in Judaism, with the realm of meaning. That is: God is the only God, not so much because he is the only God that exists (such a statement of the problem is alien to the biblical mentality, especially in the Old Testament), as because he is the only God who can produce and bestow meaning, the only one in whom reality reveals its identity and in whom the world is radiant with the beauty of the earthly paradise. When pious Jews said, morning and evening, that God is the only Lord, they were confessing and confirming that in any and every circumstance only adherence to the will ("the loving plan") of God guaranteed their freedom and fulfillment.

There must be no misunderstanding of this assertion of "singleness." God is the only Lord, not because he alone is capable of "filling the human heart," as in the Augustinian interpretation ("Our hearts are restless until they rest in you") which has struck deep roots, especially in the Catholic world. God created both the fruits of the earth and woman (see Gen 1–2) for the joy of his sons: in order to satisfy their needs and rejoice their hearts. Consequently, nothing is more alien to the biblical and Jewish tradition than to picture God as rival or adversary of human beings. No, God is the only Lord in a different sense: the only one who guarantees preservation of "the tree of life" (see Gen 2:9), the only one in whom the world, if received as gift and lived in accordance to the divine intention, becomes a house of happiness for brothers and sisters. From this point of view, Adam's sin was not that he rejoiced in things rather than in God, but that he wanted to enjoy against God's will.

God remains the only Lord, not for Israel alone but for every people and every culture, even one that may be described as "secularized" or "profane" or even "atheistic." It is from him that the water of salvation must be drawn, on him that the meaning of life must be based.

b) Acceptance of the "Yoke of the Kingdom of God"

To proclaim the oneness of God means abandoning oneself to his sovereign, providential will. This dedication is also expressed in the words: "to take on oneself the yoke of the kingdom of heaven (qabbalat malkut 'ol shamaim)."[26] The expression sums up in a felicitous way all the consequences of the shema', which the next verse of the prayer states by saying: "And you shall love the Lord your God with all your heart, and with all your soul, and with all your might" (Deut 6:5). The expression makes two basic points: that God is "king of the universe," and that his kingship is not exercised automatically but only through a deliberate response of human beings. When I speak of "kingship" here (or, more accurately, "royal lordship"), I understand it as the Bible does: this is not a worldly kingship, which is almost always woven of violence and injustice, but a divine kingship, which creates and promotes life and freedom.

Indeed, according to the biblical and Jewish tradition, the supreme signs of divine kingship are the creation of the world and the exodus from Egypt. In transforming the world from chaos to kosmos (see Gen 1) and leading the Hebrew people from slavery and oppression to the freedom of the promised land (see the Book of Exodus), God exercises his lordship and manifests his kingship. He reveals the "power" of love to give and bring into existence, the living energy that nourishes and is radiant, the ultimate, hidden purposefulness that establishes and sustains reality and removes it from the power of evil. Such is the meaning of the following passage of the Talmud, which says that the power of the shema' can banish Satan's forces from those who recite it:

> R. Jishaq said: "Phantoms depart from those who recite the shema' on their bed, as has been said: 'The sons of the lamp elevate their flight' (Job 5:7). Here the word 'fly' can only refer to the Law, in accordance with what is said: 'You let your gaze fly upon it, and it is no more' (Prov 23:5). And the word 'lamp' can refer only to phantoms, in accordance with what is said: 'Wasted by fatigue and devoured by the lamp and qeteb meriri, the midday demon' (Deut 32:24)."[27]

The thesis which the Talmud wants to prove is this: Those who recite the shema' keep the forces of evil far from them. The thesis is

proved from a series of verses that are interpreted according to the
midrashic method of the rabbis. The first biblical verse chosen is Job
5:7: "The sons of the lamp elevate their flight." But how does this
help understand the thesis that those who recite the shema' keep the
forces of evil far from them? In order to answer, it becomes necessary
to appeal to two other verses of the Bible: Prov 23:5 and Deut 32:24. In
the light of these, once they are suitably accommodated to the purpose, the Talmudic redactor explains Job 5:7: "The sons of the lamp"
are phantoms, that is, the forces of evil, while "elevate their flight"
signifies that they flee because of the "flight," that is, the "winged
word" of the Torah, of which the shema' is the key part. Thus the
thesis advanced is proved: Those who recite the shema' overcome
the forces of evil.

This kind of exegesis may make us smile; the important thing,
however, is not the method but the result, and the result is that the
praying of the shema' represented, and still represents, for Judaism
an authentic experience of victory over the powers of evil, to which
it has always refused to submit. This is also the meaning of another
Talmudic passage that is not unlike the first: "R. Jishag said: 'Those
who recite the shema' on their beds are like men with two-edged
swords in their hands, as has been said: "They glorify God with their
mouths, and a two-edged sword is in their hands" (Ps 119:6).' "[28]

c) The Jewish People, Witness to God

The Jewish people know that there is but one God, not only for
them but for the entire race. As a result, they have an important role:
the role of privileged witness. The word for "witness" in Hebrew is
'ed; it is one of the three key words in the confession of faith in the
Jewish tradition (the other two are shema' and 'ehad). Not without
point do the rabbinical commentaries observe that the word
'ed combines the last letter of shema' ('ayin) and the last letter of
'ehad (dalet).

For the same reason the two letters 'ayin and dalet are written
larger than the others in the unvocalized text of the Torah. This is an
eloquent way of showing the universal value of the shema', namely,
that God is the only guarantor of life's meaning, even when extremely tragic situations seem to deny that it has any meaning at all.

For this reason the shema' is also recited in moments of defeat
and of death. It bears witness that even in such moments (and, indeed, in such moments above all) God remains the only Lord who
has power to ensure life's meaning by turning defeat into victory, the
negative into the positive.

Among the countless Jews who in every century have faced death and execution while singing the shema', the case of Rabbi Aqiba remains the most famous and eloquent. He was condemned to death in 135 A.D., due to the failure of the revolt of Simon bar Koziba, known as bar Kochba, "Son of the Star" (in virtue of a messianic interpretation of Num 24:17), but his martyrdom was, in a true and full sense, a celebration of the shema'.

> The rising sun flooded the earth with its sweet rays, and the East was growing scarlet. Then Rabbi Aqiba placed his hands over his eyes and in a strong voice said: "Hear, O Israel: The Eternal, our God, the Eternal is one. You shall love the Eternal, your God, with all your heart, with all your soul, and with all your might."
>
> "This man is a sorcerer," shouted Tinius Rufus. "He has a talisman that makes him insensitive to pain."
>
> The disciples of Rabbi Aqiba then approached the place of torment, and Rabbi Meir addressed the martyr in these words: "Rabbi, Rabbi, our hearts bleed to see you suffering so atrociously." "My dear sons," Aqiba replied, "do not be afflicted on my account! I have at last reached the fulfillment of my greatest desire. For twenty-four years I have been consumed by the wish to give my life for the sanctification of the Name, as it is said: 'You shall love the Eternal, your God, with all your heart, with all your soul, and with all your might.' Now that moment has come. God be praised!"
>
> Then he murmured again: "Hear, O Israel: The Eternal, our God, the Eternal is one." And as he pronounced the word "one" ('ehad), he shuddered in the grip of death and, in a final burst, his soul flew to the heavenly places.[29]

This description of a martyr's death remains one of the most beautiful expressions of the Jewish religious soul, bearing witness as it does to the power of the shema' and to the optimism and hope that fill it.

3. The Three Passages from the Bible

The shema' is made up of three biblical passages from the Pentateuch and some berakot preceding and following them. Of the three passages (Deut 6:4–9; Deut 11:13–21; Num 15:37–41) the first is the

most important, whereas the second and third may be omitted or
shortened.

a) Obedience and Freedom

The first passage contains a series of commands which God addresses to his people, thus binding them to his will:

> Hear, O Israel: The Lord our God is one Lord; and you shall
> love the Lord your God with all your heart, and with all
> your soul, and with all your might. And these words which I
> command you this day shall be upon your heart; and you
> shall teach them diligently to your children, and shall talk
> of them when you sit in your house, and when you walk by
> the way, and when you lie down, and when you rise. And
> you shall bind them as a sign upon your hand, and they
> shall be as frontlets between your eyes. And you shall write
> them on the doorposts of your house and on your gates
> (Deut 6:4–9).

This passage states:
—the obligation of listening to the truth of the Lord's oneness
(v. 4);
—the duty of loving the Lord without reservation and in one's
very depths: "with all your heart, and with all your soul, and with all
your might" (v. 5);
—the obligation of having these commands impressed on one's
heart (they are to "be upon your heart"), that is, not only to observe
outwardly what they say but also to interiorize them (v. 6). Observance of the Torah is not to be merely external and mechanical but
must coincide with a spiritual and as it were connatural need. The
verse contains in a nutshell the entire prophetic message against the
various kinds of formalism and an explicit answer to those who
would claim that Judaism is a religion of fear and focused on
externals;
—the obligation of passing this spiritual heritage on to their children and their children's children (v. 7), and doing so faithfully and
continually (whether sitting or walking, whether lying down or rising). This obligation gives tradition its value and turns every father
into a teacher and every family into a school;
—the obligation of continually studying the preceding divine
precepts and adapting them to ever new circumstances (vv. 8–9). The
duty of "binding them as a sign upon your hand" and having them

"as frontlets between your eyes" (v. 8) and of "writing them on your doorposts and on your gates" (v. 9) is understood as primarily metaphorical, although the practice has become established in the Jewish tradition of fulfilling the duty in a concrete way by means of particular objects: the *tefillin*, two capsules which contain four passages of the Torah (Exod 13:1–10; Exod 13:11–16; Deut 6:4–9; Deut 11:13–21) and are tied to the left arm and around the forehead during morning prayer; and the *mezuzah*, a box containing Deut 6:4–9 and 11:13–20 and attached to the doorposts on the right of the person entering.

Since the *shema'* contains a series of commands, the character of these calls for remark. The commands are understood not as prohibitive or restrictive but as positive and revelatory. There are in fact two kinds of imperatives or commands: one is authoritarian (the commands of a master): it deprives others of their autonomy and subjects them to the master's power; the other is creative: it brings into play the interior dynamisms of the recipient of the command, thus promoting the latter's fulfillment and growth. An engineer who says: "You *have to* build the bridge thus and so," or a physician who says: "If you want to get well, you *must* do such and such," is not aiming to impose or repress but to serve and liberate. The divine commandments (not only the ten commandments but the entire Torah) are understood as being of the second kind: precepts for life and freedom, precepts outside of which meaninglessness and death flourish.

b) Abundance and Fruitfulness

The second biblical passage in the *shema'* is Deut 11:13–21, which lists the positive consequences of fidelity to the divine commands and the negative consequences of non-fulfillment:

> And if you will obey my commandments which I command you this day, to love the Lord your God, and to serve him with all your heart and with all your soul, he will give the rain for your land in its season, the early rain and the later rain, that you may gather in your grain and your wine and your oil. And he will give grass in your fields for your cattle, and you shall eat and be full.
>
> Take heed lest your heart be deceived, and you turn aside and serve other gods and worship them, and the anger of the Lord be kindled against you, and he shut up the heavens, so that there be no rain, and the land yield no fruit,

and you perish quickly off the good land which the Lord
gives you.

You shall therefore lay up these words of mine in your
heart and in your soul; and you shall bind them as a sign
upon your hand, and they shall be as frontlets between your
eyes. And you shall teach them to your children, talking of
them when you are sitting in your house, and when you are
walking by the way, and when you lie down, and when you
rise. And you shall write them upon the doorposts of your
house and upon your gates, that your days and the days of
your children may be multiplied in the land which the Lord
swore to your fathers to give them, as long as the heavens
are above the earth (Deut 11:13–21).

This passage is built around three main propositions:

—the first proposition makes a *conditional statement about the
real world*: "if you will obey . . . he will give" (vv. 13–15). The condition is obedience and love of the Lord (v. 13); the guaranteed result of
this obedience and love is fruitfulness (v. 14) and an abundant harvest (v. 15). These verses are perhaps among the most profound and
original of the Torah: first, because they promise a future of riches
and repletion; second, because they lay down the conditions for fulfillment of the promise. The abundance of "grain, wine, and oil" (see
v. 14) depends not on the "seasons" (to be propitiated in idolatrous
cults) nor on the labor of human beings (to be augmented through
greater diligence or an increase in the labor force) but on *love of the
Lord and obedience to his commandments.*

Here again we must avoid a misunderstanding of this relationship, which is not extrinsic (of the kind: "if you are good, I will
reward you") but intrinsic (of the kind: "if you water the plant, it will
blossom"). Those who obey the Lord's commandments and love him
are those who have the relationship to the earth and their fellow
human beings according to his living will. When this happens, that
is, when the "land" is accepted as God's gift and human beings as
one's brothers and sisters, one experiences the joy of fruition ("you
shall eat": v. 15) and well-being ("you shall . . . be full": v. 15). God
conceived of the human race as a "paradise," an "eden" (see Gen 2),
but the happiness and harmony which it is given human beings to
have here come to maturity only in the soil of responsibility and
obedience to the divine will. Where this docility is lacking, the "tree
of life" (Gen 1:9) turns into "thorns and thistles" (Gen 3:18);

—the second proposition consists of a *lengthy command/exhor-*

tation (vv. 16–17) which puts negatively the ideas which the preceding proposition expressed in positive terms. V. 16 in fact makes explicit the content of v. 13: we see that "obeying my commandments" and "loving/serving the Lord" mean "not to let your heart be deceived," "not to turn aside," "not to serve other gods and worship them." V. 17, for its part, further explains the content of vv. 14–15: unless you obey the Lord and love him "with all your heart and with all your soul" (v. 13), "the anger of the Lord [will] be kindled against you," "so that there be no rain, and the land yield no fruit" (v. 17);

—the third proposition consists of a *series of commands* (vv. 18–21) which in substance repeat Deut 6:6–9: the duty of having the divine commandments always in mind (v. 18), even in a corporeal way by means of the *tefillin*; the duty of teaching and transmitting them day after day to one's children (v. 19); the duty of observing them in one's home (vv. 20–21), using the *mezuzah* as an aid.

c) The "Signature" of God

The third biblical passage in the *shema'* is Num 15:37–41, which speaks of the obligation to "make tassels" in order to be more readily mindful of the Lord's commandments and of God's description of himself as God of the exodus:

> The Lord said to Moses, "Speak to the people of Israel, and bid them to make tassels on the corners of their garments, throughout their generations, and to put upon the tassel of each corner a cord of blue; and it shall be to you a tassel to look upon and remember all the commandments of the Lord, to do them, not to follow after your own heart and your own eyes, which you are inclined to go after wantonly. So you shall remember and do all my commandments, and be holy to your God. I am the Lord your God, who brought you out of the land of Egypt, to be your God: I am the Lord your God" (Num 15:37–41).

Three main statements are made in this passage which is the last of the readings making up the *shema'*:

—first and foremost, there is the order to wear the *ṭallit*, a cape in the form of a scapular that is more or less wide depending on local traditions and rites. V. 38 describes the characteristics of this garment (which was originally the ordinary garment of a Jew) and its liturgical adaptation: the tassels or fringes with their cord of blue (*ṣiṣit*);

—vv. 39–40 explain the meaning of the *tallit*, which is not a magical amulet but a reminder: "to look upon and remember all the commandments of the Lord" (v. 39). The reminder is threefold: to "do all the commandments" (vv. 39–40); "not to follow after your own heart and your own eyes, which you are inclined to go after wantonly" (v. 39); and to be "holy to your God" (v. 40). I said the reminder is threefold, but in reality it is single. The *tallit* recalls and proclaims: "You shall . . . be holy to your God" (v. 40). Those who are "holy" do not "follow after your own heart . . . wantonly" (v. 39); those who are not wanton "do all my commandments" (v. 39); and those who "do all my commandments" are the ones who "remember." Evidently, the *tallit* (like the *tefillin*—tassels or fringes— of the preceding passage) obeys a theologico-pedagogical logic, being a sign and instrument of holiness. It is not simply an aid to remembrance of what the Lord wills, but makes the wearer live in the holiness to which the Lord calls;

—v. 41 may be regarded as God's self-description that concludes not only the passage from Numbers but all three passages making up the *shemaʻ*: "I am the Lord your God, who brought you out of the land of Egypt, to be your God: I am the Lord your God" (v. 41). This divine self-description has three principal elements. First and foremost, God presents himself to Israel as *its* God: "I am the Lord your God" (said twice, at the beginning and the end of the verse, thus forming an inclusion). God here asserts his lordship over Israel which thus becomes his "possession" (Exod 19:5, *segullah*), his "inheritance" (Exod 34:9; 1 Sam 10:1; 26:19), his "people" (Is 1:3), his "servant" (Is 44:21), his "chosen" (Is 45:4), his "first-born" (Exod 4:22; Hos 11:1), his "sheep" (Ps 95:7), his "vine" (Is 5:7), his "dominion" (Ps 114:2), his "bride" (see Hos 2:4), and so on.

Second, God explains the nature of his lordship: he is Lord of Israel in the sense of being not a master but a deliverer: "who brought you out of the land of Egypt." He exercises his sovereignty not by repressing but by setting free, not by taking freedom away but by giving it, not by killing it but by awakening it to new life.

Third, God explains the purpose of this freedom: he delivers Israel from Egypt not in order to leave it to its own autonomy but in order "to be your God." He sets Israel free in order to replace Egypt's dominion over it with his own, to replace Pharaoh's power with the power of his love. This means that the Lord not only liberates Israel but is also the sole source and guarantor of its freedom. Without God, Israel is not only incapable of freeing itself from oppression (of which enslavement in Egypt was the painful paradigm and metaphor) but is also, and above all, incapable of preserving and nourishing the freedom obtained, since it is continually in danger of prostituting itself to new idols and new masters. God sets Israel free so that it may "belong to" him; but the belonging here means being nourished by him, not being subjected to a usurper. As the root belongs to the soil because the soil makes its trunk and branches fruitful, so Israel belongs to God because he is the foundation of its dignity and its life.

All this explains why, morning and evening, whether in the house or on the way, when it lies down and when it rises, Israel uses the shema' to proclaim its obedience and attachment to the God of the exodus, the God who sets it free. For it has discovered (and the discovery is valid not for Israel alone but for all peoples) that the tree of freedom and peace grows only in the soil of fidelity to God, that the messianic dream can become a reality only within the logic of the covenant.

4. The Morning Benedictions

In the morning service the recitation of the shema' is preceded by two berakot and followed by one, while in the evening service it is preceded by two and followed by two. In all, then, there are seven berakot which the rabbis love to connect with Ps 119:164: "Seven times a day I praise thee."

The two morning benedictions before the shema' are called, after their opening words, the yoṣer 'or ("Who formest light") and 'ahavah rabbah ("With abounding love"), while the one that concludes the shema' is known as 'emet we-yaṣiv ("True and firm"). The Mishnah speaks explicitly of these benedictions (Ber 1, 4), as does the Talmud, which comments on them at length (b. Ber 11b). Although the texts have received additions and amplifications in the course of the centuries, the original nucleus certainly goes back to the first century of the Christian era.

a) The Miracle of Creation

In the first blessing God is praised for the light, which symbolizes the multicolored riches of creation. Seeing the light, which daily reappears thanks to the divine benevolence, Israel blesses and glorifies the Eternal One, joining its voice to that of the heavenly angels and the entire universe:

> Blessed art thou, O Lord our God, King of the universe, who formest light and createst darkness, who makest peace and

createst all things:

Who in mercy givest light to the earth and them that dwell thereon, and in thy goodness renewest the creation every day continually. How manifold are thy works, O Lord! In wisdom thou hast made them all: the earth is full of thy creatures, O King, who alone wast exalted from aforetime, praised, glorified and extolled from days of old; O everlasting God, in thine abundant mercies, have mercy upon us, Lord of our strength, Rock of our stronghold, Shield of our salvation, thou Stronghold of ours!

The blessed God, great in knowledge, designed and formed the rays of the sun: it was a boon he produced as a glory to his Name: he set the luminaries around his strength. The chiefs of his hosts are holy beings that exalt the Almighty, and continually declare the glory of God and his holiness. Be thou blessed, O Lord our God, for the excellency of thy handiwork, and for the bright luminaries which thou hast made: they shall glorify thee for ever.

Be thou blessed, O our Rock, our King and Redeemer, Creator of holy beings, praised be thy Name for ever, O our King; Creator of ministering spirits, all of whom stand in the heights of the universe, and with awe proclaim in unison aloud the words of the living God and everlasting King. All of them are beloved, pure and mighty; and all of them in dread and awe do the will of their Master; and all of them open their mouths in holiness and purity, with song and psalm, while they bless and praise, glorify and reverence, sanctify and ascribe sovereignty to—

The Name of the Divine King, the great, mighty and dreaded One, holy is he; and they all take upon themselves the yoke of the kingdom of heaven one from the other, and give leave one unto the other to declare the holiness of their Creator: in tranquil joy of spirit, with pure speech and holy melody they all respond in unison, and exclaim with awe:

Holy, holy, holy is the Lord of hosts: the whole earth is full of his glory. . . .

He alone worketh mighty deeds, and maketh new things; he is the Lord over struggle, sowing righteousness, and reaping victory. He createth healing, and is revered in praises. He is the Lord of wonders, who in his goodness reneweth the creation every day continually; as it is said: *(O give thanks) to him that maketh great lights, for his loving-*

kindness endureth for ever. . . . Blessed art thou, O Lord, Creator of the luminaries (109–15).

The following observations will help to a better understanding of this text:

—To begin with, the beginning and the end (the words in italics) echo each other and reveal the meaning and riches of the prayer. The prayer is a solemn praise of God who is proclaimed as the one "who formest light and createst darkness" and is "Creator of the luminaries." In these sentences, then, we have the central theme of the benediction: it blesses God for the gift of *light.* The opening sentence is taken, in part, from Is 45:7: "I form light and create darkness, I make weal and create woe," with "createst all things" being substituted for "create woe," which was open to harmful interpretations. According to some commentators, the intention of the Jews in this confession of God was to oppose the Persian dualistic belief in two divinities: one of light and goodness, the other of darkness and iniquity;

—*light,* for which God is being praised in this hymn, is a symbol of creation as a whole: not only the earth and the human beings who dwell on it but also the heavens and the angelic hosts who serve God. Light is the symbol/reality of the entire universe: earthly and heavenly, material and spiritual, human and angelic. The words used to express the make-up of creation are varied: earth, world, works, riches, luminaries, hosts, angels, and so on. All of these together, symbolized by the light, constitute creation;

—creation is defined as the "work" and "riches" of God. Thanks to this view of it, Judaism neither identifies "things" with God (as in pantheism) nor opposes them to him (as in dualism) but distinguishes them from him and relates them to him. Relation and distinction are in fact the two key terms presupposed by the idea of creation. Like the work of an artist, the world is the expression of its author's intentions: of his mercy and goodness: "who in mercy (*berahamim*) . . . and in thy goodness (*beṭuvo*) renewest the creation." By means of the two italicized words, much used in rabbinical literature, the Jewish tradition established the true character of creation and expressed its true value and meaning: creation is a sign of divine love and a gift to human beings;

—this *berakah* speaks, moreover, not only of creation but even more of a *re-creation:* "in thy goodness renewest the creation every day continually." The miracle of the first creation, or the *bereshit* ("beginning") of the origins, is repeated daily. This is not verbal tri-

fling. To believing Jews the world is not part of "what has to be," of
the "necessary." Rather it is a "testimonial" of love which God offers
them daily. Thanks to it, "man can find the courage to begin life
anew each day, freed of the barnacles of yesterday's errors, burdens,
and sins, since he faces each morning a fresh new world that God has
just created!"[30]

—the surprise and joy felt at the re-creation of the world by
divine love are so great that only an exclamatory cry can express
them: "How manifold are thy works, O Lord! In wisdom hast thou
made them all." In addition to this exclamation, taken from Ps
104:24, the text also uses a series of laudatory terms, many of which
are repeated several times: "Blessed art thou. . . . O King, who alone
wast exalted from aforetime, praised, glorified and extolled."

—but human words seem insufficient for expressing the praise
and joy evoked by the re-created world. Believing Jews therefore feel
the need of turning to the angelic courts and joining them as, day and
night, "they . . . take upon themselves the yoke of the kingdom of
heaven" and sing: "Holy, holy, holy . . ." (Is 6:3). This passage about
the angels, which is especially beautiful both poetically and theologi-
cally, is not to be interpreted in a literal way. In the Jewish tradition
the angels have no autonomous and superhuman existence. They
are therefore usually thought of as inferior to human beings, and
they are not free. Their function (as indicated by their very name
"angels," which means "messengers") is to concretize in a dramatic
way certain important aspects of Jewish religious experience: for
example, God's love or his justice, Israel, the Torah, and so on. In this
benediction the role of the angels is to express the central and radical
place of the praise of God which Jews are called upon to offer each
day, every time the light of dawn reappears. Like the angels, Jews
have the duty of "taking upon themselves the yoke of the kingdom of
heaven" and glorifying, with one voice, the thrice holy God.

b) The Gift of the Torah

In the second benediction, which is known as the *birkat ha-
Torah* or, from its opening Hebrew words, as *'ahavah rabbah*, God is
praised for the gift of the Torah. This is a greater gift even than
creation, and a concrete expression of his love for Israel and the
entire human race.

With abounding love hast thou loved us, O Lord our God,
and great and overflowing tenderness hast thou shown us.
O our Father, our King, for our fathers' sake, who trusted in

thee, and whom thou didst teach the statutes of life, be also gracious unto us and teach us. O our Father, merciful Father, ever compassionate, have mercy upon us; O put it into our hearts to understand and to discern, to mark, learn, and teach, to heed, to do and to fulfill in love all the words of instruction in thy Torah. Enlighten our eyes in thy Torah, and let our hearts cleave to thy commandments, and unify our hearts to love and reverence thy Name, so that we be never put to shame. Because we have trusted in thy holy, great and revered Name, we shall rejoice and be glad in thy saving power. O bring us in peace from the four corners of the earth, and make us go upright to our land, for thou art a God who worketh salvation. Thou hast chosen us from all peoples and tongues, and hast brought us near unto thy great Name for ever in faithfulness, that we might in love give thanks to thee, O Lord, who hast chosen thy people Israel in love (115–17).

Here are some important points to be noted about this second of the berakot that precede and prepare for the shema‘:
—the meaning of the prayer as a whole is given in the formula that ends it: "who hast chosen thy people Israel in love." The prayer is an act of solemn praise of God for having loved and chosen Israel as recipient of the gift of the Torah. It also contains a rich "theology of the word" or "of revelation," that complements and completes the preceding prayer with its "theology of creation." Creation and revelation are the two pillars of Judaism; like nature and the Law in Psalm 19, the world and the divine word are not opposed but call for and require each other. Sinai (revelation) is not simply juxtaposed with Genesis (creation) but interprets and includes it. The relation between the two is therefore hermeneutical: thanks to revelation (the Torah) the world created by God reveals a meaning that calls for hearing and acceptance. Thus the Torah has two dimensions: on the one hand, it is revelatory (it tells us what creation is and what intention lies behind it), and, on the other, it is normative (it tells how we are to live as creatures and how we are to make creation bear fruit);
—contrary to a deeply rooted stereotype, the Torah (usually, though ambiguously, translated as "Law") is looked upon by Judaism as an expression of God's love. "With abounding love hast thou loved us, O Lord our God." The Torah is the concrete, effective sign of this "abounding love" that has accompanied the Israelite people from the beginning. The Torah is at the service of life (ḥayim) and reveals the

love of God, who is here repeatedly invoked as "our Father," "merciful Father, ever compassionate," full of "great and overflowing tenderness."

This emphasis on God's love calls attention to another aspect of his action: its gratuitousness, expressed in Deut 7:7–8: "It was not because you were more in number than any other people that the Lord set his love upon you and chose you, for you were the fewest of all peoples; but it is because the Lord loves you, and is keeping the oath which he swore to your fathers, that the Lord has brought you out with a mighty hand, and redeemed you from the hand of Pharaoh king of Egypt";

—Awareness of the Torah as source of life gives rise to the insistent plea that God would add to his gift the further and most important gift of understanding and plumbing the depths of the Torah: "O put it into our hearts to *understand* and to *discern*, to *mark*, *learn* and *teach*, to *heed*, to *do* and to *fulfill* in love all the words of instruction in thy Torah." This petition, which with its eight explanatory verbs describes an endless voyage, as it were, into the world of the Torah, is repeated and newly explained in other petitions: "enlighten our eyes," "let our hearts cleave," "make us go upright," "bring us in peace";

—this *berakah* brings us to the threshold of the *shema'*, having prepared us to recite it. Because God "has loved Israel *with abounding love*," Jews in turn are exhorted, in the *shema'*, to "love the Lord thy God with all thy heart, and with all thy soul, and with all thy might" (Deut 6:5). It is in this climate of covenant that the *shema'* is recited. The *shema'* presupposes and expresses, accepts and fulfills the covenant.

c) *The Yes of Obedience and Fidelity*

In the third benediction, which follows upon the *shema'* and is known from its opening words as *'emet we-yaṣiv* ("true and firm"), Judaism professes its docility to God and its "submission" to the Torah:

> True and firm, established and enduring, right and faithful, beloved and precious, desirable and pleasant, revered and mighty, well-ordered and acceptable, good and beautiful is this thy word unto us for ever and ever. It is true, the God of the universe is our King, the Rock of Jacob, the Shield of our salvation: throughout all generations he endureth and His Name endureth; his throne is established, and his kingdom

and his faithfulness endure for ever. His words also live and endure; they are faithful and desirable for ever and to all eternity, as for our fathers so also for us, our children, our generations, and for the generations of the seed of Israel his servants.

Alike for former and later ages thy word is good and endureth for ever and ever; it is true and trustworthy, a statute which shall not pass away. True it is that thou art indeed the Lord our God, and the God of our fathers, our King, our fathers' King, our Redeemer, the Redeemer of our fathers, our Maker, the Rock of our salvation; our Deliverer and Rescuer from everlasting, such is thy Name; there is no God beside thee.

Thou hast been the help of our fathers from of old, a Shield and Saviour to their children after them in every generation: in the heights of the universe is thy habitation, and thy judgments and thy righteousness reach to the furthest ends of the earth. Happy is the man who hearkeneth unto thy commandments, and layeth up thy Torah and thy word in his heart. True it is that thou art indeed the Lord of thy people, and a mighty King to plead their cause. True it is that thou art indeed the first and thou art the last, and beside thee we have no King, Redeemer and Saviour.

From Egypt thou didst redeem us, O Lord our God, and from the house of bondsmen thou didst deliver us; all their first-born thou didst slay, but thy first-born thou didst redeem; thou didst divide the Red Sea, and drown the proud; but thou madest the beloved to pass through, while the waters covered their adversaries, not one of whom was left. Wherefore the beloved praised and extolled God, and offered hymns, songs, praises, blessings and thanksgivings to the King, the living and everenduring God; who is high and exalted, great and revered; who bringeth low the haughty and raiseth up the lowly, freeth the prisoners, delivereth the meek, helpeth the poor, and answereth his people when they cry unto him; even praises to the Most High God, blessed is he, and ever to be blessed. Moses and the children of Israel sang a song unto thee with great joy, saying, all of them,

Who is like unto thee, O Lord, among the mighty? Who is like unto thee, glorious in holiness, revered in praises, doing marvels?

With a new song the redeemed people offered praise
unto thy Name at the sea shore: they all gave thanks in
unison, and proclaimed thy sovereignty, and said:
The Lord shall reign for ever and ever.
O Rock of Israel, arise to the help of Israel, and deliver,
according to thy promise, Judah and Israel. Our Redeemer,
the Lord of hosts is his Name, the Holy One of Israel. Blessed
art thou, O Lord, who hast redeemed Israel (127–29).

This benediction, which is also known as birkat ge'ulah (re-
demption/liberation) and is already attested in the Talmud,[31] is undoubtedly one of the most beautiful prayers in the religious and
liturgical literature of the world. It is a solemn profession of faith in
the abiding validity of the word of God that is proclaimed in the
shema', the word that, today as in the past, continues to save Israel as
it saved it long ago from Egypt. The prayer therefore has two parts:
the first focuses on the word of God (the shema', which was recited
before this benediction), the radiant beauty and sure effectiveness of
which it sings; the second centers on Israel's remembrance and experience of Egypt and brings to mind once again the power God exerted
on that occasion and the joyous liberation he effected.
Some points for a better understanding of the text:
—in this benediction the praying community gives its full assent
to the divine word in the shema', the word whose inexhaustible
riches and fruitfulness are suggested with the help of sixteen adjectives: true, firm, established, enduring, right, faithful, beloved,
precious, desirable, pleasant, revered, mighty, well-ordered, acceptable, good, and beautiful. The most important of these adjectives is
the first ("true"; in Hebrew, 'emet), which the tradition requires to
be recited without any pause immediately after the final two Hebrew words (four in English) of the shema': 'Adonai 'Elohekem, "The
Lord your God."
In the Jewish tradition, "truth" is less a predicate of the mind's
activity than it is a dimension of existence. An existence or life is
"true" that, "like a tree planted by streams of water" (Ps 1:3), produces fruits of meaning; a life is "false" that, though rich in ideas and
even though "proving itself truthful" at the logical and rational level,
is incapable of love and peace.
The purpose of connecting the word 'emet with the final words
of the shema' is to emphasize the point that God alone makes human
existence "true"; only in him do human beings discover and bring to
fulfillment the meaning of their lives. According to another tradi-

tion, if the 245 words of the shema' are added to the three just mentioned (the last two of the shema' and the first of the ensuing benediction), the total is 248, which is the same as the number of the parts of the human body.[32] The midrash regards this analogy as deeply meaningful: if human beings are faithful to the shema', which is as it were the body of God, God will be faithful to the human body.[33] Note well: to the "body" of the human person, and not just to the soul. Truth, in the Bible, has to do with this "body," that is, the totality of the human person and of history: spirit and matter, logos (thought) and sarx (flesh);

—God is the foundation and guarantor of this "truth." The words of the shema' are "true" because they were pronounced by the God who is "our king," "the Rock of Jacob," "the Shield of our salvation"; the God whose "kingdom" and "faithfulness" endure for ever;

—thanks to this God, the Torah (of which the shema' is the heart and summary) is "true" for ever, "throughout all generations": "as for our fathers so also for us, our children, our generations, and for all the generations of the seed of Israel his servants . . . our fathers of old . . . their children after them in every generation."

—this statement of the abiding vitality and validity of the Torah is based not on rational argument but on a particular historical experience: "From Egypt thou didst redeem us . . . and from the house of bondsmen thou didst deliver us; all their first-born thou didst slay, but thy first-born thou didst redeem; thou didst divide the Red Sea, and drown the proud; but thou madest the beloved to pass through. . . . Moses and the children of Israel sang a song unto thee with great joy." The foundational event of Israel's religious experience is the exodus, the principal stages of which are remembered in this benediction: the going out, the deliverance, the death of the Egyptians, the Passover, the crossing of the Red Sea, the song of triumph and joy after the Red Sea had been crossed, and so on;

—this foundational event created an awareness of God as one who is "near" (see "Thou hast been the help of our fathers," with which the second part of the benediction begins) and watches over human history not from without but from within, as a loving participant. This explains the numerous and varied titles by which God is from time to time described and defined: "our Redeemer," "Redeemer of our fathers," "our Rock," "the Rock of our salvation," "our Deliverer and Rescuer," "the first . . . and the last," "the Shield of our salvation";

—the memory of the exodus as foundational event not only makes possible a present time of trust and joy ("Happy is the man who hears your precepts and places your law and your word in his heart"), but also opens the heart to the certainty of messianic redemption: "O Rock of Israel, arise to the help of Israel, and deliver. . . ." Past deliverance becomes the guarantee and assurance of future liberation: as God freed us from oppression in Egypt, so he will free us (and all peoples) from new oppressions. Between past and future deliverances comes the invocation ("O Rock of Israel, arise to the help . . .") that concludes the *shema'* and prepares the way for the *tefillah*.

5. The Evening Benedictions

According to Deut 6:7, praying Jews are obliged to recite the *shema'* twice daily: "When thou liest down, and when thou risest up." In the evening recitation, as in the morning, the *shema'* proper is preceded and followed by benedictions. There are two that precede, as in the morning: the first (*ma'ariv 'aravim*, "thou who . . . bringest on the evening twilight") thanks God for the regular alternation of day and night; the second (*'ahavat 'olam*, "with everlasting love") praises God for the same reasons as in the morning, but in a shorter and more concentrated form.

After the *shema'* there are two benedictions in the evening, whereas in the morning there is only one: the first of them (*'emet we-'emunah*, "true and trustworthy") confesses God as deliverer and redeemer; the second (*hashkivenu*, "cause us . . . to lie down") asks God for a good night and for the removal of every danger. The structure, meaning, and content of these four benedictions are basically the same as in those of the morning. The differences (mostly nuances) are of two kinds: the texts are shorter, and there are more references to the evening hour at which they are recited. I shall give the text of each benediction and point out its main characteristics.

a) The Gates of Dawn and Dusk

In the first benediction God is praised for the night that has now come. Like the light of dawn, night is a "creature" of God who manifests and realizes his will by means of it.

> Blessed art thou, O Lord our God, King of the universe who
> at thy word bringest on the evening twilight, with wisdom
> openest the gates of the heavens [or: of dawn and dusk], and
> with understanding changest times and variest the seasons,
> and arrangest the stars in their watches in the sky, accord-

ing to thy will. Thou createst day and night; thou rollest away the light from before the darkness, and the darkness from before the light; thou makest the day to pass and the night to approach, and dividest the day from the night, the Lord of hosts is thy name; a God living and enduring continually, mayest thou reign over us for ever and ever. Blessed art thou, O Lord, who bringest on the evening twilight (305).

Three aspects of this prayer are especially important:

—the central theme is "night" (*lailab*), symbol of non-light and anti-creation. For this reason it is the place for the wild beasts (Ps 104:20), the pestilence that stalks in darkness (Ps 91:6), and thieves and murderers (Job 24:13–17). Even if the symbolism of the night is ambivalent (in fact it also can mean something good: rest and cessation of toil), nevertheless in the ordinary experience it is its deep and terrifying darkness which predominates.

—God is proclaimed as the one who "createst day and night," and who "at thy word bringest on the evening twilight." These two expressions, which have an unusual symbolic and theological depth, must be properly understood. When God is said to create both day and night, light and darkness, the second element in these pairs (night, darkness) is not being placed on the same level as the first, as in dualism, as though it were of equal value and dignity. The point is rather to deny night and darkness any independent status by placing them under the control of God, who vanquishes any powers they have (as he vanquishes the primeval chaos: Gen 1:1ff.) by the power of light and kosmos. When God is proclaimed creator of night, night is declared to have been dethroned; it is now not a place or phase of terror and death but of God's creative love. To believing Jews every dawn that breaks is a new creation in which, as on the first day, God chains the darkness and transforms it into order. Therefore they do not fear the night but can rest in peace and can without fear bless their Lord because he "brings on the evening twilight," "opens the gates of dawn and dusk," "varies the seasons," and "rolls away the light from before the darkness, and the darkness from before the light";

—since the *shema'* is being recited in the evening, in the darkness of night, the *qedushah* of the angels, which was part of the morning benedictions, is omitted. The reason is that according to the midrashic tradition the angels can glorify the Eternal One only by day and not by night: "The *qedushah*, which is the supreme proclamation of the divine glory, can be recited only during the day when nature manifests itself to our senses in all its richness and splendor. The qedushah is omitted at night when the world of nature hides itself from our perception."[34]

b) The Purpose of Life

In the second benediction ('ahavat 'olam, "with everlasting love") God is praised, as in the morning service, for the gift of the Torah, which gives Israel's life its purpose:

> With everlasting love thou hast loved the house of Israel, thy people; Torah and commandments, statutes and judgments hast thou taught us. Therefore, O Lord our God, when we lie down and when we rise up we will meditate on thy statutes; yea, we will rejoice in the words of thy Torah and in thy commandments for ever; for they are our life and the length of our days, and we will meditate on them day and night. And mayest thou never take away thy love from us. Blessed art thou, O Lord, who lovest thy people Israel (307).

The following remarks may help to a better understanding of this text:

—the main consideration that calls for and grounds an attitude of praise and thanksgiving of God is that "with everlasting love thou hast loved the house of Israel." Note the nuance of difference between the wording of the morning benediction ("with abounding love") and the wording of the evening benediction ("with everlasting love"). According to some commentators the difference is this: the morning benediction speaks of "abounding love," because the reference is to the present experience of God's love as it manifests itself in the recurrence of a new dawn and new life. The evening benediction, on the other hand, speaks of "everlasting love" ('olam literally means "future") because the reference is to the certain hope that God's love perdures beyond the night. The night does not contradict his love but on the contrary is illumined and vanquished by it;

—the love which God had and has for Israel is summed up in a single gift: the Torah. The benediction celebrates the beauty and power of the Torah by means of various names: "commandments," "statutes," and "judgments." The Torah is seen here as a sign of "our life";

—the Torah, for which God is blessed and invoked, is not a burden to be carried but a fountain of joy to which human beings may abandon themselves: "we will rejoice in the words of thy Torah and in thy commandments for ever; for they are . . . the length of our days." It is this consciousness—that the Torah is indeed the secret of life—which gives rise to the double invocation with which the prayer ends: "We will meditate on them day and night. And mayest thou never take away thy love from us."

c) The Fidelity of God

The third benediction, which follows immediately upon the shema', acknowledges the truth and efficacy of the divine words that have been pronounced. The text, which is attributed to Rab, basically resembles the text of the third morning benediction, but there are some variants:

> True and trustworthy is all this, and it is established with us that he is the Lord our God, and there is none beside him, and that we, Israel, are his people. It is he who redeemed us from the hand of kings, even our King, who delivered us from the grasp of all tyrants; the God, who on our behalf dealt out punishment to our adversaries, and requited all our mortal enemies; who doeth great things past finding out, yea, and wonders without number; who maintaineth us in life, and hath not suffered our feet to slip; who made us overcome and conquer our enemies, and exalted our strength above all them that hated us; who wrought for us miracles and retribution upon Pharaoh, signs and wonders in the land of the children of Ham; who in his wrath smote all the first-born of Egypt, and brought forth his people Israel from among them to everlasting freedom; who made his children pass through the divided Red Sea, but sank their pursuers and their enemies in its depths. Then his children beheld his might; they praised and gave thanks unto his Name, and willingly accepted his sovereignty. Moses and the children of Israel sang a song unto thee with great joy, saying, all of them,
> Who is like unto thee, O Lord, among the mighty? Who is like unto thee, glorious in holiness, revered in praises, doing wonders?
> Thy children beheld thy sovereign power, as thou didst cleave the sea before Moses: they exclaimed, This is my God! and said, The Lord shall reign for ever and ever.
> And it is said, For the Lord hath delivered Jacob,

and redeemed him from the hand of him that was stronger than he. Blessed art thou, O Lord, who hast redeemed Israel (311–13).

The following are the main differences from the text of the morning benediction:

—at the heart of the benediction is the memorial of Israel's deliverance from slavery in Egypt, but whereas in the morning the story is told in verbs in the past tense ("from Egypt thou didst redeem us," "thou didst deliver us," "all their first-born thou didst slay," "thy first-born thou didst redeem," "thou didst divide the Red Sea, and drown the proud," and so on). In the evening benediction the verbs are in the present tense, implying a constant and continuous action. The reason for the difference is simple:

> In the morning we are full of gratitude for having been rescued from the grip of dark night and from moral depression. In the evening, on the other hand, we think hopefully of our future redemption and are mindful of God's protection and constant watchfulness that never lessen. For this reason, the morning benediction uses the past tense, the tense of grateful retrospection; in the evening the present and future tenses are chosen, for these are the tenses proper to trustful expectation ('emunah).[35]

—in the morning benediction God is invoked as follows: "O Rock of Israel . . . deliver . . . Israel and Judah." Here, in the evening benediction, we read: "The Lord hath delivered Jacob, and redeemed him from the hand of him that was stronger than he." The rabbinical commentaries like to point out the different names used for the patriarch: in the morning benediction he is called "Israel," a name indicating power and victory (according to a popular etymology "Israel" means "he has been powerful against God"; see Gen 32:23ff.); in the evening benediction the name used is "Jacob," which suggests weakness and appeal. This is a way of saying that in the morning Jewish believers feel "strong," like Israel, because they are enriched with the gift of a new day, whereas in the evening they feel "weak" and "in need of help," as Jacob did when threatened by the darkness of night.

d) Prayer for Peaceful Repose

The fourth benediction (hashkivenu, "cause us to lie down in peace") is also called ge'ulah 'arikatah ("extended redemption"), because it is regarded as a prolongation of the third benediction. It asks God to protect us during the night by keeping the hostile evil powers from us:

> Cause us, O Lord our God, to lie down in peace, and raise us up, O our King, unto life. Spread over us the protection of thy peace; direct us aright through thine own good counsel; save us for thy Name's sake; be thou a shield about us; remove from us every enemy, pestilence, sword, famine and sorrow; remove also the adversary from before us and from behind us. O shelter us beneath the shadow of thy wings; for thou, O God, art our Guardian and our Deliverer; yea, thou, O God, art a gracious and merciful king; and guard our going and our coming unto life and unto peace from this time forth and for evermore. Blessed art thou, O Lord, who guardest thy people Israel for ever (313).

Three basic ideas are expressed in this benediction:

—first and foremost there is the prayer to God for peaceful repose: "Cause us, O Lord our God, to lie down in peace (le-shalom). . . . Spread over us the protection of thy peace (shalomekah). . . . Shelter us beneath the shadow of thy wings" (see Ps 17:8; 36:8);

—what is meant, concretely, by "peaceful" repose? It means a sleep that is free from attack by all the many and terrible specters that, according to the mind of antiquity and a primitive symbolology, people the darkness of night: "Remove from us every enemy, pestilence, sword, famine and sorrow." These negative forces are summed up in the petition: "Remove also the adversary [Satan] from before us and from behind us." Satan, the Adversary, is the supreme symbol of evil, of opposition to the divine plan. Asking God to remove Satan from us is another way of asking him to renew the work of creation each night by transforming chaos (night) into cosmos (day);

—repose is not requested for its own sake but in view of the creation of the new day, a creation in which we are called upon to collaborate: "Raise us up unto life (le-ḥayim)" and surround us with peace (shalom). God grants a new day for the sake of life and peace, which represent both a gift to be received and a task to be accomplished.

The future tense of the psalm ("The Lord will watch over your going and your coming") is here changed to: "guard our going and our coming"; the literal meaning of "going" and "coming" (which in the psalm refer to the going and coming of the pilgrims in Jerusalem) is changed to a symbolic meaning, namely, the going and coming of night. Just as God watches over not only those who live in the holy city but also those outside it, so too he protects not only during the day (symbolized by Jerusalem) but also during the night (symbolized by being outside Jerusalem). Along with these two reinterpretations (time and symbolism) the prayer adds an explanatory expression to the words of the psalm: "unto life (le-ḥayim) and unto peace (le-shalom)." The benediction begins by asking God to raise us up to life and peace; it ends by asking him to guard us "unto life and unto peace," not only when we arise but always, whether we "go out" or "come in."

The evening recitation of the shema' thus ends with the image of a God who constantly remains with his people "unto life and unto peace": day and night, in oppression and in freedom.

III. THE SECOND STRUCTURAL UNIT: THE *TEFILLAH*

The tefillah is, after the shema', the second most important moment in Jewish prayer. It consists of a series of short benedictions or prayers recited three times a day: morning, afternoon, and evening, and is the prayer par excellence of the Jewish liturgy (the literal translation of ha-tefillah is "The Prayer"). It is closely connected with the shema' and in the rabbinical tradition is recited immediately after the final benediction of the shema', without any break.

The Talmud explains the close connection with the shema' on the basis of Ps 63:5: "I bless thee, O Lord, as long as I live; in your Name I lift up my hands [in petition]." The verse has two parts, the first a benediction, the second an invocation. According to the Talmud, the first part is developed in the shema', the second in the tefillah.[36] Just as the psalm verse is a unit in which the first part prepares for the second and the second refers back to the first, so the shema' and the tefillah form a unit in which each part refers to the other and is harmoniously combined with it.

I. Three Different Names

Since the tefillah comprises eighteen benedictions (in fact there are now nineteen, since the fourteenth has been divided into two), it is also called shemoneh-'eśreh ("eighteen"), especially among the

Ashkenazi Jews. ("Eighteen," that is, "benedictions.") Although in historical fact the number eighteen was reached by pure chance, the midrashic tradition likes to see theological reasons for it: "Moses was asked: 'How are we to know the number of prayers we are bound to offer?' He answered: 'How often does the divine Name occur in Psalm 29?' They said: 'Eighteen times.' He then said: 'We must offer *eighteen benedictions.'* "[37]

Saadia Gaon (882–942), one of the first great compilers of a prayer book, found twelve reasons why the *tefillah* contains eighteen benedictions: because the patriarchs "Abraham, Isaac, and Jacob" are mentioned as a group eighteen times; because the Torah gives formulas of prayers on eighteen occasions; because there are eighteen feast days in the Jewish calendar; and so on.

A second name for the *tefillah* is *'amidah,* which in Hebrew means "standing." The prayer is therefore called the *'amidah* because it is recited while standing and facing Jerusalem, the place and symbol par excellence of holiness. To take a standing position before someone is a way of attesting one's submission and docility. By reciting the *shemoneh-'esreh* while standing, the praying community expresses its readiness to accept and obey the divine will.

The practice of standing is not only amply attested in many passages of the Old Testament (see Sir 50:13; Ex 20:21; 38:10; Neh 8:5) but is also taken over by the Christian tradition, where it becomes one of the basic postures of ecclesial prayer. In addition to symbolizing docility or availability, standing also suggests freedom. Unlike slaves, who are forced to prostrate themselves, free human beings face others on a common level of autonomy and dignity. By reciting the eighteen benedictions while standing, praying Jews manifest not only their docility but also their idea of God: a dialogical partnership by which they enter upon a communion based on respect and love.

The most commonly used name, however, for the series of prayers after the *shema'* is *tefillah,* which derives from the verbal root *pll,* meaning "judge," "observe," "study," "test." In its reflexive form, *itpallel,* the verb means "to judge oneself," that is, to submit oneself to criticism, to conduct a "self-analysis." *Tefillah* is the substantive word for this process of self-observation and self-knowledge. It is usually translated as "prayer," the word here being understood not as the expression of one's sentiments but as a confrontation with God and his Torah, whereby, as though in the light of the sun, the soul discovers its identity and frees itself from the incrustations and mystifications that keep it alienated.

Contrary to common opinion, prayer in the Judeo-Christian tradition is not an alibi or a bit of pleasant self-complacency but a stern examination of conscience that purifies the person and contributes to the person's regeneration. According to the Mekilta (14, 10), "the tefillah is stronger than arms": it is not a magical force, but the power emanating from the conscientization and responsibility bestowed by the Torah.

It is along this line that the efficacy of prayer—a theme so dear to both Jewish and Christian spirituality—is to be understood. God always hears the prayers of his servants and does not leave their cries unanswered:

> I sought the Lord, and he answered me,
>   and delivered me from all my fears.
> Look to him, and be radiant;
>   so your faces shall never be ashamed.
> This poor man cried, and the Lord heard him,
>   and saved him out of all his troubles (Ps 34:5–7).

How are these verses to be understood, and how are they to be reconciled to these other verses from Psalm 22: "O my God, I cry by day, but thou dost not answer; and by night, but find no rest" (Ps 22:3)?

The tefillah, understood as self-understanding in the light of God's word, can help to resolve this apparent contradiction: God always "hears" our prayers, not in the sense that he adjusts himself to our will but in the sense that he conforms our will to his. When we pray to God and invoke his aid we are not forcing him or bending him to our desires but rather accepting and adhering to his will. Praying persons who abandon themselves to God's will can always say: "I sought the Lord, and he answered me"; whereas those who find this abandonment difficult can say: "O my God, I cry by day, but thou dost not answer; and by night, but find no rest."

These two "voices" are hidden in everyone who prays, and it is the task of the tefillah to turn the believer gradually from the first to the second:

> Since the tefillah aims essentially at elevating the soul to
> God through knowledge of his will, every prayer carries its
> own answer with it. If believers see the prayer denied, why
> should they be upset? That prayer is no longer capable of

expressing their true will and desire, because it does not represent the will and desire of their creator. Only to the superficial glance does their prayer seem unanswered; in reality, whether accepted or denied, the prayer has achieved its purpose: it has made them aware of the presence and will of God.[38]

I have dwelt at length on this theological aspect of the term *tefillah* because, by comparison with the other two names of the prayer, it is more original and more full of meaning. When devout Jews establish a rhythm for their day through recitation of the "Eighteen Benedictions," they gradually purify their wills to the point of bringing them into harmony with the divine will.

Their wills, which thus grow transparent as crystals, become the reflection of another will: the will of God, their creator and Lord. "Thy will be done": this invocation, the first in the Lord's Prayer of Jesus of Nazareth, can be regarded as the most complete expression and summary of the entire *tefillah*.

2. Origin and Structure

The majority of scholars agree in principle that, in its general structure if not in its individual parts, the *tefillah* originated in the second century before the Christian era. Others even date it to the fourth century of the pre-Christian era and think that its main components had already become part of the liturgy of the Second Temple.

Rabbi J. H. Hertz writes as follows of the origins of the *tefillah*:

This Prayer is not the product of one mind or even of one period. The opening benedictions, the "Praises," are the work of the Men of the Great Assembly, in the fourth pre-Christian century. The concluding benedictions, the "Thanksgivings," are not so old; but they undoubtedly go back to the Maccabean age, the middle of the second century before the Common Era. Much younger are the "Petitions," though nearly all of them were in use before the end of the Second Temple. As to origin, some of the Eighteen Benedictions were taken over from the Temple; some were framed originally for private devotion; while still others seem to have arisen in the Synagogue itself. The final editing of these prayers took place about the year 100,

after the Common Era, at the direction of the Patriarch
Gamaliel II.[39]

a) The Principal Historical Testimonies

The basic text that provides the most information about the *tefillah* is Tractate *Berakot* of the Mishnah, which devotes two of its nine
chapters to it. After speaking of the *shema'* (chapters 1–3), the tractate goes on to discuss the *tefillah* (chapters 4–5), while the remaining
chapters (6–9) are given over to the benedictions, especially the benediction after meals. Chapters 4 and 5 speak of how and when the
tefillah is to be recited; they report the differing opinions of the rabbis. In 4, 3, for example, we read: "Rabban Gamaliel says: A man
should pray the Eighteen [Benedictions] every day. R. Joshua says:
The substance of the Eighteen. R. Akiba says: If his prayer is fluent in
his mouth he should pray the Eighteen, but if not, the substance of
the Eighteen" (Danby 5).

This passage provides a good deal of important information. First
of all, it gives a picture of an easily dated historical period, since
Rabban Gamaliel, R. Joshua, and R. Aquiba all belonged to the second generation of Tannaites (70–135 A.D.). The use of the *tefillah* was
already widespread in that period. Second, the passage speaks of two
versions of the *tefillah*: one complete ("Eighteen Benedictions"), the
other a summary or abstract ("the substance of the Eighteen").
Third, it shows that there was a notable flexibility and freedom in
the recitation of the *tefillah*, with some preferring the complete version (Rabban Gamaliel), others the shorter version (R. Joshua), and
still others the one or other version depending on certain conditions
(R. Akiba).

Talmudic sources also supply important information. Three
passages in particular are relevant. The first is *Meg* 17b, according to
which "one hundred and twenty elders, many prophets among
them, compiled the Eighteen Benedictions." The second is *Ber* 33a,
where we read that "the Men of the Great Assembly established for
Israel benedictions and prayers, sanctifications and *havdalah* [the
prayer for the evening of the Sabbath]." The third is *Ber* 28b, which
says that the Eighteen Benedictions were the work of one Simon the
Carder: "Our Masters tell us that Simon ha-Pakuli organized the
Eighteen Benedictions, at Jamnia, in the presence of Rabban
Gamaliel."

Although it is not easy to interpret and reconcile these passages
(especially the first two with the last), they seem to agree on two
points that can hardly be challenged: the practice of reciting these

prayers is far older than the early Christian period, and their organization and the establishment of the number eighteen took place around 70 A.D., in the Academy of Jamnia, after the fall and destruction of the Second Temple. But the work of organization that was done at Jamnia must be correctly understood: what was determined there was not the precise wording of the individual blessings, but their number, order, and general structure. The complete formulas of the *tefillah* would not come into existence until the ninth century, when the first prayer books appeared.

In light of the various points I have adduced, it is possible to distinguish three phases in the formation of the *tefillah*:

—the first is the lengthy period of the existence of the Second Temple; it was during these years that some of the principal benedictions of the *tefillah* were composed—certainly the first three and the last three, since, according to Tosefta *Ber* 3, 13, these were known to the two schools of Hillel and Shammai;

—the second phase coincides with the Academy of Jamnia, which came into existence after the destruction of the temple in 70 A.D. Here the number of the benedictions and the content of each were first established. The work done here was one of redaction and organization and not of creation. The scholars of Jamnia were not so much the authors of the *tefillah* as they were its heirs and compilers;

—the third phase begins with the prayer books, which give the full text of the Eighteen Benedictions. Here again, however, the work was one of compilation and not of creation; the formulas and words are the more or less faithful, more or less literal echo of ancient formulas and words which Jews had been using for centuries to invoke and praise their God.

b) The Tefillah on Feast Days and Weekdays

When the *tefillah* is recited on weekdays, it comprises eighteen benedictions, but the number is reduced in recitation on feast days and the sabbath. The first three (benedictions of praise) and the last three (benedictions of thanksgiving) are always recited, but the intermediate ones (benedictions of petition) are either omitted or reduced in number.

The reason for the omission or reduction is that on the sabbath devout Jews are already experiencing the divine plenitude; this is not something to be awaited and requested, as on weekdays, but a blessing to be enjoyed, as in the messianic age. An image widespread in Jewish symbolism is of the sabbath as the "bride" of Israel; when visited by the "bride," which is the *Shekinah* (the Nearness of God),

Israel no longer "asks" but is intent on enjoying, praising, and thanking. Prayer of petition is a sign of the gap between the present time, which is threatened by sin, and the messianic age, which will be filled with *shalom* and grace. The sabbath, like the other great feasts, is an image and anticipation of the messianic time and therefore cannot but set aside prayer of petition. Such prayer is meaningful when the bride is far off, for it invokes her beauty and asks her to draw near; but when she is present and urges the devout to song and rejoicing, this prayer loses its meaning.

There are, then, two types of *tefillah*: one recited on weekdays and comprising eighteen benedictions; the other recited on the sabbath and feast days and comprising seven or, at times, nine benedictions.

On the sabbath and feast days the intermediate invocations are replaced by a new one called *qedushat ha-yom* ("sanctification of the day"): "Blessed art thou, O Lord, who hallowest the Sabbath" (461) or "who hallowest Israel and the feasts." This varies only slightly according to the feast being celebrated. For example, on Rosh ha-Shanah it reads: "Blessed art thou, O Lord, King over all the earth, who hallowest Israel and the Day of Remembrance (*yom ha-zik-karon*)" (855); on the Day of Atonement: "Blessed art thou, O Lord, thou King who pardonest and forgivest our iniquities and the iniquities of thy people, the house of Israel . . . who hallowest Israel and the Day of Atonement" (903); and so on. The intermediate invocations are always replaced by a single blessing, except on the feasts of the New Year and the Day of Atonement, when they are replaced by three.

The *tefillah* for feast days is characterized not only by omission of the intermediate invocations but also by certain other details (*musaf*). For example, in the *tefillah* for the sabbath, the fourth benediction is enriched by theological reflections on the spiritual meaning of the sabbath. In the evening *tefillah*, the sabbath is described as "memorial of the creation," a description that is immediately followed by the recitation of Gen 2:1–3; in the morning *tefillah* the sabbath is associated with the gift of the Torah on Sinai and presented as a symbol of the covenant between God and Israel; and in the afternoon *tefillah* the sabbath is greeted as the day of complete rest that anticipates and already embodies the *shalom* and rest of the messianic age, "for that day shall be all Sabbath" (*Tam* 7, 4; Danby 589).

I have chosen these passages in order to bring out three different but complementary aspects of the sabbath: creation, revelation, and redemption, or the three pillars of Jewish thought and liturgy. In addition to these variations, there are others that depend on the different rites and communities.

On weekdays the *tefillah* almost never varies throughout the year, except on a few occasions during some special periods. In the rainy season, for example, to the second benediction is added: "Thou causest the wind to blow and the rain to fall" (133); on the feasts of Hanukkah and Purim there is added to the eighteenth benediction a recall of the miracles which God did during the Maccabean period; on fast days a special invocation is added to the sixteenth benediction, asking God to remain closer than ever to his people; if there are sick persons in the community, an explicit prayer for their healing may be added to the eighth benediction; and so on.

c) *The Structure of the* Tefillah

The *tefillah* is made up of nineteen benedictions (originally eighteen), which are divided into three groups or sections: 1) the first three benedictions; 2) the last three; and 3) the thirteen intermediate.

The first three benedictions are introductory and have praise of God for their theme. They glorify God for the three principal attributes that define his innermost being and deepest identity: his love (*hesed*), his power (*gevurah*), and his holiness (*qedushah*). God's love manifests itself primarily in his historical self-revelation to the patriarchs and the Hebrew people, while the signs of his power are creation out of nothing and re-creation from death, that is, the resurrection of the dead. But God is "greater" than any revelation and any creation; in relation to human beings and their history he always remains sovereignly free and transcendent; for this reason the third benediction acknowledges and proclaims him to be *ha-qadosh*, "Holy." These first three benedictions constitute a single theological and thematic unit and one of the most beautiful and deeply meaningful acts of faith in the Jewish liturgy.

The final three benedictions serve as a conclusion and focus on the theme of gratitude. As a matter of fact, only the second expressly develops this theme, while the first expresses the hope that God will restore the worship in the Jerusalem temple, and the third the hope that he will give the gift of abundant peace. The rabbinical tradition nonetheless likes to describe all three as "benedictions of thanksgiving," since thanksgiving will be complete and real only when abundant peace and the fullness of worship become a reality.

The thirteen intermediate benedictions are the heart of the *tefil-*

lah and form a series of petitions that God would grant his people all the things it needs in order to live. These benedictions are the Magna Carta of Judaism; they show us what Judaism regards as truly important. They are not a random group but are structured according to a theological and anthropological logic.

The first three have to do with values of the mind and spirit: understanding, repentance, and forgiveness. Understanding is the ability to penetrate (*intus-legere*, to read within) the meaning of things, their innermost truth and reality; repentance (*teshuvah*, return) is the ability to draw near gradually to the truth which one has discovered and loves, turning each time to slake its own thirst with its beauty and transparency; forgiveness is the ability to begin anew even when the truth has been betrayed through sin.

The next four petitions have to do with the values of freedom, bodily health, abundant fruits of the earth, and the native land. Here again, the petitions are linked and structured to form a coherent whole. Of what use are goods without bodily health? And how is bodily well-being possible without experience of freedom and a homeland? Freedom, health, goods, and homeland form, in Judaism, an indissoluble foursome in which each depends on the others.

These seven petitions are followed by six that look more to the community and society. Hitherto, those praying have prayed for themselves; now their prayer focuses on the needs of the people, the entire collectivity. The petitions here have to do with integral justice, the conquest of injustice, the reward of the just, the rebuilding of Jerusalem, the coming of the Messiah, and the hearing of prayers. Like the preceding groups, these six, despite appearances, have a strongly unified structure, since they are built upon the themes of justice (the first three) and the messianic age (the last three). When all is said and done, these praying are asking that the people may live in justice and that this justice be full and complete. A life of justice means victory over enemies and the proper reward of the just, while experience of messianic fullness implies the rebuilding of Jerusalem, a rebuilding that is not only material but moral and spiritual, in which the will of God becomes the will of human beings and every prayer is heard.

From a literary point of view, each benediction has the structure of any benediction: an opening formula that is technical and standardized ("Blessed art thou, O Lord . . ."); the reason or reasons for the benediction; and a concluding formula that resembles the opening formula and sums up the reasons alleged. But since the *tefillah* is a single long prayer, the initial formula holds for the entire series and is not repeated.

The structure and content of the *tefillah* can be summarized in the following outline:

A. Three Opening Benedictions
1. Thou art God
2. Thou art mighty
3. Thou art holy
} Praise of God

Therefore we ask:

B. Thirteen Intermediate Petitions

4. Understanding
5. Repentance
6. Forgiveness
} Spiritual blessings

7. Personal freedom
8. Health
9. Well-being
10. Reunification of the scattered
} Material blessings

11. Integral justice
12. Punishment of enemies
13. Reward of the just
14. The new Jerusalem
15. The Messiah
16. Hearing of prayers
} Social blessings

Therefore:

C. Three Final Benedictions
17. Restore worship in Jerusalem
18. Accept our gratitude
19. Grant us peace
} Thanksgiving to God

d) Manner of Recitation

The *tefillah* is to be recited standing and with the gaze directed toward Jerusalem. Furthermore, it is recited in complete silence by each individual and without interruption. The recitation of the first and next-to-last benedictions is accompanied by a bow, which is a gesture of adoration and humility. The Talmud, *Ber.* 34, bases this

precept on Gen 24:48: "I bowed and prostrated myself before the
Eternal One; I blessed the Eternal One, the God of my master
Abraham."

The bow is to be made attentively and in accordance with the
prayer; thus the head is bowed when the words baruk 'attah
("Blessed art thou") are said, and raised immediately when the word
"God" is pronounced. The reason for this is that "God raises up those
that are bowed down," that is, those carrying the burden of affliction
and sorrow. This very simple gesture thus conveys all of Judaism's
theological and spiritual wisdom. In time of suffering and oppression
Jews are humbled and "bowed down," but, however heavy the burdens that crush them, when they call upon the name of God they
receive the strength to rise up. That is why they must straighten
their heads as they pronounce the name of God, for to say "God" is to
say "freedom"; calling upon the one renders the other present.

In addition to being recited by individuals and in silence, the
tefillah is also recited a second time, aloud, when there is a sufficient
number of participants (a minyan or group of ten). This second recitation is performed as follows: a reader repeats the tefillah, while the
congregation participates partly by listening and partly by appropriate responses. In this repetition (which is motivated by the need of
helping those who do not yet know the tefillah by memory to learn it)
the text of the Eighteen Benedictions is basically unchanged, although some of the benedictions may be enriched by more explicit
contents and more dialogical formulas. This is the case, for example,
in the third benediction, which in the first recitation simply calls
God "holy," but in the second develops the theme by including several references to Is 6:3 and Ez 3:12. Compare the two formulas:

a) the individual formula: "Unto all generations we will proclaim the lordship of God, for he alone is most high and holy. May thy
praise, O our God, not lessen on our lips for ever, for thou art a great
and holy God and King. Blessed art thou, O Lord, the holy God."

b) the congregational formula:

Reader: We will sanctify thy Name in the world even as
they sanctify it in the highest heavens, as it is written by
the hand of thy prophet: And they called one unto the
other and said,
Cong.: Holy, holy, holy is the Lord of hosts: the whole earth
is full of his glory.
Reader: Those over against them say, Blessed—

Cong.: Blessed be the glory of the Lord from his place.

Reader: And in thy Holy Words it is written, saying

Cong.: The Lord shall reign for ever, thy God, O Zion, unto all generations. Praise ye the Lord.

Reader: Unto all generations we will declare thy greatness, and to all eternity we will proclaim thy holiness, and thy praise, O our God, shall not depart from our mouth for ever, for thou art a great and holy God and King. Blessed art thou, O Lord, the holy God (135–37).

A comparison of the two formulas shows both the new theological content and the new literary structure of the second in relation to the first.

There is one further change when the *tefillah* is thus repeated; it occurs in the eighteenth benediction. Here, when the reader begins to recite the formula of thanksgiving, the congregation does not listen in silence but instead recites, in an undertone, a different prayer of thanksgiving. This seemingly strange practice is justified on the grounds that thanksgiving cannot be delegated to another but can only be personal.

3. The Text and a Commentary

From both the theological and the anthropological point of view, the *tefillah* is evidently a carefully structured prayer. Furthermore, it is connected with the *shema'* and complements it. The *shema'* is God's address to Israel, which is summoned to hear and obey; the *tefillah* is Israel's response of invocation and thanksgiving. Precisely because God has spoken to Israel, Israel can thank him and call upon him.

a) The Three Benedictions of Praise

The first three benedictions are called "benedictions of praise" because their dominant theme is the glorification of the Name of God. The first benediction is known as *'avot* ("fathers") because it speaks of God as "God of our fathers." The second is known as *gevurot* ("mighty acts"), because it celebrates the great works in which God manifests his power and might. The third is known as *qedushat ha-shem* ("sanctification of the Name"), because it speaks of God's holiness and sovereign freedom.

1. Blessed art thou, O Lord our God and God of our fathers, God of Abraham, God of Isaac, and God of Jacob, the great,

mighty and revered God, the most high God, who bestowest
lovingkindness, and art Master of all things; who remem-
berest the pious deeds of the patriarchs, and in love wilt
bring a redeemer to their children's children for thy Name's
sake (131). O King, Helper, Saviour and Shield. Blessed art
thou, O Lord, the Shield of Abraham.

2. Thou, O Lord, art mighty for ever, thou revivest the dead,
thou art mighty to save. [In the summer add: Thou makest
the dew to fall; in the winter: Thou causest the wind to blow
and the rain to fall.] Thou sustainest the living with lovingkindness, revivest the dead with great mercy, supportest
the falling, healest the sick, freest the bound, and keepest
thy faith unto them that sleep in the dust. Who is like unto
thee, Lord of mighty acts, and who resembleth thee, O King,
who orderest death and restorest life, and causest salvation
to spring forth? Yea, faithful art thou to revive the dead.
Blessed art thou, O Lord, who revivest the dead (133–35).

3. Unto all generations we will proclaim the lordship of
God, for he alone is most high and holy. Let your praise, O
our God, never lessen on our lips for ever, for thou art a great
and holy God and King. Blessed art thou, O Lord, the
holy God.

These three benedictions give answer to two questions: Who is
God for human beings, and what is a human being in God's sight?
The answer to the first question is given by recalling and explaining
the three fundamental attributes of God: *gaddol* (great), *gibbor*
(mighty), and *qadosh* (holy). The first benediction develops the
theme of God who is great in love, as the story of the patriarchs
shows; the second, the theme of God who is mighty in works, as is
shown by creation and especially by the resurrection of the dead,
which is a new and more wonderful creation; the third, the theme of
God whose Name is holy, as is shown by the very court of heaven, in
whose chant of "Thrice Holy" the congregation is urged to join.

According to one probable explanation, *qadosh* (holy) means
"separated" and is a synonym for transcendence, otherness, irre-
ducibility. After having been described as "great in love" and
"mighty in works," God is proclaimed "holy," thereby suggesting
that any descriptions given of him must always be relative and par-
tial. He is always greater than the "names" given to him, names

which reflect our names rather than his Name. It is for this reason that in the Jewish tradition the true Name of God cannot be spoken. This consciousness is at the heart of all true religion; when it disappears or weakens, human beings begin to make use of God instead of serving him, and religion degenerates into ideology. We can and must speak of God; we do it by giving names and coming up with definitions, but on one condition: that after saying what we have to say, we have the courage to proclaim him "holy."

The answer to the first of the two questions is thus given by explaining the principal divine attributes (*gadol, gibbor,* and *qadosh*). The answer to the second ("What is a human being?") can be put thus: a human being is one who must acknowledge the reality of God by proclaiming his "greatness," "power," and "holiness." In the third blessing, those praying (the plural is used because even when an individual is alone, he or she is united to the community) say: "Unto all generations we will proclaim the lordship of God."

The proclamation is not simply verbal but is primarily existential. We acknowledge God's "greatness" when we accept his love (*hesed,* a word which occurs twice in the first benediction) by interpreting our life as his gift and living it in covenant with him. We acknowledge his "power" when we renounce our own will to power and reinterpret life and death in the light of his will. We acknowledge his "holiness" when we confess his unfathomable greatness and inexhaustible depth (see Rom 11:33–35) and adore the mystery instead of manipulating it.

The theological riches contained in these benedictions will become clearer in the light of some more detailed observations.

—In the first benediction God is described in the light of Ex 3:15 and Deut 10:17. When he reveals himself to Moses, the latter urgently asks for his Name. God answers: "Say this to the children of Israel: the Eternal, the God of your fathers, the God of Abraham, the God of Isaac, the God of Jacob sends me to you. This is my name for ever" (Ex 3:15). The rabbinical tradition likes to ask why "God" is repeated with the name of each patriarch; the answer given is that Isaac and Jacob were not satisfied with an indirect knowledge of God, passed on to them by their ancestor Abraham, but made this knowledge their own through personal searching. The experience of God can be attested and handed down but not delegated; each person is always called upon to have and renew this experience.

The second biblical citation is from Deut 10:17, where God is defined by three attributes: *gadol* (great), *gibbor* (mighty), and *norah* (venerable; to be feared; terrible), this last being a synonym of *qa-*

dosh. According to the rabbinical tradition, these three are the most appropriate names for the divine reality. In practice, the first three benedictions of the *'amidah* develop these three attributes.

The semantic focal point of the first benediction is the word *ḥesed* (good will, favor), which is twice repeated. If God is *gadol* (great), the sign of this greatness is his love, which he reveals in revealing himself to human beings and for the sake of which he created the world. This first benediction glorifies the "God of history" rather than the God of creation because in the Jewish view creation is primarily a sign of God's love rather than of his power and its meaning can be grasped only in the setting of revelation. Awareness of this love leads to the splendid triple invocation in which God is called *'ozer* (he who helps), *moshyah* (he who saves) and *magen* (he who defends; whence the word "shield").

—In the second blessing the dominant theme is the mighty acts of God whereby he manifests his love: the gift of dew, wind, and rain, the gift of food, the support of the weak ("thou supportest the falling"), the healing of the sick, the liberation of prisoners, and, above all, the raising of the dead. This last is mentioned five times and is the act that sums up all the others.

There are three thematic foci of greater importance in this benediction. The first is expressed in the term *jeshu'ah*, "salvation": "Thou art mighty to save," "Who resembleth thee, O King, who . . . causest salvation to spring forth?" In keeping with Jewish thinking, the salvation meant here is an integral salvation embracing the entire human person, and not simply a spiritual salvation. That is why it includes such elements as dew, wind, and rain, the healing of illnesses, and deliverance from slavery.

The second thematic focus is expressed in the phrase *meḥaiah ha-metim,* "to revive the dead." While the repetition of the thought may be due in part to apologetic motives (to exclude from the community those who, like the Sadducees, questioned the reality of the resurrection), the deeper meaning of it emerges only at the theological level. In Judaism, resurrection and creation are not opposed but are convergent signs of the same divine love. For this reason the benediction speaks of God as one who "sustainest the living with lovingkindness (*be-ḥesed*) and revivest the dead with great mercy (*be-raḥamim rabbim*)."

Creation and resurrection thus spring from the same soil: the *ḥesed* and *raḥamim* of God. When God makes "the dew fall" and "the wind blow" and when he "raises the dead," these are all parts of

the same creative activity by which the chaos of nothingness is overcome by the harmony of cosmos. If, then, our minds are prone to
separate these various "operations" of God and to think of the first
two as obvious and natural and the last alone (the resurrection of the
dead) as miraculous and supernatural, this is due not to our greater
penetration and farsightedness but to our lack of wisdom and our
blindness.

The third thematic focus is expressed in the word "fidelity":
"Faithful (ne'eman) art thou to revive the dead." God's creative activity, of which the raising of the dead is one of the most important
expressions, is utterly free on his part and guaranteed only by his
fidelity. If the sun shines anew every morning and the spring returns
every year to make the earth bear its fruits, this is not due, except at
the phenomenological level, to human effort or a law of nature but to
God's fidelity. Believers see the work of creation as sustained by the
"divine fidelity," and the raising of the dead is only the final degree
of the fidelity that daily gives us new moral and physical strength,
new youthfulness and freshness.[40]

—In the third benediction the dominant note is the attitude and
response of human beings before God: the qedushah or sanctification
of the divine Name, of which Rabbi E. Munk writes:

[The qedushah] is Israel's daily proclamation of the divine
holiness. . . . It is recited in a most solemn manner, with
reader and congregation alternating, and can be said only in
the presence of ten adults. . . . This prayer is the high point
of public prayer. Its content is the glorification of the unfathomable oneness of the divine essence. . . . Israel does
not have a qedushah of its own that is distinct from that of
the heavenly choirs, nor does it look for formulas different
from theirs. On the contrary, it attunes its glorification to
that of the angels.[41]

A careful analysis of the qedushah (in its congregational form;
above, p. 88) shows that there are three thematic terms of theological
importance. The first is qadosh, which, in various forms, occurs nine
times. Around this pole three principal actors move in concentric
circles as it were: the reader, the congregation, and the heavenly
hosts. All three speak with a single voice that is earthly and heavenly, human and divine, and proclaim "unto all generations," that is,
"for ever," that God is "holy, holy, holy." That voice originates in

eternity itself and does not so much describe God as evoke his supreme majesty, his freedom, and his unfathomable sovereignty over
the universe.

The second term is *kavod*, which is translated as "glory":
"Heaven and earth are full of thy glory." Whereas *qadosh* defines the
innermost mystery of God, *kavod* unveils the deepest nature of creation: creation is neither identical with God nor opposed to him, but
is pure transparency and a luminous reflection of him.

Those who are skilled in looking at the world through the eyes of
faith see beyond phenomena and even the contradictions visible in
the world; they glimpse in and through it the limitless beauty and
inexhaustible mystery of God himself.

Does not a similar witness come from the unwearying explorers
of matter, whether at the microscopic or macroscopic level, as they
gaze, enchanted, at its inextricable complexity?

The third term is *hll* (*halleluyah*, "praise the Lord"), the expression par excellence of joy and praise. Whereas *qadosh* defines the
nature of God and *kavod* the nature of the world, *hll* establishes
proper relationship of human beings to both God and the world. The
task of human beings is to praise God for the things of the world.
Thus the two poles—God and world—are linked to praise: God as the
recipient (God is praised), the world as the motive (God is praised
because of the world). Praise requires both, and human beings are
the ideal interpreters.

b) The Thirteen Intermediate Petitions

The three benedictions of praise, which form as it were a great
overture for the *tefillah*, are followed by thirteen "benedictions of
petition," so called because they contain requests. After defining
God in his relationship to human beings and the latter in their relationship to God, the praying soul now trustfully opens its heart and
formulates a series of personal and communal petitions that represent the best of Jewish wisdom and spirituality. This section of the
tefillah may be regarded as the fundamental charter of Jewish
values:

> 4. Thou favourest man with knowledge, and teachest mor-
> tals understanding. O favour us with knowledge, under-
> standing and discernment from thee. Blessed art thou, O
> Lord, gracious Giver of knowledge.

> 5. Cause us to return, O our Father, unto thy Torah; draw
> us near, O our King, unto thy service, and bring us back in

perfect repentance unto thy presence. Blessed art thou, O Lord, who delightest in repentance.

6. Forgive us, O our Father, for we have sinned; pardon us, O our King, for we have transgressed; for thou dost pardon and forgive. Blessed art thou, O Lord, who art gracious, and dost abundantly forgive.

7. Look upon our affliction and plead our cause, and redeem us speedily for thy Name's sake; for thou art a mighty Redeemer. Blessed art thou, O Lord, the Redeemer of Israel.

8. Heal us, O Lord, and we shall be healed; save us and we shall be saved; for thou art our praise. Grant a perfect healing to all our wounds; for thou, almighty King, art a faithful and merciful Physician. Blessed art thou, O Lord, who healest the sick of thy people Israel.

9. Bless this year unto us, O Lord our God, together with every kind of the produce thereof, for our welfare; give [dew and rain for] a blessing upon the face of the earth. O satisfy us with thy goodness, and bless our year like other good years. Blessed art thou, O Lord, who blessest the years.

10. Sound the great horn for our freedom; raise the ensign to gather our exiles, and gather us from the four corners of the earth. Blessed art thou, O Lord, who gatherest the dispersed of thy people Israel.

11. Restore our judges as in former times, and our counsellors as at the beginning; remove from us sorrow and sighing; reign thou over us, O Lord, thou alone, in lovingkindness and tender mercy, and clear us in judgment. Blessed art thou, O Lord, the King who lovest righteousness and judgment.

12. And for slanderers [and heretics] let there be no hope, and let all wickedness perish as in a moment; let all thine enemies be speedily cut off, and the dominion of arrogance do thou uproot and crush; cast down and humble speedily in our days. Blessed art thou, O Lord, who breakest the enemies and humblest the arrogant.

13. Towards the righteous and the pious, towards the elders of thy people, the house of Israel, towards the remnant of their scribes, towards true proselytes, and towards us also may thy tender mercies be stirred, O Lord our God; grant a good reward unto all who faithfully trust in thy Name; set our portion with them for ever, so that we may not be put to shame; for we have trusted in thee. Blessed art thou, O Lord, the stay and trust of the righteous.

14. And to Jerusalem, thy city, return in mercy, and dwell therein as thou hast spoken; rebuild it soon in our days as an everlasting building, and speedily set up therein the throne of David. Blessed art thou, O Lord, who rebuildest Jerusalem.

15. Speedily cause the offspring of David, thy servant, to flourish, and lift up his glory by thy divine help because we wait for thy salvation all the day. Blessed art thou, O Lord, who causest the strength of salvation to flourish.

16. Hear our voice, O Lord our God; spare us and have mercy upon us, and accept our prayer in mercy and favour; for thou art a God who hearkenest unto prayers and supplications; from thy presence, O King, turn us not empty away; for thou hearkenest in mercy to the prayer of thy people Israel. Blessed art thou, O Lord, who hearkenest unto prayer (137–47).

These invocations, despite the differences among them, form in fact a single coherent and rigorously structured petition that asks God for complete, messianic salvation. The several requests represent the basic elements in this integral salvation.

—The fourth benediction, known as da'at (knowledge) from its principal term, asks God for the gift of intelligence (from intus-legere, to read things in depth, penetrating to their radical truth). The content of this "intelligence" is expressed by three words: da'at (knowledge), binah (understanding), and hasekel (discernment). The intelligence or insight in question here is not simply rational but existential, that is, insight that grasps the meaning of things in light of the intentionality that underlies and dynamizes them. It might be said that "knowledge" here is equivalent to "wisdom" that urges human beings to seek the good and feeds the passion for truth (see 1

Kgs 3:9; Jer 9:23). It is with this interpretation in mind that the *havda-lah* prayer is introduced at this point on the evening of the sabbath. That prayer emphasizes the essential difference between light, symbolized by the sabbath, and darkness, represented by what is non-sabbath. A grasp of this difference, gained by living the former and vanquishing the latter, is a gift of *da'at* or the insight that enables human beings to see and enjoy things from the viewpoint of God, their creator and sustainer. Where this kind of "intelligence" is lacking, the world is as it were deprived of light and remains indifferent and mute, whether one knows it rationally or possesses it with greedy passion.

This benediction, then, expresses the first and most important of all the petitions, the one that precedes and gives meaning to all the others. That is why the Talmud could say: "How important knowledge must be if it has been placed at the beginning of the weekday prayers!" (*Ber.*33a).

—The fifth benediction, known as *teshuvah* (repentance), asks God for the gift of conversion, of a return to his truth. This benediction is connected with the preceding, which it picks up and completes by explicitating its content and purpose. In other words, true "knowledge" is knowledge that leads human beings back to the Torah and to the service of God. "Cause us to return . . . unto thy Torah . . . (and) unto thy service ('*avodah*)." *Teshuvah, Torah,* and '*avodah* are the three thematic words that give this petition its structure. *Torah* is the expression of the divine will and '*avodah* is the sign of the human person's readiness and availability, while *teshuvah* (which in the vocabulary of the Bible means to go back to the proper starting point, to re-turn) signifies the gradual correspondence of the second to the first. As human beings gradually discover truth, thanks to the gift of "knowledge," they cannot but conform themselves to the Torah by placing themselves at its service. This slow and gradual process of conformity, which lasts a lifetime, is the real favor being requested in this benediction.

—The sixth blessing, which is called *selihah* (forgiveness), asks God not to consider our sins and infidelities. Once again, this benediction picks up and completes the preceding. For in their gradual conformity to the truth human beings do not follow an undeviating path but experience moments of uncertainty and even betrayal. Therefore they pray: "Forgive us . . . for we have sinned; pardon us . . . for we have transgressed." *Teshuvah* and *selihah* go together: where the former is deficient, the latter restores confidence and hope; where the former even fails completely, because based on human effort, the latter is always victorious, because guaranteed by God: "Thou dost pardon and forgive. Blessed art thou, O Lord, who art gracious, and dost abundantly forgive." God forgives human beings not because they are good but because he is good (hanun). This is the certainty Jews carry with them on their search for the truth; it gives them the strength they need in order not to succumb to any defeat or any sense of inevitability.

—The seventh benediction, known as ge'ulah (redemption), asks God to keep far from us the affliction that hinders the exercise of freedom. It was probably composed during the time of persecution by Antiochus Epiphanes (215–163 B.C.) and, in its present setting, begins a new series of more concrete and material petitions: for personal freedom, health, well-being, and native land. The first of all these more concrete blessings is indeed personal freedom, for without this the others would be insufficient and unreliable. While all individuals and all peoples respond to the theme of freedom, this is especially true of the Jewish people, for they came into existence through the exodus from Egypt, a deliverance willed and ensured by God.

A basic characteristic of Judaism is its assertion of this personal freedom as utterly radical, because it is directly linked to the will of God, from which it flows. That is why this benediction calls God go'el, "he who sets free": "Blessed art thou, O Lord, the Redeemer of Israel." Precisely because God is the source of freedom, the latter is extremely important to human beings and is invoked and sought as the greatest personal value and the value that is the condition for all the others. For how could health, wealth, and native land have meaning without the savor given to them by interior and personal freedom?

—The eighth benediction, known as refu'ah (healing), asks God for complete bodily health. The key word in this benediction is the verb rf', which means to restore health, to cure infirmities. God is twice invoked as rofe', literally "physician," in this case a physician who, unlike any other, is ne'eman (faithful) and rahaman (merciful). We might be tempted to smile at the application of "physician" to God, and yet nothing is so dear to him as the human body, which is his "image and likeness" (Gen 1:27). He cares for this "body" in his tender providence, as we are told by Jesus of Nazareth, one of Judaism's most penetrating and faithful interpreters: "Do not be anxious about your life, what you shall eat or what you shall drink, nor about your body, what you shall put on. Is not life more than food, and the body more than clothing? Look at the birds of the air:

they neither sow nor reap nor gather into barns, and yet your heavenly Father feeds them. Are you not of more value than they?" (Mt 6:25–26). After freedom, health is the most valuable blessing to have and to pray for.

—The ninth benediction, known as *birkat ha-shanim* (benediction for the years), asks God for fruitful seasons and abundant harvests. The petition has two parts, the first general, the second specific. God is first asked to bless "this year unto us, together with every kind of produce"; the petition is then made more specific: "give dew and rain for a blessing upon the face of the earth."

Anyone familiar with the Middle East knows how necessary rain is and how life and survival depend on it. To pray for rain is to pray for the fruits of the earth, that they may be sufficient to feed all its inhabitants. The second benediction also mentioned rain when celebrating God as the one who "causest the wind to blow and the rain to fall." Rain was there seen as a sign of God's creative activity that elicits human admiration and praise; here it is the object of a petition that God would meet the needs of human beings.

It is important not to overlook the thematic word in this benediction, namely, *brk*, which is used four times but with a meaning different from its usual one: "Bless this year . . . give dew and rain for a blessing. . . ." Here the subject who does the blessing is God, whereas in the standardized formula "Blessed art thou, O Lord," the unexpressed subject is human beings. There are in fact two kinds of benediction: that of God, directed to human beings, and that of human beings, directed to God. There is an essential difference between the two, for God "blesses" human beings through the concrete gifts of creation (rain, here, is a part that stands for the whole), whereas human beings bless God by acknowledging and praising him. God's blessing is primordial and creative, that of human beings is responsive and laudative. The latter arises as a response to the former and is inspired by realization of it. The relation between the two kinds of blessing emerges with clarity in the concluding sentence: "Blessed art thou, O Lord, who blessest the years." God is blessed because he blesses us, and does so not by words but by the "years," that is, the riches of the world and the fruits of the earth.

—The tenth benediction asks for the reunification of the Jewish people, in accordance with Is 11:12 ("He . . . will assemble the outcasts of Israel, and gather the dispersed of Judah from the four corners of the earth") and Is 27:13 ("In that day a great trumpet will be blown, and those who were lost in the land of Assyria and those who were driven out to the land of Egypt will come"). The key word in this benediction is qbs, "to gather" (whence qibbus, kibbutz), which occurs three times.

This gathering or reunification, which according to Jewish symbology is both proclaimed and brought to pass by the blowing of the shofar (trumpet), has for its first object the Jewish people, now scattered to the four corners of the earth; but it also has for its object the whole human race, of which the Jewish people is a representative part. According to many, the prayer uttered in this benediction has been answered by the founding of the new state of Israel, in which Jews from 102 countries and speaking over 80 different languages are now gathered. The claim may be true, but the benediction and its prayer remain timely, not only because the gathering of the Jews calls for the reunification of the entire human race, but also and above all because, especially from the spiritual point of view, the gathering of Israel is never complete but always still to be realized.

The prayer for a native land is not to be understood either in a nationalist or in an exclusive sense. As a place that bestows an identity and promotes socialization, and not as a place opposed to that of others, a land is a precious possession, like freedom, health, and well-being.

—The eleventh blessing, called ṣedaqah (justice), asks God to establish social relations based on solidarity and love; the prayer thus completes the preceding. Of what use, after all, is a native land if in it dominion belongs to the strongest, who oppress it, exploit it, and do violence to it? The prayer has two steps or stages. First, it asks the Lord to send courageous and loyal governors like those who led Israel prior to the monarchy and whom popular tradition remembered as holy and heroic: "Restore our judges as in former times."

But even honorable individuals like the judges were not immune to the temptations of injustice and errors. Therefore the prayer passes from the historical plane to the eschatological and asks God to become himself the ruler of Israel: "Reign thou over us, O Lord, thou alone." The text not only calls for the reign of God but also tells us what that reign will be like. Unlike the rule of human beings, which is marked by injustice and violence, God reigns "in lovingkindness (ḥesed) and tender mercy (raḥamim), and . . . in judgment (mishpat)."

—The twelfth benediction, known in the Talmud as birkat haminim (benediction of the heretics), asks God for the radical elimination of evil as personified by "slanderers," "heretics," and "enemies." "For slanderers and heretics let there be no hope . . . let all thine enemies be speedily cut off."

Of all the benedictions this one poses the most problems, as is shown by the many changes and corrections it has undergone down the centuries and by the adaptations of it in the new prayer books, especially those of the Reform, some of which eliminate it entirely.[42]

There are two considerations that make this benediction problematic, one historical, the other theological. If, as seems probable, the birkat ha-minim originated as a prayer against Jewish Christians, whose conception of Torah and Messiah threatened the survival of Judaism, then we must ask: Is the benediction still meaningful today in a profoundly changed historical and cultural climate in which, even if slowly, the principles of respect, dialogue, and tolerance are being professed and asserted?

But it is above all at the theological level that this benediction causes difficulties. Can we properly ask God to "cut off" our enemies. Do not execratory prayers, even though common in the Bible (see, for example, Num 10:35; Ps 69:25–29; 59:14–15; 137:9), contradict the true meaning of prayer and even belief in God?

I shall try to answer these questions later on. For the moment it is enough to point out that rather than being directed against "enemies" understood as real individuals, the benediction looks to the elimination of evil, the action of which hinders the coming of God's reign. The prayer is for the victory of love and not the defeat of enemies. That this is the primary thought in the Jewish mind when using this benediction (and other execratory texts) is shown by the following passage from the Talmud in which Beruria, the wise wife of Rabbi Meir, challenges a prayer in which her husband has asked God for the death of two criminals: "Is it perhaps written that 'criminals must be eliminated'? No, on the contrary it is written: 'Let sins be done away with.' It is so written in order that you may ask mercy for them and that they may repent and be converted. Only thus will the wicked vanish while saving their lives" (Ber. 10a).

—The thirteenth benediction asks God for the victory of goodness as represented by three categories of persons: the "righteous" (ṣadiqim), the "pious" (ḥasidim), and the "proselytes" (gere ha-ṣedeq, literally, "strangers who have become righteous"). This benediction expresses in positive terms that which the preceding benediction had put negatively, for a society of "the righteous, the pious, and true proselytes" is the opposite of one containing "slanderers, heretics, and enemies." Here, as in the preceding benediction, the categories are symbolic in that they stand for all Jews and—why not?—the entire human race.

The purpose of the prayer is to ask God for a world in which there will be only righteous persons, persons whose love and behavior reflect that of God himself: "Toward the righteous and the pious . . . may thy tender mercies be stirred." This very beautiful formula expresses the ideal of every human society, for a society is truly human when the human beings making it up act with mercy, like God, allowing his way of acting (ḥesed) to shine through them, so that they will deserve to be called ḥasidim (literally: full of ḥesed).

This benediction concludes the petitions having to do with the native land: that God would reunify it (10), make it just (11), and render it capable of overcoming evil (12) and doing what is good (13).

—The fourteenth benediction asks God to rebuild Jerusalem and make it once again his city: "And to Jerusalem, thy city, return in mercy . . . rebuild it soon . . . as an everlasting building." Even though today Jerusalem has become once again the city of the chosen people, this benediction retains its value, for its reference is not only historical but also, and primarily, eschatological. Before being a city of stone, the Jerusalem which God is asked to rebuild is a city of the heart; it is a city built by God rather than by human beings, in accordance with Zechariah 8:3: "Thus says the Lord: I will return to Zion, and will dwell in the midst of Jerusalem."

According to a midrashic story, the Shekinah had gradually distanced itself from human beings as they sinned, but with the coming of the patriarchs it reversed its course and gradually drew nearer to human beings according to their merits and goodness. Thus, while evil drives the Shekinah away, goodness draws it back.[43] Israel bears witness that in the going and coming of the Shekinah the latter wins out over the former; in the end the Shekinah will return and never depart again.

It is not without meaning that this eschatological horizon appears at the end of the petitions previously formulated. God has been asked for many things (a good year, a native land, justice, the conquest of evil, and so on). The praying community knows, however, that all these "things" will not automatically be given to us simply for the asking; difficulties, ambiguities, and struggles remain as before. Despite everything, however, the community will continue to live, work, and love thanks to its certainty that God will "return to Jerusalem" and "rebuild it as an everlasting building."

—The fifteenth benediction, which asks God to bring in the messianic age, is so closely linked to the preceding that the Palestinian Talmud, unlike the Babylonian, regards them as a single benediction. Drawing its inspiration from Is 11:1, this benediction speaks of the "offspring of David" and asks that he may "flourish" as before, thereby introducing the fullness of salvation: "And lift up his glory by thy divine help, because we wait for thy salvation." In the messianic age human activity will become a pure reflection of the divine; God, who is "salvation," will be welcomed by human beings, and salvation will turn into "strength." While this benediction poses several problems of interpretation, especially regarding the person of the Messiah (so that Reformed liturgies prefer to alter the text), there can be agreement on at least one point: to pray for the "offspring of David" is another of the ways of asking God for a human world in which life will be radiant with meaning, as it was in the earthly paradise.

    —The sixteenth benediction, the last of the petitions, asks God to hear prayers: "Hear our voice . . . accept our prayer." It seems strange, does it not, that such a benediction should come at the end of the petitions and not at the beginning?[44] The answer is that the benediction must be interpreted in relation to the Messiah, in accordance with Is 56:6-7: "Every one who holds fast to my covenant—these I will bring to my holy mountain, and will make them joyful in my house of prayer." Thus far the community has prayed by asking God for various things. But while it prayed, its gaze was fixed on the messianic age, the only place where prayer (every prayer) is truly heard, since the human will is there in perfect accord with the will of God. Only in the "place" which Isaiah describes as a "house of prayer" does life reveal its identity and is filled with joy. It is for that "place" that this benediction prays, describing God as him "who hearkenest unto prayer." It is with an invocation of God so described that the series of petitions ends and the final benedictions begin.

c) The Three Benedictions of Thanksgiving

    The three final benedictions are called "benedictions of thanksgiving" because their dominant theme is thanksgiving and gratitude to God. In fact, only the second of the three explicitly develops the theme of thanksgiving, while the other two are rather petitions, asking God for the restoration of the Temple worship and the granting of *shalom*, peace. The three had their historical origin in the liturgy of the temple, which explains their unity and dynamics. The first was an appeal to God to accept the sacrificial offerings. When the temple was destroyed in 70 A.D., the benediction was substantially changed and became an appeal to God to accept the prayer offered in the synagogue and to restore the priestly service. The second benedic-

tion remained a prayer of thanksgiving, while the third picked up
and concluded the blessing which the kohanim (priests) gave to the
people at the end of the sacrificial offerings.

17. Accept, O Lord our God, thy people Israel and their
prayer; restore the service to the inner sanctuary of thy
house; receive in love and favour both the offerings of Israel
and their prayer; and may the worship of thy people Israel
be ever acceptable unto thee. And let our eyes behold thy
return in mercy to Zion. Blessed art thou, O Lord, who restorest thy divine presence unto Zion (149–51).

18. We give thanks unto thee, for thou art the Lord our God
and the God of our fathers for ever and ever; thou art the
Rock of our lives, the Shield of our salvation through every
generation. We will give thanks unto thee and declare thy
praise for our lives which are committed unto thy hand and
for our souls which are in thy charge, and for thy miracles
which are daily with us, and for thy wonders and thy benefits, which are wrought at all times, evening, morn and
noon. O thou who art all-good, whose mercies fail not; thou,
merciful Being, whose lovingkindnesses never cease, we
have ever hoped in thee. Blessed art thou, O Lord, whose
Name is all-good, and unto whom it is becoming to give
thanks (151–55).

19. Grant peace, welfare, blessing, grace, lovingkindness
and mercy unto us and unto all Israel, thy people. Bless us,
O our Father, even all of us together, with the light of thy
countenance; for by the light of thy countenance thou hast
given us, O Lord our God, the Torah of life, lovingkindness
and righteousness, blessing, mercy, life and peace; and may
it be good in thy sight to bless thy people Israel at all times
and in every hour with thy peace. Blessed art thou, O Lord,
who blessest thy people Israel with peace (155)

The first of these benedictions is called 'avodah (service) because it asks God to reestablish divine worship in Jerusalem. The
second is called hodayah (thanksgiving), because it develops the
theme of gratitude for the divine blessings received. The third, finally, is called birkat ha-shalom (benediction for peace), because it

asks God for prosperity and well-being. But because this final benediction is sometimes preceded by the priestly blessing (recited nowadays by a reader), it is also called *birkat kohanim* (benediction of the
priests).

Although the three have different themes, the Jewish tradition
likes to think of them all as "benedictions of thanksgiving." The
reason is that any spirit of thanksgiving is necessarily linked to the
hearing of prayer and the gift of peace. Only they can be truly grateful whom God has heard and has flooded with his peace. The middle
benediction is therefore regarded as the gravitational center of these
final three; its meaning is captured and summed up in the word
modim (from the root *ydh*): "We give thanks unto thee, for. . . ." The
commentators like to point out that the word has three principal
meanings. First and foremost, *modim* means "to prostrate oneself,"
"to bow down"[45] (whence the prescribed bow at the beginning and
end of this benediction); secondarily it means "to acknowledge," "to
confess"; and, finally, it means "to be grateful," "to thank." Having
reached the end of its *tefillah*, the community repeats its gesture of
adoration, acknowledgement, and thanksgiving, the single/three-
fold attitude that finds expression in every true prayer.

With regard to each of the benedictions in particular:

—The seventeenth benediction asks God to accept the prayers
that have been offered to him. The key word is *rṣh* which means to
adopt/accept with love and sympathy. Indeed, how could prayers be
heard if not by reason of God's free and unmerited good will? The
praying community has thus far offered its petitions, but it knows
that if its prayers are to be heard, it will not be because of its merits
but by reason of the divine favor: "Accept, O Lord our God, thy
people Israel and their prayer."

From the present moment the community mind turns to the past
and then back to the future: "Restore the service to the inner sanctuary of thy house" and "let our eyes behold thy return in mercy to
Zion." The prayer for the *tefillah* being offered here and now stimu-
lates remembrance of the prayers offered during the sacrifices in the
temple, as well as prayer asking for the eschatological day when the
Shekinah will return to Jerusalem.

The Reformed liturgies have chosen to eliminate the references
to the temple and the restoration of Zion and to keep only the plea
that God would accept the prayers raised up to him. But even in
liturgies that keep the text in its entirety, it is always possible to
move beyond the literal interpretation to the eschatological. To ask
God for the "restoration of the temple" and the "return to Zion" is a

way of asking him to manifest in the midst of Israel and of human beings generally.

—The eighteenth benediction develops at length the theme of thanksgiving, and does so in a summarizing way that brings the *tefillah* toward its end. We thank God because he is "the Lord our God" (*'Elohenu*) and "the God of our fathers"; because he is "the Rock of our lives"; because God is a God who works "miracles," "wonders," and "benefits"; and, above all, because he is an "all-good" and "merciful" God whose kindness never ceases. All of these motives are summed up in the closing formula: "Blessed art thou, O Lord, whose Name is all-good and unto whom it is becoming to give thanks." We do not know the Name of God, for his being is an unfathomable mystery. One thing, however, we do know: that this Name is *ha-tov*, the supreme Good and the source of all good. For this reason, the sole task of human beings is to praise (*le-hodot*).

—The nineteenth benediction asks God for the gift of peace and is connected with the priestly benediction in Num 6:23–26, which ends with this wish: "The Lord lift up his countenance upon you, and give you peace." The congregation picks up these final words and answers them with a prayer for peace: "Grant peace, welfare, blessing, grace, lovingkindness and mercy unto us and unto all Israel." The key word in this benediction is therefore *shalom*, which, according to the rabbinical commentaries, is the final request of the *tefillah* and its crown and completion. The word occurs four times and is explained and enriched by numerous synonyms and by some exemplifications: "Grant peace (*shalom*), welfare (*tovah*), blessing (*berakah*), grace (*hen*), lovingkindness (*hesed*) and mercy (*rahamim*)." It is clear, then, that in the Jewish tradition "peace" has a number of meanings and is a sum total of all good things rather than a simple absence of war. It is no accident the root of the word means "entire," "integral,"[46] for peace exists where there is wholeness and integrity.

In addition to deploying a rich set of synonyms, the benediction offers two explanations of the reality signified by "peace"; one explanation relates peace to the vision of God, the other to the gift of the Torah: "Bless us . . . with the light of thy countenance; for by the light of thy countenance thou hast given us . . . the Torah of life (*Torat hayim*)." "To see God" (the biblical image for dialogue with him) and to carry out his will, which is manifested in the Torah, are the secret and root of the peace that springs up and gives its fruits where the Lord is acknowledged as Lord of the covenant and where his word is received and obeyed. *'Adonai* (Lord), *shalom*, and *Torah* form a trio that are inseparable and necessary, since one of them cannot exist without the others.

4. *The* Birkat ha-minim

One of the nineteen benedictions—the twelfth—merits special attention. Of this benediction Rabbi E. Munk writes: "No passage in the ritual has been so often misunderstood as this one. In the course of history the text has been so often altered and corrected, it is highly unlikely that the original tenor of it will be reconstructed with certainty."[47]

This benediction is known as the "benediction of heretics" because it ends with praise of God who destroys heretics. In our modern languages, however, the prayer is likely to be ambiguous, since one might think of God blessing the heretics or the heretics blessing God. To avoid misunderstandings, it would be better to use a different translation. Jacob J. Petuchowski translates "curse on heretics," while Schalom Ben Chorin prefers "prayer against heretics,"[48] since this wording lends itself to a less negative and more qualified assessment of the situation.

The basic problems posed by the *birkat ha-minim* can, by and large, be reduced to two, one historical, the other theological. The first can be formulated as follows: Who are the *minim* (heretics) of whom the benediction speaks? Are they Jewish Christians, who are being excommunicated, or are they "heretics" and wicked people generally? The second problem is this: What justification is there for introducing curses and anathemas into prayers? Is not such a procedure a contradiction of faith in God and in his universal love? It is not easy to respond to these questions (especially the first), and scholars continue to give different answers.

a) *The Rabbinical Source and Its Interpretation*

The earliest text supplying data on the *birkat ha-minim* is Ber. 28b-29a in the Babylonian Talmud:

Our Rabbis taught: Simeon ha-Pakuli arranged the eighteen benedictions in order before Rabban Gamaliel in Jabneh. Said Rabban Gamaliel to the Sages: Can anyone among you frame a benediction to the Minim? Samuel the Lesser arose and composed it. The next year he forgot it and he tried for two or three hours to recall it, and they did not remove him (from the lectern). Why did they not remove him seeing that

Rab Judah has said in the name of Rab: If a reader make a
mistake in any of the other benedictions they do not remove
him, but if in the benediction of the Minim, he is removed
because we suspect him of being a Min?—Samuel the
Lesser is different, because he composed it. But is there not a
fear that he may have recanted?—Abaje said: we have a
tradition that a good man does not become bad. But does he
not? Is it not written, "But when the righteous turneth away
from his righteousness and committeth iniquity" (Ez 18:24)?
Such a man was originally wicked, but one who was originally righteous does not do so. But is that so? Have we not
learned: Believe not in thyself until the day of thy death?
For Johanan the High Priest officiated as High Priest for
eighty years and in the end he became a Min.[49]

The passage is not easy to interpret; Maimonides has this to say
about it:

In the time of Rabbi Gamaliel apostates were multiplying in
Israel; they grew insolent and tried to incite Israel to abandon the Eternal One. The Rabbi saw that this situation was
very dangerous, indeed the most dangerous possible; therefore he and his Beth-Din intervened and composed a new
berakah which asked God to destroy the apostates. This
prayer was made part of the ritual in order that all might
become familiar with it. That is why the prayers in the she-
moneh-'esreh number nineteen instead of eighteen.[50]

Maimonides' interpretation was subsequently repeated and further refined by others, including some modern scholars like J.J. Petuchowski, who writes:

Here is the development in its broad lines. In the beginning
there were eighteen benedictions. But when the Jewish
Christians became a danger (they were suspected of collabo-
rating with the Romans), people no longer trusted the Jew
who stood beside them in the synagogue, for he might be a
Jewish Christian and therefore a "traitor." A way had to be
found of barring such individuals from entering the synagogue, but this was not easy because Jewish Christians
looked like other Jews and followed the same way of life. An
execratory formula was then introduced which Jewish

Christians would be unable to approve with their "Amen,"
for they would then be cursing themselves.[51]

In this type of interpretation, the birkat ha-minim was composed
at the Synod of Jamnia (90–100 A.D.) by Samuel the Lesser, on orders
from Patriarch Gamaliel II. The prayer was directed against Jewish
Christians and meant to show them to be separated and
excommunicated.

C. Thoma offers a more nuanced interpretation. In his view, the
prayer against heretics was not composed at Jamnia with the Jewish
Christians in mind; rather, like the other benedictions, it had been in
existence and use in a more generic and varied form. Instead of being
created new at Jamnia, it was simply given a set place in the sequence of prayers. Samuel the Lesser's task was to "actualize" the
prayer so that it would allude to and, if need be, include Jewish
Christians. But the latter were neither the original nor the sole objects of the prayer, this being formulated against apostates and unbe-
lievers generally.[52]

From this interpretation the author concludes: "No excommunication of Jewish Christians by all of the rabbis ever took place. According to the various versions of the blessing against heretics, they
were not even perceived everywhere as particularly dangerous
apostates. Neither, therefore, was the separation between Judaism
and Jewish Christians irrevocable."[53] All may not agree with the first
part of this conclusion,[54] but they can and should agree with the
second: even if the birkat ha-minim came into existence historically
as an express excommunication of Jewish Christians, it is by no
means to be regarded as irrevocable. Condemnations and excom-
munications always originate less in love of the truth than in misunderstanding and fear. Therefore they can always be set aside, and in
this case are being set aside, as the many courageous pioneers of the
Jewish-Christian dialogue bear witness.

b) Variations in the Text

Many versions and paraphrases of the birkat ha-minim have
come down to us. The oldest and most deserving of attention is the
so-called Palestinian recension, a text discovered by Solomon
Schechter in the Cairo Genizeh at the end of the nineteenth century:

For the meshummadim (apostates, traitors, or even: bap-
tized ones?) let there be no hope. Uproot the kingdom of
wickedness (malkut zadon) speedily in our days. Let the

Nazarenes (noṣrim) and the minim (heretics, degenerates) perish as in a moment. Let them be obliterated from the book of life. Let them not be inscribed with the righteous. Blessed are you, O Lord, who humbles the arrogant.[55]

In addition, there is the Babylonian version, which goes back to the third century A.D.: "For the meshummadim let there be no hope. Let all heretics (minim) and traitors (noṣrim) perish as in a moment. Uproot and destroy the kingdom of wickedness speedily in our days. Blessed are you, O Lord, who breaks the enemy and humbles the arrogant."[56]

The two texts are evidently similar. The only difference is the absence from the Babylonian version of the reference to Jewish Christians (noṣrim), who are expressly mentioned in the Palestinian version. The reason for the omission is that while Jewish Christians were present and important in Jerusalem, they were not in Babylon. The formulas used in the synagogues vary from country to country and according to the kind of Jewish thinking they represent. For example, in the Einheitsgebetbuch Deutschlands (1929), which is a product of Liberal Judaism, the text reads as follows: "Grant that the erring may return to the path which leads to you; grant that in our time violence may disappear from the earth and wicked pride may be put to rout. Blessed are you, Eternal One, who sweep away violence and humble pride."[57]

The new edition of the American Reformed ritual, Gates of Prayer (New York, 1975), has chosen a more radical solution and simply omitted the birkat ha-minim. But in most contemporary rituals the prayer reads as follows:

And for slanderers let there be no hope, and let all wickedness perish as in a moment; let all thine enemies be speedily cut off, and the dominion of arrogance do thou uproot and crush; cast down and humble speedily in our days. Blessed art thou, O Lord, who breakest the enemies and humblest the arrogant (Hertz, 143–45).[58]

c) Intolerance of Evil

The greater difficulty posed by the birkat ha-minim is theological: How is it possible to ask God: "Let all wickedness perish as in a moment; let all thine enemies be speedily cut off; cast down and humble speedily in our days"? How is it possible to pray: "Blessed art thou, O Lord, who breakest the enemies"? There is no doubt that such expressions are a stumbling block for modern sensibilities and make room for dangerous ambiguities. That is why many Reformed liturgies prefer to replace them with others that are more general and impersonal. But, whatever the validity of substituting abstract terms (wickedness) for concrete (the wicked), the basic problem, that of interpretation, remains. Only a correct hermeneutic can safeguard their tenor and truth while avoiding either reduction or falsification. In developing a correct hermeneutic of these execratory texts two basic principles must never be forgotten.

First of all, any and every purely literal interpretation must be avoided. Execratory expressions are often to be found in the Bible (see, for example, the execratory psalms such as Ps 21 or 89), but, whether placed in God's mouth or requested of him, they are, like all images applied to the godhead, anthropomorphic, that is, analogical. This means that they are partly "true" and partly "false"; that they contain a "truth," but this truth is not a truth found in the literal sense, for no sooner is the latter affirmed than it must be transcended and left behind.

From this first principle it follows that a prayer asking God to curse "slanderers," "the wicked," "enemies," and so on does not call down his vengeance against them (God does not will the death of sinners but that they be converted and live!); rather it expresses his and our "anger" against evil and injustice. God is radical love and fathomless transparent purity, light undimmed and vital energy beyond our comprehending. Because he is such, he cannot but hate "evil." An execratory prayer expresses this irreducible opposition between God and every historical form of suffering, injustice, and oppression, for these contradict the mystery of his love. It expresses the ontological and utterly unbridgeable distance between the holiness of God and human sin. It is a prayer that the former may triumph and the latter dwindle and disappear; that the powers of life advance and those of death be silenced.

The second basic principle is this: that while avoiding a literal interpretation, we must not fall back into abstract generalizations. No one experiences evil as an abstraction; the evil that oppresses and is bloodstained is something concrete and part of everyday life, something that takes flesh in history. Moreover, it bears a concrete name. "Hebrews" and "Egyptians," "blacks" and "whites," "minorities" and "controlling groups," "third world" and "rich countries," "weak" and "strong," "tortured" and "torturer": the members of these pairs cannot be put on the same level, for if "evil" is universal, it is so because of its agents and not because of its victims. Execratory prayers remind us that evil is dramatically concrete; they put us on guard against the danger of reducing it to a disembodied concept.

Is it possible, however, in face of evil (and of the execratory prayers that attest to its existence) to maintain this twofold attitude of universal love and awareness of concrete evil, the only attitude that can keep us from either instrumentalizing evil or emptying it of its content? The experience of people who are truly men and women of prayer shows that it is indeed possible. In these individuals, intolerance of concrete evil and the struggle against it are always accompanied by a great love that is both real and universal. One proof of this is the following prayer of Leo Baeck, the last Chief Rabbi of Germany and a witness from 1943 to 1945 of the horrors of the Holocaust in the concentration camp at Theresienstadt:

> Peace be to men of ill will, and let there be an end to all vengeance and all desire to punish and chastise. . . . O God, keep an account of all the victims and all their love . . . of all those devastated, tortured hearts that, in spite of everything, remained courageous in the face of death. . . . All this, my God, should be a ransom in your sight for the forgiveness of sins, so that justice may be born anew as you take account of all this good and not the evil.[59]

IV. THE THIRD STRUCTURAL UNIT: THE QERI'AT TORAH

In addition to the shema' and the tefillah, the Jewish liturgy has a third key part: the qeri'at Torah or "reading of the Torah;" which takes place in the synagogue on Mondays, Thursdays, and Saturdays and on festal and semifestal days. Among the several commands contained in the shema' one is especially important: "And thou shalt teach them (the words of the Torah) diligently unto thy children, and shalt talk of them when thou sittest in thine house, and when thou walkest by the way, and when thou liest down, and when thou risest up" (Deut 6:7). The purpose of the biblical command is to inculcate love for God's word in every generation; the purpose of the qeri'at Torah in the synagogue, on set days and according to specified procedures, is to satisfy the command, for through the qeri'at Torah the Jewish people are nourished by the word of God that is read and commented on.

a) *The Tree of Life*

Judaism is unintelligible apart from the Torah, which is its soul and substance, its secret and fascination. In the Jewish tradition, the centrality of the Torah finds expression less in rational argument than in language of images. One of the most beautiful of these is "the tree of life." According to a midrash,[60] when Adam and Eve left the earthly paradise, God gave them the Torah in place of the tree of life. The Torah thus becomes the new Eden, not only because it shows the existence of a new Eden to be possible but also because it sets down the conditions whereby the new Eden becomes a reality and whereby human beings may enter it. The Torah is *eṣ ha-ḥayim*, "the tree of life," because it contains it and shows the way to it, expresses it and makes it a reality.

A second image showing the central place of the Torah is that of a foundation. In the *Pirke Aboth*, a tractate of the Mishnah containing the most important maxims of the teachers of Judaism, we read the following: "Simeon the Just was [one] of the survivors of the Great Synagogue. He used to say:—Upon three things the world standeth; upon Torah, upon Worship and upon the showing of kindness."[61] There is really only one foundation and not three, namely, the word of God in its three inseparable expressions: Torah (the revealed word), worship (the word reactualized and given ritual form), and the actions of love (the word as lived out, inspiring human lives).

These images are important also by reason of their universality; that is, they refer not only to Israel but also to *'adam*, that is, every human being, the entire world. The word of God is the foundation not only of Israel but of all peoples and the whole of reality.

b) *The* Qeri'at Torah *Three Times Weekly*

Because of its importance, the Torah is read and commented on in the synagogue several times each week. The practice is a very ancient one, and the Talmudic tradition assigns its origin to Moses himself. When the Talmudic teachers comment on Ex 15:23–25 ("They [the Israelites] went into the wilderness . . . and found no water. . . . And the people murmured against Moses, saying 'What shall we drink?' "), they take "water" as a synonym for the Torah: "When Israel had wandered in the wilderness for three days without the Torah, it began to complain. Therefore prophets arose and ordained that the Torah be read on the sabbath, Monday, and Thursday, so that the people might never be deprived of the reading of the Torah for three days in a row."[62] Whatever the historical value of this midrash, its theological and spiritual meaning is clear: just as human beings suffer and are in danger of death if deprived of water for three days, so Israel will forget the meaning of life if for three days running it is not fed by the Torah, which, like water, slakes thirst and brings about growth.

The three images which I have mentioned are enough to show how unfounded is the prejudice of those who identify the Torah with legalism and formalism. According to some authors, the root of the word "Torah" is yrh, which can mean, among other things, "to make fruitful," "to generate."[63] The Torah is the "seed" that begets human beings and brings them to maturity, to the adult state. Torah, therefore, might best be translated as "wisdom" or "life" rather than "law"—that is, by two words which were among the main descriptions applied to Jesus by the early Church (see 1 Cor 1:24; Jn 6:35). Despite the polemical overtones which came after the New Testament texts and were read back into the latter at the redactional stage, Christianity did not originally challenge the value of the Torah, which it understood according to its true intention, but rather loved it to the point of seeing it personified in Jesus.

Because the Torah is wisdom and life, it is also the focal point of the entire synagogal worship: "The synagogue service is based on the reading of the Torah. The parts of the liturgy that precede and follow this reading are as it were the jewel case whose function is to make the diamond shine more brightly."[64] In other words, the reading of the Torah is the most crucial and important of the three structural units making up the Jewish liturgy, not only because the shema‘ and the tefillah are collections of passages from the Torah but also and above all because both of these attained to their fullness in the soil of the Torah. In the measure that the Torah is studied and unveiled, the believing community learns to obey its Lord, loving him "with all its heart, with all its soul, and with all its might" (the shema‘), and to live in trusting abandonment to his will, praying to him and invoking his help in its needs (the tefillah). If the Torah is a tree, then the shema‘ and the tefillah are its ripest fruits; they are supported and fed by the tree, but they also express its riches and fruitfulness.

c) Torah, Targum, and Midrash

The Torah needs to be studied and investigated rather than simply read or listened to, for it reveals its meaning only slowly and through patient effort in personal and communal application. The Torah is not to be viewed as a "magical word" that descends from on high, but as a seed that must be cultivated and made to bear fruit: "The commandment [the Torah] which I command you this day is not too hard for you, neither is it far off. It is not in heaven . . . neither is it beyond the sea. . . . But the word is very near you; it is in your mouth and in your heart, so that you can do it" (Deut 30:11–14).

The rabbinical tradition inquired carefully into the meaning of these words; two main interpretations prevailed, one accentuating the magical and sacral approach, the other the effort of communal hermeneutic. In the first interpretation, the statement that the word "is not in heaven" was understood to mean that the Torah is "near to us" in the sense of being immediately intelligible without the need of any study and investigation. In the second interpretation, to say that the Torah is "near to us" means that its understanding requires an effort of the community and a dedication to study. Of these two interpretations the second is to be accepted, as is clear from the following midrash which tells of a great controversy between Rabbi Eliezer ben Orkanos and Rabbi Yermeya regarding the passage from Deuteronomy we have been discussing.

That day, Rabbi Eliezer gave all possible and imaginable answers [to explain the words: It is not in heaven], but the Masters did not accept them. He said to them: "Let this carob tree decide whether the law is as I have interpreted it." The carob tree moved a distance of a hundred ells or, according to some, four hundred. But they replied: "You cannot prove your point with a carob tree." He then said to them: "Let this stream of water decide whether the law is as I interpret it." The water began to run backwards. They said: "You cannot prove your point with a stream of water." He persevered and said: "Let the walls of this school decide whether the law is as I interpret it." The walls tilted and were on the point of falling. Rabbi Jeoshua reproached them, saying: "What business is it of yours when scholars argue about the law?" Out of respect for Rabbi Jeoshua the walls did not fall, but out of respect for Rabbi Eliezer neither did they straighten up but remained tilted.

Rabbi Eliezer persevered and said to them: "Let the heavens decide whether the law is as I interpret it." A divine voice came from heaven and said: "What is it that all of you have against Rabbi Eliezer? In every question, the *halakah* represents my opinion!" Rabbi Jeoshua stood up and said: " 'It is not in heaven' (Deut 30:12). What does this mean?" Rabbi Yermeya said: "We cannot set store on a divine voice, for You have written in the Torah: Follow the

majority (Ex 23:2)." Rabbi Natan then sought out the
prophet Elijah and asked him: What did God do at that moment (that is, when the Masters answered: We pay no attention to a voice from heaven)? Elijah answered: "He smiled
and said: 'My sons have vanquished me, my sons have vanquished me.' "[65]

The meaning of the midrash is clear. Rabbi Eliezer defends his
interpretation by recourse to supernatural proofs, but the Masters
are not convinced by these and reject them as unacceptable. In their
view an interpretation of the Torah is true when it is conveyed by
reasonable arguments and does not depend on supernatural inter-
ventions. And when Rabbi Eliezer stands firm and refers his case to
God himself, who then takes his side, Rabbi Yermeya, a representative of the tradition, opposes even the Eternal One, who allows the
challenge and admits he was mistaken.

The purpose of the midrash, then, is to teach that interpretation
of the Torah is not the privilege of a few "magicians" or "wizards,"
but is the right of all who study and love it, in keeping with a maxim
in the Pirke Aboth that says: "To whom does the Torah belong? To
him who studies it more."[66] The midrash also teaches that the only
authority which can guarantee the interpretation of the Torah is that
of rational argument and communal consensus ("follow the majority"). The story serves as a great caution against all forms of interpretation that are exaggeratedly fundamentalist (the interpretation is
ensured by the "letter") or sacral (the true interpretation is provided
solely by the "hierarchy").

Precisely because the Torah belongs to those who "study it
more," the Jewish tradition has always made it the subject of inquiry, investigation, and examination. The Talmud, an encyclopedic
work of the fourth and fifth centuries A.D., is the most extensive
witness to this activity of interpretation (haggadah) and actualization
(halakah) which occupied Judaism for almost a thousand years. The
word "Talmud" is, in fact, short for "Talmud Torah," meaning
"study/teaching of the Torah."

This vast study of the Torah made use especially of two privileged instruments: the targum and the midrash.

"Targum" (from the root trgm = translate, explain) means
"translation," "explanation," "interpretation"; the reference is to
the translation of the books of the Bible from Hebrew into Aramaic.
After the return from the Babylonian exile, classical Hebrew was
gradually replaced by Aramaic; as a result, the biblical text needed

to be translated if it was to be understood by all. The reading of the Torah and its translation into Aramaic went on simultaneously, verse by verse, through the agency of an official reader (qore') and a translator (meturgheman). According to a tenth-century source that probably reports a pre-Christian practice, a targum proceeded as follows:

> The one called to the Torah reads and another translates, verse by verse . . . and a third person stands between the reader and the translator . . . to help the reader and the translator, and to prompt them before they read or translate. . . . If there is one who does not know how to read well, or is shy, then the third one helps him. But if he doesn't know at all how to read, he may not be called to read or to translate. . . . And if the reader erred, the translator may not correct him. Similarly if the translator erred, the reader may not correct him. Only the third one may correct the reading or the translating.[67]

The introduction of the targum into the synagogal liturgy was not unattended by difficulties: there were those who thought Aramaic incapable of expressing the beauty of the Hebrew (see b. Sot. 33a); others considered it to be equal in dignity to Hebrew (see b. Sanh. 21b). The solution adopted was a kind of translation that was neither too literal nor too free ("They who translate a verse in its literal form are falsifiers, and they who add anything are blasphemers": Meg. 4, 41). In any case, the targumic literature attests to something very important, namely, that in Judaism the Torah must be understood and interpreted by all.

The targums (later written down at periods not easily datable, including some that may have been pre-Christian) represent the first level of commentary and interpretation of the Torah. They contain a variety of materials, both haggadic and halakic, that not only help in understanding difficult and controverted passages of the scriptures but also draw on other sources: the Mishnah and the midrashim.

The principal tool for the study of the Torah was, however, the midrash, which was the method of exegesis used by the Scribes (400 B.C. to 10 A.D.), the Tannaim (to 220 A.D.), and the Amoraim (ca. 500 A.D. to the end of the Gaonate, 1040 A.D.). The word midrash is derived from the root drsh, "to investigate," "to inquire." The purpose of the inquiry is to find the hidden meaning of the passages of the Torah by showing their deeper, present intentionality that floods

personal and communal events with its light. The midrash owes its
existence not to rational questioning (how did the biblical text take
shape?) but to existential pressures (how does the biblical text help
us to live and survive?).

Looked at in this light, midrash is a method of exegesis that may
be called "spiritual," to distinguish it from the modern historico-
critical method practiced in academic circles, especially in the West.
For example, in dealing with the great problem of suffering, one
teacher had this to say: "It is written: 'He gives food (ṭeref) to those
who fear him; he is mindful of his covenant' (Ps 111:5). Rabbi Jeoshua
ben Levi said: 'In this world he has given lacerations (ṭeruf) to those
who fear him, but in the next world he will be for ever mindful of his
covenant' " (Bereshit Rabba 40, 2). The darshan (exegete) changes
the vowels and turns ṭeref, "food," into ṭeruf, "lacerations." He thus
gives the verse a new meaning that enables him to supply a convinc-
ing explanation of human suffering: The just may suffer in this world
and be as it were "lacerated," but God does not forget them; he is
mindful of his covenant. The tragedy of suffering and injustice is
thus stripped of its inevitability, its sense of unavoidable necessity,
and placed in an interpretive context that opens the way to a possible
renewal of its meaning and a probable surmounting of it.

Another example: commenting on the verse "The writing of God
was engraved on the tablets," the exegete says: "The reading should
not be ḥarut (engraved) but ḥerut (freedom), for the 'writing of God,'
that is, the Torah, bestows true freedom on human beings."[68] The
exegete does two things with the word ḥarut: first, he removes it
from its immediate context; then he substitutes e for a, thus obtaining a new word, ḥerut, which means freedom. Why the change? In
order to teach and show that God's word is the source and guarantee
of freedom.

But what justification is there for such interpretations? What
keeps them from being arbitrary and even bizarre? There can only
be one answer: the justification comes not from correct rational argument but only from mature spiritual experience. Because the darshan is in constant contact, day and night, with the Torah, he discovers its life-giving and liberating thrust; this enriches and
transforms him and enables him in turn to change ṭeref into ṭeruf and
ḥarut into ḥerut, thereby opening new horizons and creating new
meanings.

Since the darshan's purpose is to provide motives for life and
hope, his language is deliberately figurative, imaginative, and para-
doxical; his comments consist of stories, parables, plays on words,

anecdotes, and proverbs, all of which attract the masses and hold their attention. To ensure success in this area he even makes extravagant, absurd, or foolish claims. The story is told of Rabbi Jehuda Hannasi, compiler of the Mishnah, that in order to waken an audience that was falling asleep, he suddenly said: "It happened once in Egypt that a woman gave birth on a single occasion to 600,000 children." Once they were awake and interested, the audience heard the rabbi continue: "The woman was Jochebed, mother of Moses, whose greatness was equal to that of 600,000 human beings."[69]

d) The Reading of Scripture in the Synagogue

The Torah was not read according to the divisions of it that are now followed (chapters and verses) but according to a different system in which the text was divided into a series of passages called *parashot* (plural of *parashah*), which means "parts," "sections" (etymologically: "quantities," "masses"). In Palestinian usage there were 153 passages, and the cycle covered three years; in Babylonian usage (which finally won out) there were 54 passages and the cycle ran for a year, the passages being read once a week (the mornings of Monday, Thursday, and the Sabbath; feasts days; semifestal days and days of fasting). The *parashot* (which the Ashkenazi Jews call *sidrah* from *seder*, "order") derive their individual names from the opening word, or one of the opening words, of the section. Thus the *parashah* Noah begins with the words "These are the generations of Noah" (Gen 6:9) and continues to the end of Gen 11.

The first *parashah*, known as *bereshit*, begins on śimḥat Torah ("joy of the Torah"), which is celebrated on the twenty-third of Tishri (September-October), at the end of the feast of *sukkot* (tabernacles). The last parashah, known as *we-zot ha-berakah*, is read during the same festal period a year later, so that beginning and end coincide, as in a circle. Many commentators like to see in this fact a symbol of the Torah itself, which is not a burden to be carried but a royal crown to be worn as an ornament.

In the morning services on the sabbath, feast days, and the ninth of Av (July–August), and in the afternoon services of feast days and some days of fasting, the reading of a section of the Torah is followed by the reading of a second passage, this one from the prophets. The latter is known as a *haftarah*. The term is not easily explained. It is currently interpreted either as "conclusion" or "opening" (*ptr* = to open), the sense being that those taking part in the synagogue service are obliged to remain silent during the reading of the Torah and the

Prophets, but are released from this obligation after the *haftarah*. According to another explanation, the reading from the prophets was called *haftarah* because it supposedly replaced the reading of the *parashah*, which Antiochus Epiphanes (168–164 B.C.) has prohibited; Jews were thereby exempted (another possible meaning of *ptr*) from the obligation of reciting it.

The *haftarah* for a given day was not chosen at random but in relation to the *parashah*, with which it was linked by a phrase or a word or one or several common themes. For example, when the *parashah Noah* was to be read (Gen 6–11) the passage chosen as the *haftarah* was Is 54, because it speaks of Noah in v. 9: "For this is like the days of Noah to me: as I swore that the waters of Noah should no more go over the earth, so I have sworn that I will not be angry with you and will not rebuke you." The choice of *parashot* and *haftarot*, as far as length and the criteria for linking them were concerned, differed from region to region and synagogue to synagogue. Only later on were the readings standardized and an almost universal liturgical practice imposed.

The *parashah* from the Torah and the *haftarah* from the prophets were followed by a third important element, the *derashah* or homiletic commentary intended to actualize the two biblical passages by explaining them and adapting them to the needs of the community. The *derashah* normally followed a set pattern: the homilist tried to connect the *parashah* (the first verses of which he cited by way of introduction) and the *haftarah* by means of biblical verses from the Writings and the Psalms. These verses were called *petihtot* (from the root *pth*, "to open"), because with their aid he "opened," that is, showed, the meaning of the passages heard. In this way, the homilist effected, in a concrete manner, the union of Torah, Prophets, and Writings (the three collections making up the Hebrew Bible) by using the whole of scripture.

C. Perrot, author of a well-known study on the reading of scripture in the ancient synagogues, writes: "The *seder* [that is, the *parashah*], the *haftarah*, and the homily, in which the *petihtot* are used, are the three pillars of the scriptural liturgy. The elements are closely interrelated to form an organic unity that gives a distinctive character to each sabbath and an original aspect to the entire cycle."[70] No citation could better bring out the importance of the synagogal reading of the Bible and its fruitfulness for the Jewish tradition and the Jewish liturgy, to which the Christian liturgy has remained closely linked, especially in the first part of the Mass.

e) Historical Problems

The practice of reading the Torah in public is certainly ancient and of pre-Christian origin. On the other hand, the sources do not enable us accurately to date that origin or the subsequent developments; as a result, the views of scholars vary greatly. The historical data of which we are sure are these:

a) *Deut 31:10–13:* "Moses commanded them, 'At the end of every seven years, at the set time of the year of release, at the feast of booths, when all Israel comes to appear before the Lord your God at the place which he will choose, you shall read this law before all Israel in their hearing. Assemble the people . . . that they may hear. . . .' " This passage may be regarded as the earliest reference to a public reading of the Torah; it was to take place every seven years, at the feast of booths. Nothing is said, however, of the passages chosen or of the manner in which they were to be read.

b) *Neh 8:1–8:* "And when the seventh month had come . . . Ezra the priest . . . read from it [the Torah] facing the square. . . . They [Ezra and the Levites] read from the book, from the law of God, clearly; and they gave the sense, so that the people understood the reading." Ezra, "a scribe skilled in the law of Moses" (Ezra 7:6) and, with Nehemiah, a major figure in the political and religious restoration of Israel after the Babylonian exile, decreed an historic public assembly on the feast of booths (perhaps in 444 B.C.), at which he read the law, translated it ("gave the sense"), and explained it to the people. Many authors see in these verses the origin of the targum and midrash.[71] Even apart from the precise meaning of the verses, many hold that, in all likelihood, the practice of reading the Torah at the principal Jewish feasts became common from Ezra's time on.

c) *Lk 4:16–19 and Acts 13:15:* Since I have already cited and analyzed the passage in Luke,[72] it will be enough here to cite the passage from Acts: "After the reading of the law and the prophets, the rulers of the synagogue sent to them [Paul and his companions], saying, 'Brethren, if you have any word of exhortation for the people, say it.' " This passage makes it certain that in the first century of the Christian era the practice of having *parashah, haftarah,* and *derashah* was widespread in the synagogues. Paul's address (Acts 13:16–41) is the oldest datable example of a homily in the synagogue; it is a tissue of citations from the psalter (Ps 2:7; 66:10) and the prophets (Is 55:3; Hab 1:5). Unfortunately, we do not know the precise *parashah* and *haftarah* for which Paul composed his *derashah;* nor, contrary to what some maintain,[73] is this passage in Acts enough to prove that in the time of Jesus and Paul, a fixed and standard cycle of synagogue readings was already in existence.

d) *Mishnah, Meg. 3, 4–6*: this and other passages attest the regular reading of the Torah on Monday, Thursday, and the sabbath, on feast days, including Hanukkah and Purim, and on days of fasting. It seems, however, that the length of the passages was not set but left to the discretion of the authorities in the various synagogues. The Mishnah (*Meg. 4, 1–2*) also attests to the existence of the *haftarah*.

e) *Babylonian Talmud, Meg. 29b*: "The Jews of the West [Palestine] read the Torah in the course of three years." This passage alludes to a three-year cycle of readings consisting of 153, 155, or 167 *sedarim* (pericopes or sections). Since, however, the Talmud refers to the cycle, while the Mishnah does not (though the latter is full of careful and detailed information), it may be thought that practice referred to was of recent origin (third century of the Christian era).[74]

f) *Babylonian Talmud, Meg. 31b*: "Rabbi Simon ben Eleazar says: 'Ezra ordered Israel to read the curses in Leviticus (26:15–31) before the feast of *shavu'ot* and the curses in Deuteronomy (27:16–26; 28:15–68) before *rosh ha-shanah.*' " According to this testimony of Rabbi Simon ben Eleazar, who was a contemporary of Judah ha-Nasi, not only was an annual cycle of 54 passages observed in Israel but the practice went back to Ezra himself.

The scanty information available to us attests to an ancient custom of reading and commenting on passages of the Torah and the prophets on particular feasts and specified days. It also attests to the probable existence of two cycles, one annual, the other triennial, the development and real origin of which, however, remain undetermined. But even though so many questions remain[75] and the views of scholars are so many and divergent, especially regarding the use of a continuous reading of the Torah and of the cycles connected with the reading,[76] one thing is certain: the *Qeri'at Torah* occupies a central place in the synagogue; here the Bible is read, translated, and commented on, as the two passages from the New Testament clearly show (Lk 4:16–19; Acts 13:15ff.). Furthermore, though the origin of the practice is difficult to date, it certainly goes back many centuries before the Christian era.

f) The Benedictions for the Torah

The *Qeri'at Torah* is preceded and concluded by two special benedictions. The first reads: "Blessed art thou, O Lord our God, King of the universe, who hast chosen us from all peoples, and hast given us thy Torah. Blessed art thou, O Lord, Giver of the Torah" (487). The second: "Blessed art thou, O Lord our God, King of the universe, who hast given us the Law of truth, and hast planted everlasting life in our midst. Blessed art thou, O Lord, Giver of the Torah" (487).

In these two blessings believing Jews proclaim God as *noten ha-Torah*, "giving/bestowing the Torah." The present participle (*noten ha-Torah*) brings out the continuity of God's speaking and revealing activity, which takes place neither in the past nor in the future but here and now. When Jews take part in the reading in the synagogue, it is as though they set aside all temporal distance and were present at the making of the covenant on Sinai, where God gave the Torah to Moses.

In addition to stating the divine origin of the Torah, the two benedictions describe the quality and purpose of its contents. The content is described as *Torat 'emet* (the Torah of truth), and its purpose is to give *ḥayye 'olam* (everlasting life). In the Bible, "truth" is predicated not so much of ideas (true or false) as of persons or objects (solid or not). The root of *'emet* is *'mn*, which means "to be strong/steady," whether in a passive sense (to be set on one's feet) or an active (to support something or someone). A few passages from the Bible shed light on the meaning. 2 Kgs 18:16 speaks of the columns of the temple as *'omenot* (structures that support) and 2 Sam 4:4 uses for "nurse" the word *'omen*, which means, literally, "one who holds in her arms and is able to ensure maternal care." When the Torah is described as *'emet*, its existential value is being asserted: the Torah, like the columns of the temple, supports life; like the hands of a nurse, it gives and enriches life.

Torat 'emet, the word of God, is given to human beings so that they may have *ḥayye 'olam*, everlasting life. In later Christian tradition, few expressions have been so misunderstood and misinterpreted as *ḥayye 'olam*. In the Bible, the word *'olam* (eternity) is not opposed to historical time but is rather its content and fulfillment. "Everlasting life" is therefore not life that comes after death but life that rises above the sheer factuality of external, chronological time and reveals all the beauty and meaning of our earthly life. As some authors meaningfully observe, the root of *'olam* is *'lm*, "to hide," so that *'olam* means, properly speaking, "hidden time," "concealed time." "Everlasting" life is life grasped in the "hidden" intentionality that underlies it, as distinct from life seen as purely material and extended in time. "Everlasting" life is life filled with meaning that is objective as well as subjective, as distinct from life experienced as empty.

Everlasting life is complete life as opposed to incomplete (as a work or picture is said to be complete or incomplete); life that is fulfilled as opposed to scattered and fragmented life; life that is fruit- ful as opposed to life that is barren and arid. It is this everlasting life which, according to the benediction, God has "planted in our midst."

The image of "planting" shows that "everlasting life" (or, to use a parallel expression, the "earthly paradise") is a real possibility for human beings, one that depends on their freedom and personal re- sponsibility. Just as a tree does not in fact bear fruit unless human beings tend it and work on it, neither does life become "everlasting" without human commitment and collaboration. The role of the Torah is not only to show the possibility of everlasting life but also to point out the conditions for attaining to it. Coming into existence, as it does, between the deliverance from Egypt and the entry into the promised land, the Torah shows the way that leads human beings out of the wilderness and into "a good and broad land, a land flowing with milk and honey" (Ex 3:8).

A final point to be noted in the benedictions is the theme of election: "Blessed art thou, O Lord our God . . . who hast chosen us from all peoples." Few ideas have been, and are, as open as this to mischievous and sometimes even dangerous interpretations. The benediction in fact gives the meaning and extent of the election: "Thou hast chosen us from all peoples and hast given us thy Torah." God chose Israel as depositary of the Torah; his purpose therefore is not that Israel should dominate over others but that it should bear fruit; nor did he choose it in an exclusive sense (Israel alone, and not others) but in an inclusive sense (Israel also is chosen, like all others). Thus understood, Israel's election is not so much a distinctive privi- lege as it is the radical self-consciousness proper to human beings, for human beings are not neutral ground, foreign to the divine, but rather the native place of the divine; over them sounds the voice of God who challenges them and calls them to a relationship of cove- nant. Human existence develops its full being and beauty only when it is lived in accord with the logic of the covenant and with the divine intentionality that dynamizes it.

The reading from the prophets (the *haftarah*) is likewise pre- ceded and followed by benedictions. One of these, the last of the four recited after the *haftarah*, says:

> For the Torah, for the divine service, for the prophets, and for this Sabbath day, which thou, O Lord our God, hast given us for holiness and for rest, for honour and for glory— for all these we thank and bless thee, O Lord our God;

blessed be thy Name by the mouth of every living being
continually and for ever. Blessed art thou, O Lord, who hallowest the Sabbath (497–99).

The *Qeri'at Torah* ends with this fine prayer said by the congregation as the scroll of the Torah is replaced in the ark: "I have given
you a perfect doctrine; do not abandon my Torah. It is a tree of life to
them that grasp it, and of them that uphold it every one is rendered
happy. Its ways are ways of pleasantness, and all its paths are peace"
(see 493–95). This song, which is made up of expressions from the
Book of Proverbs (3:17; 3:18; 4:2), sums up very well the theological
and anthropological meaning of the Torah in Judaism: it is the "tree
of life" (*eṣ ḥayim*) that shows the possibility and reality of Eden.

g) Example of a Midrashic Homily

Jews read and listen to the Torah not out of intellectual curiosity
but for existential reasons. Like "a light to our path" (Ps 119:105), it
discloses the meaning of events by providing keys for reading them,
as well as alternative interpretations. The Torah and everyday life
are not two unrelated poles; on the contrary, each is to be understood
in function of the other: the first interprets the second, and the second embodies the first. Apart from the Torah life becomes as dark as
night and as arid as the wilderness; separated from life, the Torah
becomes a soul without a body, an idea without a referent.

It is the task of the *derashah*, or midrashic homily, to keep the
two poles united while preventing both their separation and their
identification. I shall offer an example of such a homily from the
Pesikta of Rab Kahana, a compilation of commentaries or discourses
on some passages of the Bible that were read during the synagogue
service on particular occasions.[77] The compilation, which is attributed to Rabbi Kahana (fifth century of the Christian era), cites numerous homiletic texts produced over a period of about 500 years, from
the School of Hillel and Shammai (about a century before the Christian era) to about the fourth century of the Christian era. The first
chapter (Piska 1) of the collection reproduces some homilies for the
feast of Hanukkah, at which a section of the Book of Numbers was
read that began with the words: "On the day when Moses had finished setting up the tabernacle, and had anointed and consecrated it
with all its furnishings . . ." (Num 7:1). The passage goes on to tell of
the offering of the wagons and oxen which the leaders of the tribes of
Israel presented to Moses after the building and consecration of the
tabernacle.

Why was this passage read on the feast of Hanukkah, and how was it interpreted? To answer these questions I shall conduct the reader through a few pages of Piska 1.[78]

The *darshan* (homilist) begins his commentary by citing a verse from the Song of Solomon: "I have come [back] into My garden, My sister, My bride" (5:1). In the homilist's view, the meaning of Num 7:1 is revealed by the meaning of Song 5:1. But what connection can there be between two texts that seem so different in content and context?

The *darshan* will answer this question only at the end of his homily, after having roused the curiosity of his audience and having kept them alert, attentive, and expectant from the beginning of the conversation to its end.

"I am come [back] into My garden, My sister, My bride" (Song 5:1). R. Azariah, citing R. Judah bar R. Simon, told the parable of a king who became so angry at his wife that he deposed her and cast her out of his palace. After a time when he was willing to bring her back and restore her to her place, she said: Let him first renew for my sake his former practice [of accepting from my hand whatever I offered him], then let him bring me back and restore me to my place. Thus in the past [when the Holy One had withdrawn far from men into heaven], yet from above He would still accept their offerings, as it is said of Noah's offering "[From above] the Lord smelled the sweet odor" (Gen 8:21). Now, however, He will renew His ancient practice of accepting their offerings while close to them here on the earth below: "I am come [below] into My garden, My sister, My bride." Thus incidentally, according to R. Hanina, Torah teaches one good manners, as that a groom is not to enter the bridal bower until his bride gives him leave: "Let my Beloved come into His garden" (Song 4:16), and only after that "I am come into My garden" (Song 5:1).

[With regard to God's presence on earth at the beginning of time], R. Tanhum, the son-in-law of R. Eleazar ben Abina, citing R. Simeon ben Yosne, noted that the Song does not say "I am come into a garden" but "I am come into My garden." [For *ganni*, "My garden"], read *ginnuni*, "My bride's bower," My and man's dwelling place where at the beginning of time the Divine Root was implanted—yes, originally the root of the Presence was fixed in the regions of the earth below. The verse "They used to hear the voice of the Lord God as [Adam] would walk in the garden" (Gen 3:8)[79] proves God's presence on earth at the beginning of time, for, as R. Abba bar Kahana noted: The text does not really say "would walk in" but "walked away from" [and refers not to Adam] but to God, who, [after Adam had sinned, was angered] yet in reluctance walked away from [him towards heaven]. Thereupon "Adam and his wife were all but hid" (ibid.) because, as R. Aibu explained, in that instant Adam was deposed from his high place and his stature was diminished to no more than a hundred cubits (komah).

[As to who brings about God's return to the earth], R. Isaac said: It is written "The righteous shall inherit the earth, and dwell thereon in eternity" (Ps 37:29). And where will the wicked dwell? Are they to fly about in the air? The concern of the verse, however, is not the dwelling place of the righteous or the wicked: by "shall . . . dwell thereon in eternity" is meant that the righteous bring it about that the Eternal shall dwell on the earth.

At the beginning of time, accordingly, the root of the Presence was fixed in the regions of the earth below. After Adam sinned, the Presence withdrew to the first heaven. The generation of Enosh arose: they sinned; the Presence withdrew from the first heaven to the second. The generation of the flood arose: they sinned; the Presence withdrew from the second heaven to the third. The generation of the dispersion of the races of man arose: they sinned; the Presence withdrew from the third heaven to the fourth. The Egyptians in the days of our father Abraham arose: they sinned; the Presence withdrew from the fourth heaven to the fifth. The Sodomites arose: they sinned; the Presence withdrew from the fifth heaven to the sixth. The Egyptians in the days of Moses arose: from the sixth heaven to the seventh.

Over against these wicked men, seven righteous men arose and brought it about that the Presence came back to the earth. Our Father Abraham arose: the merit he earned brought it about that the Presence came back from the seventh heaven to the sixth. Isaac arose: the merit he earned brought it about that the Presence came back from the sixth heaven to the fifth. Jacob arose: the merit he earned brought it about that the Presence came back from the fifth heaven to the fourth. Levi arose: the merit he earned brought it about that the Presence came back from the fourth heaven to the third. Kohath arose: the merit he earned brought it about that the Presence came back from the third heaven to the second. Amram arose: the merit he earned brought it about that the Presence came back from the second heaven to the first. Moses arose: the merit he earned brought it about that the Presence came back to the earth. Hence [the reference to Moses] in the verse "It was on Israel's bridal (klt) day that Moses brought to a conclusion (klwt) [the coming back to earth that God had begun in the days of Abraham] (Num 7:1).

I shall offer a few remarks that will help understand the content of this derashah, as well as passages that at first reading may remain obscure or disjointed.

a) The aim of the darshan is to explain the meaning of the feast of Hanukkah in the light of the passage from Numbers that is read on this occasion. He focuses his attention on a single verse of the reading: "On the day when Moses had finished (kallot) setting up the tabernacle" (Num 7:1). In these words the darshan sees hidden the deeper meaning of the event being celebrated. His task is to reveal this meaning by passing from the literal meaning of the verse to a more comprehensive and spiritual meaning. The shift is effected by means of special techniques which the synagogue audience knew about and appreciated. One of the most used of these techniques was to connect kallat (bridal feast) with kallot (bring to completion, finish) and to interpret the second in light of the first.

The procedure is neither bizarre nor based on chance, but is a complex, intuitive, and original operation. Thanks to his special knowledge of the Torah, which he has continually read, studied, examined closely, and investigated, the homilist glimpses a new aspect of the feast of Hanukkah. Like a poet or an artist, he breaks through the veil of appearances and grasps the luminous essence of things. It is this kind of sensibility (and not caprice) that is the basis for the homilist's hermeneutical activity and enables him to connect two seemingly unrelated words.[80]

b) The darshan begins with a verse from the Song of Solomon: "I am come [back] into My garden, My sister, My bride" (5:1). This verse has no explicit connection with the verse in Numbers on which he is commenting, but in fact a connection is there, even though the congregation is not in a position to know it; the connection will become clear only at the end of the *derashah*. As a result, the congregation will remain attentive throughout the homily, because it is trying to make out the connection between the verse of Numbers and the verse of the Song and to solve the riddle that has caught its interest. Evidently, this method is not only theological but also, and above all, psychological and pedagogical, for it stretches the receptive capacity of the audience and its ability to remember. That the procedure must have fascinated audiences is shown by not a few testimonies. For example, it is told of Rabbi Johanan (who lived ca. 250 A.D.) that the people came running from their homes in order to secure a seat in the synagogue or hall where he was teaching. And of some preachers Chrysostom says, with a trace of bitter hostility, that the enthusiasm and applause they elicited reminded him of an audience in the theater.[81]

c) Instead of explaining the verse of the Song which he has quoted, the *darshan* seems to forget it or sets it aside and then, seemingly without connection, tells the story of a king and a queen, how their relationship of love was broken and how they were reconciled. The emphasis is on the reconciliation: before returning to her husband, the king, the woman lays down a specific condition: as in the past, he must accept and appreciate all that she gives him with her own hands.

At the beginning of time, the human race lived in the Garden of Eden like a queen; its position was truly royal, for it enjoyed the privilege of living with the divine Presence (Shekinah). But the sin of Adam and later generations compelled God gradually to withdraw from the human race, which thus lost its royal status. But the loss was not irreparable. Once good men like Abraham, Isaac, Jacob, and others appeared, God began to return to earth. The last of these just men was Moses, thanks to whom the Shekinah returned to earth definitively and for good.

d) But how is this parable connected with the verse from the Son ("I am come [back] into My garden, My sister, My bride") with which the homily begins? At this point the solution of the riddle begins. The subject of "I am come" is God, who returns to earth, thanks to the actions of good men and especially of Moses; the "garden," thanks to the reading of *ganni* (my garden) as *ginnuni* (bridal chamber), symbolizes the relationship of love that existed between God and humankind at the beginning of creation; finally, Israel represents the human race in the midst of which God reestablishes his covenant of love. The parable tells of a king and queen who, after a break in their relationship, decide to live together once again; now, if the king is God and the queen is Israel, then the verse of the Song, with the addition of "back" to "I am come" effectively expresses the new situation in which, like a husband, God returns to his bride, Israel, which symbolizes the human race.

e) Once the connection between the verse of the Song and the parable becomes clear, the connection between all this and the verse of Numbers on which the homilist is commenting also begins to be clear. In the verse "On the day when Moses had finished setting up the tabernacle," the "tabernacle" is none other than the new relationship of love between God and the human race, a relationship comparable to that of marriage. The connection between the verse of the Song and the verse is Numbers is thereby explained; the verse of the Song, with *ginnuni* (bridal chamber) substituted for *ganni* (my garden), becomes the key for interpreting the verse in Numbers. The "tabernacle" now takes on the meaning of "my bridal chamber," for it is the place where God is reunited to the human race.

f) But the connection between the verses in Numbers and the Song is not simply thematic. The verse in Numbers is not simply read for its content as it stands; rather there is a textual rereading as well. The word *kallot* (bring to completion) is revocalized and interpreted as *kallat* (wedding feast), and the verse which formerly read "On the day when Moses had finished (*kallot*) setting up the tabernacle" is changed to: "On Israel's bridal day . . . Moses brought to a conclusion [the coming back to earth that God had begun in the days of Abraham]."

g) But what has all this to do with the feast of Hanukkah? In the case of an audience that was familiar with the origin of this feast (the reconsecration of the temple that had been desecrated by Antiochus Epiphanes in 167 B.C.), the answer was easy: as the completion of the tabernacle by Moses signified the return of the Shekinah to the midst of the human race, so the purification of the temple that had been desecrated meant the return of the Shekinah to the midst of Israel, its bride. This parallel between the completion of the tabernacle by Moses and the restoration of the temple by the Maccabees is the basic idea developed in the homily. The parallel is evidently not only historical and literal but also, and above all, theological and spiritual; its purpose is to teach the love of God for Israel and, through Israel, for the human race. Even though he (God) may from time to time distance himself from human beings because of their sins, their good actions will always impel him to return and dwell in their midst.[82]

h) Within this basic framework the *darshan* takes other exegetical steps and offers other interesting information. For example: to show that after Adam's sin God no longer accepts the offerings of the human race directly, Gen 8:21 is cited; to bring out the decisive role of Israel, the homilist cites first the words of Song 4:16, "Let my Beloved come into His garden," which are put on the lips of the chosen people, and only then the words of Song 5:1, "I am come into My garden," which are put on the lips of God; to prove that Israel is the nuptial "place" of God, the statement "I am come into My garden" is changed into "I am come into My bride's bower"; to show that God withdrew from the earth after the sin of Adam, the homilist has recourse to a citation from Rabbi Kahana, according to which Gen 3:8 says not that God "walked" in the garden but that he "walked away from" it; and to show that the Shekinah has returned to the earth because of the good works of the just, the homilist relies on the interpretation of Ps 27:29 given by Rabbi Isaac.

This lengthy analysis shows that a midrashic homily was, on the one hand, simple and allusive, and, on the other, complex and carefully developed. It is simple by reason of its narrative form made up of stories and parables; it is complex because of the weaving in of biblical verses that are linked and interpreted in various ways. The midrashic homily in this way thus honored its double fidelities: to the Jewish people and to the word of God, to human needs and to the depths of the Torah. Thanks to its parabolic language, the homily spoke to the hearts of all, educated and uneducated alike, by shedding light on everyday life; at the same time, however, it communicated the inexhaustible and always actual riches of the divine word, thanks to the many interconnections it established among passages of the Bible that were on each occasion read and interpreted anew. This twofold fidelity is needed today as in the past: in order that human beings may not be deprived of God's word and in order that they may not betray this word.

Chapter 3

Private and Communal Phases
of Jewish Prayer

The influence of the shema' Yiśra'el, the tefillah, and the qeri'at Torah is not limited to a restricted segment of time; rather, these activities dynamize the entire range of Jewish life, both public and private. In saying this, we already glimpse the several spheres in which Jews live out their religious life: the individual, the familial, and the communal. Each of these spheres, while having its special nuances and characteristics, follows the same theological and spiritual logic.

In the following pages I shall speak first of prayers offered by individuals, the prayers which each Jew recites in the course of the day; then of familial prayers, those recited daily at meals, weekly during the sabbath, and annually at the feast of Passover; and finally, of prayers in the synagogue, those recited in congregational form on weekdays, feast days, and special occasions.

As we move from sphere to sphere, we will often find the same words recurring and echoing, sometimes in a repetitive way, sometimes in an innovative manner. But we shall quickly come to see that there is never mere repetition but always a new perspective. Prayer, like life itself, is in one way always the same and in another always new.

I. BENEDICTIONS BY INDIVIDUALS

A benediction as formula or expression of prayer is a manifestation and translation into words of berakah as an interior attitude in relation to God. In the analysis of the shema', the tefillah, and the qeri'at Torah we saw many of these benedictions, some lengthy with complex structures, others brief and to the point, but all sharing one characteristic: they are public and official. In addition to these, however, believing Jews have other benedictions connected with rising and retiring and with special events in the course of the day.

I. On Waking in the Morning

The act of getting up, in which one turns from the night to the day, is to be accompanied by a series of blessings. The Babylonian Talmud describes in detail the various phases in the passage from sleep to wakefulness: 1. awakening; 2. hearing the cock crow; 3. opening the eyes; 4. rising to a sitting position; 5. putting on the first garment; 6. rising from the bed; 7. touching the floor; 8. standing up; 9. putting on the shoes; 10. tieing the belt; 11. putting on the head-dress; 12. putting on the tassels; 13. putting on the phylacteries; 14. washing the hands; 15. washing the face. Each of these actions is accompanied by a special benediction:

When he awakens, let him say: "O my God, the soul which thou gavest me is pure; thou didst create it, thou didst form it, thou didst breathe it into me. Thou preservest it within me, and thou wilt take it from me, but wilt restore it to me hereafter. So long as the soul is within me, I will give thanks unto thee, O Lord my God and God of my fathers, Sovereign of all works, Lord all souls! Blessed art thou, O Lord, who restorest souls unto the dead" (Hertz, 19).

When he hears the cock crow, let him say: "Blessed is he who gave the cock understanding to distinguish between day and night."

When he hears the cock crow, let him say: "Blessed is he who makes the blind see."

When he sits up in bed, let him say: "Blessed is he who sets prisoners free."

When he puts on his garment, let him say: "Blessed is he who clothes the naked."

When he starts to rise, let him say: "Blessed is he who straightens those who are stooped."

When he gets down from his bed and touches the floor, let him say: "Blessed is he who stretched out the earth over the waters."

When he stands upright, let him say: "Blessed is he who directs the steps of human beings."

When he has put on his shoes, let him say: "Blessed is he who satisfies my needs."

When he tightens his belt, let him say: "Blessed is he who girds Israel with strength."

When he wraps the covering around his head, let him say: "Blessed is he who crowns Israel with majesty."

When he dons a garment with tassels, let him say: "Blessed is he who has sanctified us by his commandments and has bidden us wear garments with fringes."

When he puts the phylacteries on his arm, let him say: "Blessed is he who has sanctified us by his commandments and has bidden us wear the phylacteries"; (when he puts the phylacteries on his head:) "Blessed is he who has sanctified us by his commandments and has given us the precept of the phylacteries."

When he washes his hands, let him say: "Blessed is he who has sanctified us by his commandments and has ordered us to wash our hands."

When he washes his face, let him say: "Blessed is he who removes the bands of sleep from my eyes and slumber from my eyelids. May it be your will, O Lord my God, to accustom me to your law. Make me attached to your commandments; let me not come under the power of sin, evildoing, temptation, and shame, but bend my nature to submission to you. Keep me from the wicked, from evil companions, and teach me to be attached to natures that are good and to good companions here in your world. Grant that this day and every day I may find favor, love, and mercy in your eyes and in the eyes of all who see me, and do good works in my behalf. Blessed are you, O Lord, who do good works in favor of the people of Israel."[1]

The most important of these fifteen benedictions are the first and the last. The latter blesses God for having freed the body from "the bonds of sleep" (in antiquity sleep was regarded as an anticipation and image of death), and asks his help and protection during the new day. The first blessing thanks him for restoring to the body the soul that is the principle of the divine life from which human beings benefit. To believing Jews, the act of awakening and returning to life is not a natural occurrence nor an acquired right but a miracle of which each day is the witness and beneficiary. Every morning God renews creation as in the beginning, when he "formed man of dust from the ground, and breathed into his nostrils the breath of life; and man became a living being" (Gen 2:7). This interpretation does not contradict the scientific explanation (and therefore cannot be contradicted by it) which explains the passage from sleep to waking by cerebral and neuro-chemical mechanisms; rather it is the foundation for the scientific explanation and makes this possible.

When we wake in the morning and renew our relations with the world, the important thing is not to know how this comes about but to know that if it occurs, it is due to the love of the God who creates and re-creates. When we regain consciousness, God is "restoring the soul to the physical body." When the cock crows, God is redistributing time and setting its rhythm. When we open our eyes, he is "making the blind see." When we arise, he is restoring our freedom of movement. When we clothe ourselves, he is "clothing the naked." When we touch the floor with our feet, he is "stretching out the earth over the waters." When we put on our shoes, he is "satisfying our needs," and so on. To begin the day with this "key to its interpretation," this act of faith, is not to indulge in poetic fancy. For believers, these actions embody a luminous, foundational certitude of which the berakah is the ontological echo and literary expression.

The benedictions I have cited are to be recited privately by every Jew in passing each morning from sleep to wakefulness. Many Jews, however, did not know them by heart nor could they learn them easily because they did not have access to written texts. As a result, the custom arose of reciting them in the synagogue at the beginning of the liturgical service. A reader said them aloud, and those present answered with the traditional Amen; the practice gave the participants an opportunity to memorize them. This practice was kept up even later on when written texts were available, such as the prayer books. Even today the benedictions are recited in the synagogue and form the introductory part of the service; this section is called birkat ha-shakar (benediction for the dawn) and has been variously enriched and divided depending on the several rites and communities. Nowadays this introductory section begins almost everywhere with the hymn 'adon 'olam, which is attributed to the great Spanish poet, Solomon ibn Gabirol (1021–1058).

> Lord of the world, He reigned alone
> While yet the universe was naught,
> When by His will all things were wrought,
> Then first His sovran name was known.
>
> And when the All shall cease to be,
> In dread lone splendour He shall reign,
> He was, He is, He shall remain
> In glorious eternity.
>
> For He is one, no second shares
> His nature or His loneliness;

Unending and beginningless,
All strength is His, all sway He bears.

He is the living God to save,
My Rock while sorrow's toils endure,
My banner and my stronghold sure,
The cup of life whene'er I crave.

I place my soul within His palm
Before I sleep as when I wake,
And though my body I forsake,
Rest in the Lord in fearless calm.[2]

It is with this poetic text, which celebrates, on the one hand, the infinite greatness of God and, on the other, his radical closeness to every human being, that believing Jews begin the day. Conscious of God's transcendence and immanence, they take up the work of creation in order to bring it to completion.

2. On Retiring in the Evening

Evening prayer is made up of two basic parts: the recitation of the *shema'* and a special benediction. The Babylonian Talmud explicitly attests to both parts. Of the *shema'* it says: "Even if the *shema'* has been recited during the synagogue service, it is an act of devotion to recite it again in bed."[3] The text prescribed for the special benediction is as follows:

Blessed art thou, O Lord our God, King of the universe, who makest the bands of sleep to fall upon mine eyes, and slumber upon my eyelids. May it be thy will, O Lord my God and God of my fathers, to suffer me to lie down in peace and to let me rise up again in peace. Let not my thoughts trouble me, nor evil dreams, nor evil fancies, but let my rest be perfect before thee. O lighten mine eyes, lest I sleep the sleep of death, for it is thou who givest light to the apple of the eye. Blessed art thou, O Lord, who givest light to the whole world in thy glory.[4]

This prayer is at once a profession of faith and a plea for help. In the morning God is invoked as the one who "removes the bands of sleep from my eyes and slumber from my eyelids": here he is in-

voked as the one who "makes the bands of sleep to fall upon my eyes
and slumber upon my eyelids." God is the source of both wakefulness and sleep, of day, which is the symbolic place of involvement
and responsibility, and of night, which is the symbolic place of the
suspension of all activity.

The petition is twofold: it asks for sound rest ("May it be thy will
to suffer me to lie down in peace") and that sleep be not disturbed by
"thoughts" and "evil dreams." Night is everywhere a symbol of dark
and malignant powers: the forces of chaos and nothingness, of opposition to creation and to love. By placing these under the sovereignty
of God (who "makes the bands of sleep to fall upon my eyes"), believing Jews change night from a symbol and place of fear and danger to
one of rest and coziness. For them night is no longer a metaphor of
chaos gaining the upper hand over the "day of creation," but rather
of the recovery of the energies that will enable them in the morning
to take up once more the "work of creation" and bring it to completion in accordance with God's plan. Admittedly, they too can always
be tempted to fall back into the power of night by forgetting its true
meaning and peopling it with specters. Therefore they pray, because
prayer, according to rabbinical teaching, is like "a two-edged sword"
(see Ps 149:6) that is victorious against all enemies, not only those of
the daytime but also and especially those of the night.

3. During the Day

There are also benedictions for other moments, whether of work
or of relaxation, that occur each day. There is no thing and no action
that is not to be transfigured by a *berakah*; this is true even of physiological needs, as the following benediction shows:

> Blessed art thou, O Lord our God, King of the universe, who
> hast formed man in wisdom, and created in him many pas-
> sages and vessels. It is well known before thy glorious
> throne, that if but one of these be opened, or one of these be
> closed, it would be impossible to exist and stand before thee.
> Blessed art thou, O Lord, who art the wondrous healer of all
> flesh (11).[5]

This benediction thanks God for having created the human person "in wisdom" (*be-ḥokmah*), a wisdom that consists concretely in
providing the person with "passages and vessels" that ensure health
and well-being. We may smile at such a prayer and even think it

unseemly. That is not the reaction of Jews, who see the divine love and perfection mirrored in the harmonious functioning of the human body. That is why the Talmud has a lengthy discussion of this benediction and the prayer book includes it among the benedictions that precede the morning service in the synagogue, in order that all may become familiar with it and commit it to memory.

During the day God is thanked for evil as well as good, since, according to the principle set down in the Talmud, "everything that God does he does for a good purpose."

> Rab Huna said, speaking in the name of Rab and in the name of R. Meir, and thus giving a teaching attached ultimately to the name of R. Aqiba: A person should develop the habit of saying always: "Everything that God does he does for a good purpose." On one occasion when R. Aqiba was on a journey, he came to a town and asked for hospitality, but did not receive it; he then said: "Everything that God does he does for a good purpose." He went off and spent the night in the open. He had with him a cock, an ass, and a lantern. A wind arose and extinguished the lantern; a cat came and ate the cock; a lion came and ate the ass. Yet he said: "Everything that God does he does for a good purpose." During the night, invading troops came and took the townspeople prisoner; and he said to them: "Did I not tell you: 'Everything that God does he does for a good purpose?' "[6]

The parable of R. Aqiba, a parable of innocent simplicity, shows that seeds of meaning are hidden in even the most adverse circumstances. Being forced to spend the night in the open and losing one's only possessions are not irreparable occurrences but are the outward form of an unexpected rescue. There is no "evil" in the depths of which a "good" does not lurk, for God is Lord even of "evil." If evil comes under the sovereignty of God, then its power, however widespread and destructive, is never definitive; it may have the next-to-last word, but never the last.

4. On Special Occasions

God is also blessed on special occasions, such as a journey or sickness or the approach of death.

A dying person who feels the end to be near is obliged to make a profession of faith such as the following:

I acknowledge unto thee, O Lord my God and God of my
fathers, that both my cure and my death are in thy hands.
May it be thy will to send me a perfect healing. Yet if my
death be fully determined by thee, I will in love accept it at
thy hand. O may my death be an atonement for all the sins,
iniquities and transgressions of which I have been guilty
against thee. Bestow upon me the abounding happiness that
is treasured up for the righteous. Make known to me the
path of life: in thy presence is fullness of joy; at thy right
hand bliss for evermore.[7]

Although this prayer is rather recent, being made up of expressions taken for the most part from the *Shulkan 'aruk* (sixteenth century), its content reflects the most authentic Jewish tradition, from
Abraham to Jesus and on down to the present day. Unconditional
abandonment to God's will, in the realization that in it is contained
all meaning and the seed of salvation, is the very heart of the Jewish
religious outlook; the abandonment is inspired not by fatalistic resig-
nation but by the unshakable hope that God is stronger than death
and able to overcome and conquer it. That is precisely the theme of
the exultant cry of Paul of Tarsus as he reflected on the experience of
Jesus of Nazareth and on his resurrection:

Death is swallowed up in victory.
O death, where is thy victory?
O death, where is thy sting? (1 Cor 15:54–55).

Just as Abraham on Mount Moriah did not lose his son but received him back and as Jesus found resurrection in the depths of his
defeat on Calvary, so believing Jews paradoxically see life within
their death: "Show me the path of life: in thy presence there is fullness of joy, at thy right hand are pleasures for evermore" (Ps 15:11).
    In time of sickness, too, believing Jews bless God:

In my sickness, Lord, I turn to you because I am the work of
your hands. Your strength and courage are present in my
heart, and your healing power within my body. May it be
your will to restore me to health. My sickness has taught me
what is important and what unimportant. I realize how de-

pendent I am on you. Pain and suffering have taught me. Once healed, may I never forget this precious insight.

Strengthen me, O Lord, and protect me with your love. Heal me, and I shall be healed; save me, and I shall be saved. Blessed are you, O Lord, the faithful and merciful healer.[8]

So too there are benedictions for an anniversary, an operation, a journey, a peril survived, a decisive meeting, a significant event, and so on.

II. THE DOMESTIC LITURGY

The primary sacred place in which the Jewish liturgy is celebrated is in the home, which is looked upon as a "shrine":

This is not a poetic exaggeration, for the Jewish home was, in a sense, a little sanctuary. The family table was regarded as an altar, each meal was a holy ritual, and the parents were the officiating priests. Family worship accompanied many of the daily activities and transformed the biological and social relationships of the family into a spiritual kinship.[9]

In this "sanctuary" of the family there are three principal celebrations: one is daily and connected with meals; the second is weekly and connected with the sabbath; the third is annual and connected with the feast of Passover. These "celebrations" refer to and complete one another, with each explaining and enriching the other two.

1. *The* Birkat ha-mazon

In Judaism the family meal is the religious action par excellence. Therefore, like, and to a greater extent than, every other daily activity, it is accompanied by a series of special benedictions. Christianity followed Judaism in assigning a central place to the meal and, in its celebration of the Eucharist, even made bread and wine its basic symbols. (I must add, however, that Christianity removed the Eucharist from the setting of the family and located it in the framework of priesthood and "temple.") Why is the family meal regarded as so important?

a) *The Symbolism of Eating*

Eating is the most primordial and regular action performed by human beings. Not only does it satisfy their basic needs and ensure their survival, but it is also the indispensable condition for any further mental or even spiritual activity. Those who lack the food with which to satisfy their hunger are also deprived of the very possibility of praying. As the psalmist says, only the living can praise God; those that have gone down into the grave cannot praise him (see Ps 115:17).

But eating is for Jews something more than a pleasurable way of satisfying the bodily need for nourishment. They regard bread, and food generally, as really and not only metaphorically a gift from God. In bread, which serves as a symbol of all good things, they apprehend a benevolent intention at work that gives it its truth and meaning; that intention is the love with which God feeds his creatures, and it finds marvelous expression in Ps 104:

> Thou dost cause the grass to grow for the cattle,
>   and plants for man to cultivate.
> that he may bring forth food from the earth.
>   and wine to gladden the heart of man,
> oil to make his face shine,
>   and bread to strengthen man's heart (vv. 14–15).

The psalmist here describes God as a generous benefactor who gives human beings the garden of the world for their sustenance and joy.

The benedictions to be recited before and after meals have a poetic and transfigurative function: to open a breach in the materiality of the good things that nourish human beings, so that they may glimpse the divine "thou" who creates them and gives them meaning. All the great religious traditions have approached food in the same way; that is why they speak of "sacred meals" or "sacred banquets." When one eats with the realization that things come to us from God's unmerited generosity, one does more than simply renew one's vital energies; one also realizes, down deep, that an interpersonal event is taking place in which two subjectivities reveal themselves and enter into dialogue: the beneficent and loving "thou" that is God, and the satisfied and thankful "thou" that is the human being. The prayer of blessing creates this communion; it creates the miracle that is the encounter of God and human beings.

Looked at from this point of view, the *berakah* expresses in words the same message that sacrifices in the temple expressed in gesture. The offering to God of firstfruits or the first-born of a flock is a way of acknowledging him as source of the fruits of the earth, receiving them with love, and proclaiming them as free gift. Thus sacrifices, like the *berakah*, effect a communion. "The understanding of 'offering' has been falsified and distorted by a terminology derived from Latin. 'Offer' is from the Latin *offerre*, whereas the Hebrew *qorban* is from *qarov*, 'near.' Buber and Rosenzweig therefore translate it as 'drawing near.' For in fact those who eat the offerings draw near to God in a communion."[10]

Through "bread" that, thanks to *berakah* and sacrifice, is received as a gift, human beings draw near to God and God to them; the two parties meet and live out, or revive, their covenant.

The act of eating evokes the symbolism not only of gift but also of sharing, for to acknowledge God as source of the fruits of the earth is to assert the universal destination of these fruits and bar any individual from possessing and hoarding them.

If "bread" is from God, then human beings may not take it for themselves but may only enjoy it together with others, for since others are beneficiaries of the same divine favor they are not our enemies or rivals but our friends. Explaining the reason for the obligation of *zimun* (the communal recitation of the *birkat ha-mazon*), Rabbi S. Hirsch writes:

> There is nothing like the struggle for daily bread to make individuals self-centered and cause them to regard others as rivals. . . . For this reason, the rabbis attributed special importance . . . to meals taken in common. They ordained that when two or three persons share a meal one of them must invite the others to recite the *berakah* with him. In this way they will become accustomed to the idea that they are all equals because they are loved by the same God and that this solicitous love is the stay of their existence. This joint prayer to the one God who is equally near to each in the form of a beneficent Providence, does away with all thought of jealous competition and, on the contrary, inspires a sense of brotherhood. We do not feel diminished by the prosperity of our neighbor, for we know that the Father is so mighty in love that he can give to each what is useful and good for each.[11]

Finally, the act of eating has a third symbolism: that of responsible activity. If it is true that God "causes the grass to grow for the cattle" and gives "wine to gladden the heart of man, oil to make his face shine, and bread to strengthen man's heart" (Ps 104:14–15), it is also true that this divine activity calls for human toil. When the *berakah* interprets things as gifts and calls for them to be shared, it does not do away with human effort but rather frees this of anxiety by giving it a new meaning: it is no longer a Promethean self-projection that builds the world out of nothing, but a responsible acceptance of a work of collaboration. "Bread" is the result of two intentions, the divine and the human, the former exclusive and foundational, the latter receptive and obedient. "Bread" is abundant where these two intentions meet and enter into dialogue; where, as in works of art, human beings accept and transform the material given to them. Work is the place where this creativity is exercised; it is a human activity, but one that accepts and concretizes the divine intention; as a result, the divine plan reaches completion, making "grow every tree that is pleasant to the sight and good for food" (Gen 2:9).

b) *The* Birkat ha-moṣi

A meal is accompanied by two benedictions: one, very short, before it; the other, longer and more complex, at its end. The first, known as the *birkat ha-moṣi* (from the root *yṣh*, to go out; here in the causative participle: that which makes to go out), runs as follows: "Blessed art thou, O Lord our God, King of the universe, who bringest forth bread from the earth (*ha-moṣi lehem min ha-'areṣ*)" (963). In these words, taken from Ps 104:14, God is acknowledged and thanked as the one who "bringest forth bread from the earth."

The key word in this benediction is *lehem*, a term rich in meanings. The basic meaning is "bread" in the sense of the food we make out of grain. In a broader usage, though still connected with the first, *lehem* can mean "food" in general. The word is still used in this sense by modern Arabs for whom *laḥma*, which corresponds etymologically to the Hebrew *lehem*, means "meat to be eaten," this being the most widespread and abundant part of their meals. To thank God for "bread" is therefore to express thanksgiving and gratitude for all the fruits of the earth that give human beings nourishment and joy.

But in the Jewish tradition as recorded in the Bible *lehem* also signifies the flesh of sacrificed animals, which are called "the bread of God (*lehem 'Elohim*)" (Lev 21:6), and it recalls the manna, *lehem min-ha-shamaim* ("the bread from heaven"). Rather than being opposed to the two preceding senses, these last two explain them and give us a deeper understanding, for both the sacrifices and the manna help us to recognize and make our own the divine intention behind the fruits of the earth. These fruits are at the disposal of human beings and are meant for their sustenance, but they achieve their true meaning and display their potentiality only when they are accepted in a way that corresponds to the dynamism at work in them. To promote this acceptance is the purpose of the *berakah*, which repeats and expresses anew the logic of sacrifice and the manna. Whenever human beings acknowledge, before their meals, that God is the source of the "bread" they are about to eat, they perform a sacrificial act and relive the miracle of the manna.

c) *The* Birkat ha-mazon

The most important benediction connected with a meal is the one that follows and is known as *birkat ha-mazon*, "benediction over food," *mazon* meaning foods.

Of all the benedictions in the Jewish ritual this is regarded as the oldest and the most important, because it alone is expressly commanded in the Torah: "And you shall eat and be full, and you shall bless the Lord your God for the good land that he has given you" (Deut 8:10). It is made up of three benedictions (presently four), in which God is thanked for the food, for the land, and for Jerusalem. These benedictions almost certainly go back to the period of the Second Temple, although the Talmudic tradition attributes them to Moses, Joshua, and Solomon respectively:

> The first benediction of the *birkat ha-mazon*, which begins with the words "thou who feedest," was instituted for Israel by Moses at the time when the manna dropped from heaven. The second was instituted by Joshua when the Hebrews took possession of the land. Finally, David and Solomon instituted the third, which ends with the words "thou who rebuildest Jerusalem."[12]

The first of these benedictions reads thus:

> Blessed art thou, O Lord our God, King of the universe, who feedest the whole world with thy goodness, with grace, with lovingkindness and tender mercy; thou givest food to all flesh, for thy lovingkindness endureth for ever. Through thy great goodness food hath never failed us: O may it not fail us for ever and ever for thy great Name's sake, since thou nourishest and sustainest all beings, and doest good unto all, and providest food for all thy creatures whom thou

hast created. Blessed art thou, O Lord, who givest food to
all (967–69).

This benediction, known as *birkat ha-zan* ("benediction for
food"), praises God as "host" of the universe, who in his love feeds all
creatures. The emphasis in the text is on the idea of "all" (Hebrew:
kol), which is repeated six times. The benediction thus celebrates the
universal reach of God's love, not only to the human race (he feeds
not only Israel but all other peoples) but to the cosmos (he feeds every
living thing, animal or vegetable, in the macrocosm and the micro-
cosm). When believing Jews sit down to table in order to eat, they feel
themselves to be in communion with all living things. Eating is for
them more than a simple material activity, for before the fruits of the
earth feed them, these same fruits already speak to them of God and
his favor; the fruits speak to the heart and spirit before they feed the
body. The *berakah* expresses this movement and brings about this
metamorphosis by turning "bread from the earth" (*lehem min ha-
'ares*) into "bread from heaven" (*lehem min-ha-shamaim*), the bread
that is manna.

Thanks to the benediction the bread becomes a heavenly gift
and reproduces the miracle of the manna (Ex 16). This is why the
Talmudic tradition attributes this benediction, the first and oldest
Jewish prayer, to Moses, who was thought to have composed it on
occasion of the fall of the manna from heaven.

The second benediction, known as *birkat ha-'ares* ("benediction
for the land"), thanks God for the fine and spacious land that was
given to Israel:

We thank you, O Lord our God, because thou didst give as
an heritage unto our fathers a desirable, good and ample
land, and because thou didst bring us forth, O Lord our God,
from the land of Egypt, and didst deliver us from the house
of bondage; as well as for thy covenant which thou hast
sealed in our flesh, thy Torah which thou hast taught us, thy
statutes which thou hast made known unto us, the life,
grace and lovingkindness which thou hast bestowed upon
us, and for the food wherewith thou dost constantly feed
and sustain us on every day, in every season, at every hour.

For all this, O Lord our God, we thank and bless thee,
blessed be thy Name by the mouth of all living continually
and for ever, even as it is written, And thou shalt eat and be
satisfied, and thou shalt bless the Lord thy God for the good

land which he hath given thee [Deut 8:10]. Blessed art thou,
O Lord, for the land and for the food (969).

After being universal and cosmic (in the *birkat ha-zan*), the benediction after meals here becomes historical and particular. God is thanked for the promised land, the deliverance from Egypt, the gift of the covenant, and circumcision. Why is reference made, in a prayer of thanksgiving after meals, to theological themes that are so rich and so remote from the setting? The reason goes deep, even if it is not immediately identifiable. If it be true (as the first benediction claims) that God feeds all living beings, it is also true that in this activity he calls for the responsible action and the solidarity of human groups. The mention of the Torah in this second benediction emphasizes this point, which is extremely important: the bread that gives joy and alleviates hunger is not bread that is selfishly accumulated and hoarded but bread that is shared in accordance with the logic of the covenant, which prohibits injustice and is the basis of brotherhood and sisterhood.

In a similar fashion, the land for which this second benediction thanks God is not a simple geographical entity but a gift of God following upon the deliverance from Egypt and the striking of the covenant. Within the logic thus established, "the good and ample land" of which Exodus speaks is not a land that bears fruit miraculously as a result of privileged natural conditions, but a land that bears fruit for all because those that till it take joint responsibility for it, are content with what they need, and are capable of sharing. The land becomes "good and ample" and is able to feed and give joy, when the covenant is kept and the Torah obeyed therein.

The third benediction, known as *boneh Jerushalaim* ("thou who rebuildest Jerusalem"), invokes God as "rebuilder" of Zion and thanks him for this:

Have mercy, O Lord our God, upon Israel thy people, upon Jerusalem thy city, upon Zion the abiding place of thy glory, upon the kingdom of the house of David, and upon the great and holy house that was called by thy Name. O Lord our God, our Father, feed us, nourish us, sustain, support and relieve us, and speedily, O Lord our God, grant us relief from all our troubles. We beseech thee, O Lord our God, let us not be in need either of the gifts of mortals or of their loans, but only of thy helping hand, which is full, open, holy and ample, so that we may never be put to shame nor humiliated.

And rebuild Jerusalem the holy city speedily in our days. Blessed art thou, O Lord, who in thy compassion rebuildest Jerusalem. Amen (971–73).

While the first benediction thanks God for food and the second for the land, which is to be received and worked in accordance with the Torah, the third benediction asks God to be always merciful (*rahem*, "have mercy") to the people of Israel. This petition has three objects: the protection of Jerusalem, its rebuilding, and in the interval before the rebuilding, the satisfaction of individual needs ("nourish us, sustain . . . grant relief from all our troubles"). What is the point of all these petitions in a prayer of thanksgiving after meals? The clear understanding of Israel that the bread which satisfies hunger is the bread of responsibility and solidarity is accompanied by a no less clear consciousness of Israel's sins of selfishness and infidelity. Therefore the petition for forgiveness: "have mercy." If the bread eaten has been unjustly hoarded, "have mercy"; if it has been taken from the poor, "have mercy"; if others die of hunger while we eat, "have mercy." In other words, make us understand how abominable these things are; and as you are *rehem* to us (*rehem* points to a vital place, the womb), make us the same to others. This is the point of the words: "Let us not be in need of the gifts of mortals . . . but only of thy helping hand, which is full, open, holy, and ample." The intention is not to do without others in a haughty attitude of superiority, but rather to be companion and friend to every other person, because we are all fed equally from "the full, open, holy, and ample" divine hand.

Until the end of the first century of the Christian era the *birkat ha-mazon* comprised the three benedictions cited, which were looked upon as a single detailed prayer (that is why the third ends with an "Amen"). A fourth *berakah* was then added, which became known as *ha-tov we-ha-metiv* ("who art kindly and dealest kindly with all"). It was composed at Jabneh by Rabbi Gamaliel on occasion of the permission obtained from the Romans to bury those who had died at Bethar after the revolt of Bar Kochba.

Blessed art thou, O Lord our God, King of the universe, O God, our Father, our King, our Mighty One, the Holy One of Jacob, our Shepherd, the Shepherd of Israel, O King, who art kind and dealest kindly with all, day by day thou hast dealt kindly, dost deal kindly, and wilt deal kindly with us; thou hast bestowed, thou dost bestow, thou wilt ever bestow benefits upon us, yielding us grace, lovingkindness, mercy and relief, deliverance and prosperity, blessing and salvation, consolation, sustenance and support, mercy, life, peace and all good: of no manner of good let us be in want (973–75).

It is surprising that, despite the brutal failure of the revolt of 135, the rabbis should have added to the *birkat ha-mazon* this benediction which is a hymn to divine love. One explanation is that it was intended as an example for

those who were discontent or disappointed that their wishes were not granted and who thought they could stop expressing gratitude to divine Providence. The benediction reminds them of a period when their ancestors were so deeply unhappy that permission to bury their dead was enough to make them burst into words of ardent thanksgiving.[13]

The fourth benediction, then, teaches us that we must learn to "be content." Contentment does not mean renouncing things but rather adopting a different attitude toward them. It is from this attitude, and not from things, that joy and gratitude spring. These four benedictions form the basic structure of the *birkat ha-mazon*, to which additions—introductory, intermediate, and final—have been made in various circles and rites.

The introductory addition, which is perhaps properly a part of the basic structure, consists of a kind of dialogue between the master of the house (or an honored guest) and the others at table.

Turning to the others, the master says: *Rabbotai nevarek*, "Sirs, let us say grace." The others answer: "Blessed be the Name of the Lord from this time forth and for ever." The sayer of the grace continues: "With the sanction (of the master of the house and) of those present, we will bless him of whose bounty we have partaken." The others answer: "Blessed be he of whose bounty we have partaken, and through whose goodness we live" (965–67). Then come the benedictions of the *birkat ha-mazon*, provided there be a minimum of three persons (men or women) present.[14]

Of the intermediate additions, an especially fine one is known as *ha-rahamon* ("the merciful one"), which consists of a series of assertions and wishes:

The All-merciful shall reign over us for ever and ever. The All-merciful shall be blessed in heaven and on earth. The

All-merciful shall be praised throughout all generations, glorified among us to all eternity, and honoured among us for everlasting.

    May the All-merciful grant us an honourable livelihood. May the All-merciful break the yoke from off our neck, and lead us upright to our land. May the All-merciful send a plentiful blessing upon this house, and upon this table at which we have eaten. May the All-merciful send us Elijah the prophet (let him be remembered for good), who shall bring us good tidings, salvation and consolation. May the All-merciful bless my honoured father, the master of this house, and my honoured mother, the mistress of this house, them, their household, their children, and all that is theirs; us also and all that is ours, as our fathers Abraham, Isaac and Jacob were blessed each with his own comprehensive blessing; even thus may he bless all of us with a perfect blessing, and let us say, Amen (975–77).

The additions at the end of the *birkat ha-mazon* consist of some psalm verses to be recited by each person in silence. Among these are verse 11 of Ps 34 and verse 25 of Ps 37, which together say: "Those who seek the Lord lack no good thing. I have been young, and now am old; yet I have not seen the righteous forsaken or his children begging bread."

2. The Feast of Shabbat

The first focus of the domestic liturgy is on "bread," as symbol both of the table and of the fruits of the earth. The second, to which I turn now, is on the sabbath as summary and symbol of all the blessings given to Israel for its enjoyment.

It is impossible to understand Jewish spirituality unless we can enter into the light-filled and fascinating labyrinth of *shabbat*, which is at once the faithful expression and effective source of that spirituality. The celebration begins with a *berakah* pronounced by the mother of the family and ends with others known as the *havdalah* and recited by the father. The culminating point of the celebration is the recitation of the *qiddush*, which is said over a cup of wine before the family meal. The lighting of lamps, the *qiddush*, and the *havdalah* are the three main rites of a Jewish family on the sabbath. By means of them the sabbath reveals its luminous nature and, "like a lamp to our feet" (see Ps 119:105), once again illumines the path of the Jewish people by revealing their identity to them and strengthening their sense of who they are.

a) The Image of the Bride

Only through midrash have the Jewish people succeeded in bringing out the deeper meaning of the sabbath:

> Genibah said: A king had prepared and adorned a bridal canopy. What was lacking? A bride to lead under it. In like manner: what did the world lack? The sabbath. Our teachers said: A king had a ring made for himself. What was lacking? A seal. In like manner: what did the world lack? The sabbath.[15]

This parable, which the *Midrash Rabba* tells in order to explain Gen 2:2 ("On the seventh day God finished his work"), establishes the relationship between the first six days of the week and the seventh: the relation is not one of temporal succession (the sabbath comes after the other six days) but one of interpretation and justification (the sabbath interprets and gives meaning to time). In fact, according to the parable, the same relationship exists between the sabbath and the other six days of the week as between bridal canopy and bride or between the king's ring and the seal on it.

The bridal canopy precedes the bride in time, but teleologically it is ordered to the bride and derives its purpose from her. In a similar way, a ring is not such in itself but only in view of someone putting it on to serve as a seal. In its naive simplicity this midrash sums up a whole treatise on the philosophy of time. Why does time exist, and how is it to be filled with meaning? Unlike the gloomy pessimists in the several forms of modern existentialism, who are filled with dread by the threat of an emptiness that swallows up and obliterates all things, Judaism experiences time as having a positive content, as being a place of meaning and a source of fulfillment. "What did the world lack? The sabbath," for just as a bride fills a house with her presence, since she is its purpose and cause, so the sabbath justifies the world, being its foundation and meaning. In the experience of the people of the Bible, time is "lacking" in itself; it is therefore a space that threatens and swallows up if it lacks the "sabbath." On the other hand, time receives definition and completion when related to the sabbath. The sabbath is non-time (we would say "eternity") insofar as it is the foundation of time; it is the time of origins insofar as it is the origin of time; it is the being that is at the heart of becoming.

If we were to attempt a translation into conceptual terms of what the images of bride and royal ring are expressing symbolically, we would have to say that the meaning of time is contained in the root of the word *shabbat*. In Hebrew this has two meanings: "to cease from toil" and "to take one's rest." On the negative side, it signifies the absence of toil and suffering; on the positive, the fullness of fruition and enjoyment. The fruition meant, however, is not subjective, which is based on personal resources, but objective, which grounds rather than is grounded on something else: "On the seventh day God finished his work which he had done, and he rested on the seventh day from all his work which he had done. So God blessed the seventh day and hallowed it, because on it God rested from all his work which he had done in creation" (Gen 2:2–3). By making the divine sabbath the basis of the human sabbath and the latter a mimesis of the former, the Genesis story defines time as an objective possibility of meaning of which human beings are the beneficiaries before they use it as a medium of self-projection.

This emphasis on the objective meaning of time does not cancel out the responsibility of human beings but rather calls for it and even heightens it, as another story from the *Midrash Rabba* shows:

> Rabbi Simon ben Johaj said: "When the work of creation was complete, the Seventh Day (the Sabbath) complained: Lord of the universe, everything you created comes in pairs, and to every day of the week you have given a companion. Only I am left alone. And God replied: The community of Israel will be your companion."[16]

Commenting on this midrash A.J. Heschel writes: "Despite its dignity the sabbath is not self-sufficient; its spiritual reality calls for human participation. An ardent longing pervades the world: the six days need space, the seventh needs human beings. It is not good for the spirit to be left alone; for this reason Israel was destined to be the companion of the sabbath." Time, which undergirds human becoming, reveals its luminous reality only to those who seek it and conform themselves to it. The sabbath, as quantitative time, becomes *shabbat*, or qualitative time, only for those who know how to be its "companions." *Shabbat* (which is a feminine noun in Hebrew), being bride of the world, reveals her treasures of love and beauty only to those who can welcome her with the openness and passion of a bridegroom.

b) The Lighting of the Lamps

The sabbath begins, in the home, with the lighting of two candles by the mother of the family. Light, which is never exhausted, is a material expression of the beauty and meaning hidden in everyday time; its radiance and warmth suggest the radiance and warmth of the sabbath that is to be welcomed and participated in.

Before lighting the candles, the mother, accompanied by her smaller children (the father and older sons have gone to the synagogue to join the community in welcoming the sabbath), says the following prayer:

> Lord of the universe, I am about to perform the sacred duty of kindling the lights in honour of the Sabbath, even as it is written: "And thou shalt call the Sabbath a delight, and the holy day of the Lord honourable." And may the effect of my fulfilling this commandment be, that the stream of abundant life and heavenly blessing flow in upon me and mine; that thou be gracious unto us and cause thy Presence to dwell among us.
>
> Father of Mercy, O continue thy lovingkindness unto me and my dear ones. Make me worthy to (rear my children so that they) walk in the way of the righteous before thee, loyal to thy Torah and clinging to good deeds. Keep thou far from us all manner of shame, grief and care; and grant that peace, light, and joy ever abide in our home. For with thee is the fountain of life; in thy light do we see light. Amen (343).

After this prayer the mother of the family lights the candles and then immediately says the blessing: "Blessed art thou, O Lord our God, King of the universe, who hast hallowed us by thy commandments, and commanded us to kindle the Sabbath light" (345). There are two motives for this benediction: sanctification (thou "hast hallowed us by thy commandments") and the lighting of the candles (thou hast "commanded us to kindle the Sabbath light").

Sanctification (from the root qdsh) signifies separation or differentiation, and it is because of this that Israel blesses the Lord. But the separation is to be understood not in relation to other peoples but in relation to time: Israel is different or unlike ("holy"), not because it is superior to other peoples but because it is able to interpret and enjoy time in a luminous way, not as the face of an enveloping nothingness but as the face of a fullness and perfection that are laden with meaning.

"Holiness" does not consist in an accumulation of good works which improve the doers morally (this is simply a consequence) but in access to the foundations of time, wherein is hidden, and whence flows, the lightsomeness of being. The lighting of the lamps, which is given as the second reason for the benediction (thou hast "commanded us to kindle the Sabbath light"), is not something different from sanctification (thou "hast hallowed us by thy commandments") but rather an explicitation of it and its translation into a material form: the light that shines around us is a symbol of the objective meaning that dwells in time.

The lighting of the candles, which is almost certainly pre-Maccabean in origin,[17] serves as a real introduction to the sabbath, providing a language for it and allowing its meaning already to emerge. Thanks to the lighting of the candles, the sabbath brings "heaven in[to] every Jewish home, filling it with long-expected and blissfully-greeted peace; making each home a sanctuary, the father a priest, and the mother who lights the Sabbath candles an angel of light."[18]

c) The Qiddush

The qiddush, which rabbinical tradition traces back to the Men of the Great Assembly (ca. fifth century B.C.), is recited by the father of the family at a festively laid table whereon the mother has previously lit the candles.[19] It consists of a benediction and the sharing of a cup of wine and another benediction and the sharing of a loaf of bread; after this comes the meal proper, which is eaten with joy and to the accompaniment of song. This qiddush is one of the most important prayers of the Jewish liturgy. It proclaims the holiness of the sabbath (qiddush ha-yom) and the difference, which is qualitative and substantial, between this day and the other days of the week.

The text comprises three berakot: in the first and third God is blessed for the fruit of the vine and for the bread which the earth yields; the second, which is more specific and more detailed, blesses him for the gift of the sabbath, the various meanings of which are recalled:

> Blessed art thou, O Lord our God, King of the universe, who createst the fruit of the vine.
> Blessed art thou, O Lord our God, King of the universe,

who hast hallowed us by thy commandments and hast taken pleasure in us, and in love and favour hast given us thy holy Sabbath as an inheritance, a memorial of the creation—that day being also the first of the holy convocations, in remembrance of the departure from Egypt. For thou hast chosen us and hallowed us above all nations, and in love and favour hast given us thy holy Sabbath as an inheritance. Blessed art thou, O Lord, who hallowest the Sabbath.

Blessed art thou, O Lord our God, King of the universe, who bringest forth bread from the earth (409).

According to the second and central *berakah*, God is blessed because he "hallows the Sabbath" (*meqaddesh ha-shabbat*), that is, declares its radical newness in relation to the time before and after it. The content of this newness is expressed symbolically by the cup of wine over which the first benediction is pronounced. In the biblical tradition (see Gen 9:20) and in Hellenistic culture wine had an important place as a symbol of gratuitousness or unmerited gift and as source of joy. Unlike bread, which is necessary for life, wine is sought for the joy and freedom of spirit that it bestows. As the psalmist says, wine "gladdens the heart of man" (Ps 104:15) and reminds us of that dimension of the human where there is something more than mere physiological needs: the dimension of direction, of plenitude, of meaning. The sabbath is all these things: it expresses the fundamental goodness of the real world, which, for all its absurdity and all the defeats it inflicts, can nonetheless continue to be loved and enjoyed; it lets us see that the destiny of human beings is not brutalizing work but the enjoyment of fellowship; it opens a breach in the walls of the factual and inevitable by showing the possibility of a completely renewed world.

For this reason the sabbath is "a memorial of the creation": it calls to mind the world as it was created, when it emerged for the first time, harmonious and resplendent, from the hands of God, before human beings sinned. But the sabbath also serves as a "remembrance of the departure from Egypt." Beyond counting though the errors of human beings may be, they cannot destroy that morning of the first creation; they can obscure it but not do away with it. The departure from Egypt, that foundational event for Jewish spirituality and culture, expresses this certainty, and the sabbath, which memorializes the departures, repeats the certainty and confirms it.

Because the *qiddush* proclaims the sabbath holy and makes it the metatemporal reality that is the foundation of all times, it can be

thought of as a voice arising from the depths of being and revealing
that in the final analysis this being is salvation.

This explains why the Falashas of northern Ethiopia, who for
centuries were cut off from all contact with other Jewish communities, were accustomed to answer, when asked who their savior was:
"The Saviour of the Jews is the Sabbath." For the same reason,
Acham Ha-am has rightly said: "Far more than Israel has kept the
Sabbath, it is the Sabbath that has kept Israel." And—we may add—
has preserved the world. For, as long as it makes the Sabbath its
foundation, nothing will be able to shake it.[20]

The beginning of the sabbath is marked not only by the qiddush
but by other prayers, some introductory, others coming at the end of
the ceremony. Among the former, three are especially beautiful: the
father's blessing of his children; the hymn Shalom 'alekem to the
angels; and the hymn to the wife and mother.

When the father returns from the synagogue and enters the
house he lays his hands on the head of each child in turn and blesses
them as the patriarchs were already doing two thousand years before
the Christian era. For centuries, the words of the blessing have been
those of the priestly benediction: "The Lord bless thee and keep thee:
the Lord make his face to shine upon thee, and be gracious unto thee:
the Lord turn his face unto thee, and give thee peace" (Num 6:24–26).
Few actions bring out so fully the priestly character of the Jewish
father and the deep sense of security which he passes on to his
children.

Next comes the hymn to the angels: "Peace be unto you, ye
ministering angels" (405), which was introduced by the Cabalists in
the sixteenth century and is based on a Baraita which relates that:

> two ministering angels escort a man home from the syna-
> gogue on Sabbath Eve, one good and one evil. When the
> good angel comes [to a] home and finds the candles lit and
> the table set, he says, "May it be His will that the next Sab-
> bath be [also] thus." And the evil angel answers, "Amen,"
> against his will. And if not [if nothing is prepared for the
> Sabbath], the evil angel says, "May it be His will that the
> next Sabbath be also thus." And the good angel answers,
> "Amen," against his will.[21]

This parable keeps alive in Jewish memory the importance of pre-
paring for the sabbath and welcoming it in a spirit of love and festal joy.

Finally, the father expresses good wishes and admiration for his wife, using the words of Prov 31:10–31: "A woman of worth who can find? For her price is far above rubies . . ." (405).

The concluding prayer, which precedes the traditional *birkat ha-mazon*, consists of Ps 126, *shir hamma'alot*: "When the Lord restored the prosperity of Zion, we were like unto them that dream . . ." (965). So great was the joy of the Babylonian exiles as they returned to their homeland in 537 B.C. that they thought they were dreaming. Jews experience the same joy, the same atmosphere, on Friday evenings as they enter into the "land" of the sabbath. As Jerusalem was for the exiles, the sabbath is the true native land of human beings, for it protects them against dispersion and ensures their identity.

d) *The* Havdalah

Like the beginning of the sabbath, its end too is marked by certain rites. The ceremony is called *havdalah* (separation, differentiation) because it signals the difference between the sabbath, which is now ending, and the weekdays that are beginning. It is also very ancient and has been attributed to the Men of the Great Assembly.[22] It consists of four short benedictions that are said over a cup of wine, a box of spices, the lights, and again over the cup of wine; the wine, spices, and lights are three symbols of the beauty and transfiguring power of the sabbath. The benedictions are preceded by a prayer composed of biblical verses from Isaiah, Esther, and the Psalms:

> Behold, God is my salvation; I will trust, and will not be afraid: for God the Lord is my strength and song, and he is become my salvation. Therefore with joy shall ye draw water out of the wells of salvation [Is 12:2–3]. Salvation belongeth unto the Lord: thy blessing be upon thy people [Ps 46:12]. The Lord of hosts is with us; the God of Jacob is our refuge [Est 8:16]. The Jews had light and joy and gladness and honour. (So be it with us.) I will lift the cup of salvation, and call upon the Name of the Lord [Ps 116:13] (745–47).

The four benedictions follow directly:

> Blessed art thou, O Lord our God, King of the universe, who createst the fruit of the vine.
> Blessed art thou, O Lord our God, King of the universe, who createst divers kinds of spices.

Blessed art thou, O Lord our God, King of the universe, who createst the light of the fire.

Blessed art thou, O Lord our God, King of the universe, who makest a distinction between holy and profane, between light and darkness, between Israel and the heathen nations, between the seventh day and the six working days. Blessed art thou, O Lord, who makest a distinction between holy and profane (747–49).

As the sabbath draws to a close, Jews like to remind themselves that God is the creator of the sacred, the light, Israel, and the sabbath; in other words, that reality is filled with light (this is the point of the sacred-profane and light-darkness polarities) for those who are able to perceive and respect it (this is the point of the Israel-other peoples and sabbath-other days polarities). To use a different terminology: Jews like to remind themselves that God has created human beings for a life rich in meaning, for the Garden of Eden (the spice box is an allusion to the earthly paradise) and that the duty of human beings is to realize this possibility by avoiding the temptation of taking the quantitative as an end in itself and by promoting the quest of quality, which is the fruit of an existence focused on justice and fraternity. The *havdalah*, which separates sacred time from profane time, "empty" time from "full" time, bids us resume our lives with a sense of responsibility and commitment, in the realization that what gives life meaning is not the material succession of hours and work but the interior project that dynamizes and sustains it.

When this project reflects the divine plan, life produces abundant fruits, as the vine produces wine, lamps warmth, and herbs their perfume.

In the Sephardic rite the *havdalah* ends with this beautiful prayer for the new week that will begin shortly:

Sovereign of the Universe, Father of mercy and forgiveness, grant that we begin the working days which are drawing nigh unto us, in peace; freed from all sin and transgression; cleansed from all iniquity, trespass and wickedness; and clinging to the study of thy Teaching, and to the performance of good deeds. Cause us to hear in the coming week tidings of joy and gladness. May there not arise in the heart of any man envy of us, nor in us envy of any man. O, our King, our God, Father of mercy, bless and prosper the work of our hands. And all who cherish towards us and thy people Israel thoughts of good, strengthen and prosper them, and fulfill their purpose; but all who devise against us, and thy people Israel, plans which are not for good, Oh frustrate them and make their designs of none effect; as it is said, "Take counsel together, and it shall be brought to naught; speak the word, and it shall not stand; for God is with us." Open unto us, Father of mercies and Lord of forgiveness, in this week and in the weeks to come, the gates of light and blessing, of redemption and salvation, of heavenly help and rejoicing, of holiness and peace, of the study of thy Torah and of prayer. In us also let the Scripture be fulfilled: How beautiful upon the mountains are the feet of him that bringeth good tidings, that announceth peace, the harbinger of good tidings, that announceth salvation; that saith unto Zion, Thy God reigneth! Amen (753).

3. The Passover Seder

We turn now to "the most impressive, the most joyous, the most memorable of all domestic rituals in Judaism."[23] It celebrates the event that is the basis of Jewish history and spirituality, the event that marked the end of slavery and the beginning of freedom. The celebration takes the form of participation in a symbolic meal (followed by a real meal) in which every dish recalls some aspect of the night when God "with mighty hand and powerful arm" led his people from Egypt and brought them into the promised land. Thus the bitter herbs recall the sufferings of the forebears of old under the tyranny of their Egyptian bosses; the leg of roast lamb recalls the sacrifice of the Passover lamb that compelled the angel of death to "pass by" the doors of the Hebrews; the haroset, a sweet compote of apples and nuts, recalls the joy and sweetness of freedom; and so on.

The text that describes in detail everything that is to be said and done during the Passover supper is called the haggadah, which means a story or narrative (from the root ngd, "to recount, relate"). The haggadah is the most often printed Jewish book and, unlike all others, is almost always illustrated. One can hardly say one really knows Judaism unless one has taken part, at least once, in a Passover seder. The seder sums up, very tersely but with unrivaled beauty, the faith and history, the thought and folklore, the heart and mind of the Jewish people of every age.

a) The Structure of the Seder

The meal taken on the night of Passover is the most solemn and richest of all Jewish meals; it includes three parts in particular: 1) the supper proper, which is abundant and eaten in joy; 2) a lengthy symbolic and ritual phase, which precedes the supper proper and in which the abiding meaning of the Passover night is experienced anew and explained, especially to the children; and 3) other symbolic and ritual moments devoted chiefly to thanksgiving and song. So important is this meal that every part of it is carefully anticipated, described, and justified. The rabbinical tradition distinguishes fourteen parts and provides a mnemonic formula (difficult to translate) in which each word sums up a part of the ritual:

1. *Qaddesh.* This marks the beginning of the Passover celebration and consists of a *berakah* recited over a cup of wine that will be drunk at the end of the prayer. The benediction says that Jews now live in a time of freedom, separated from the period of oppression and enslavement (recall that the root of *qadosh* means "to separate"); the freedom is symbolized by the cup of wine and will be celebrated throughout the period of Passover. Here is the benediction:

> Blessed art thou, Lord our God, King of the universe, who createst the fruit of the vine.
>
> Blessed art thou, Lord our God, King of the universe, who has chosen and exalted us above all nations, and hast sanctified us with thy commandments. Thou, Lord our God, hast graciously given us holidays for gladness and festive seasons for joy, this Feast of Unleavened Bread, our Festival of Freedom, a holy convocation in remembrance of the exodus from Egypt. Thou didst choose and sanctify us above all peoples; in thy gracious love, thou didst grant us thy holy festivals for gladness and joy. Blessed art thou, O Lord, who hallowest Israel and the festivals.[24]

2. *Urḥaṣ* (washing of hands). Those present wash their hands, but without the usual blessing because the time has not yet come for the meal proper.

3. *Karpas* (they sit down). A bit of greens dipped in vinegar is eaten as a reminder of the bitterness of slavery.

4. *Yaḥaṣ* (to divide). The middle one of the three matzahs is broken in two, half being put back between the other two, and half being hidden somewhere, for example, under the tablecloth.

5. *Maggid* (narrator). A second cup of wine is filled, but before it is drunk the narrator tells the story of the deliverance from Egypt, explaining its meaning and abiding relevance with the help of passages from the Bible, midrashic stories, hymns, songs, and psalms.

This is the most characteristic and important part of the Pass-over seder.

6. *Roḥṣah* (washing). All wash their hands, this time with the usual blessing since they are about to begin the meal proper.

7. *Moḥsi' maṣṣah* (blessing of the unleavened bread). The usual benediction is said over the bread, which on this occasion is unleavened; a piece of it is eaten.

8. *Maror* (bitter herbs). A piece of the bitter greens is eaten together with a bit of *ḥaroset*, the sweet compote of grated apples and nuts that recalls how by their courage and love of freedom the Jews managed to ease the burden of their enslavement in Egypt.

9. *Korek* (to roll up). Another piece of bitter herbs is eaten, this time with a piece of the unleavened bread.

10. *Shulḥan 'Orek* (supper). The meal begins, starting with an antipasto consisting of an egg and some other special foods, all of them rich in more or less universal symbolism.

11. *Ṣafun* (hidden). The company eats the piece of unleavened bread that had been hidden and that is known as the *afıqoman* (a name of uncertain origin). It is eaten in memory of the Passover lamb; after its consumption no further food may be eaten until the next day. This is an especially important moment for the children, who are urged to look for the hidden half piece of unleavened bread.

12. *Barek* (benediction). The meal being completed, the participants wash their hands as usual and recite the traditional *birkat ha-mazon*; they fill a third cup and drink it at the end.

13. *Hallel* (praise). They thank the Lord for the Passover meal at which they have relived the miracle of freedom. A fourth cup of wine is prepared and drunk after the recitation of Psalms 115–118, known as the "Hallel." At the end the door is opened to allow for the entrance of Elijah, the messenger announcing the messianic age.

14. *Nirṣah* (acceptance). The leader announces the end of the Passover seder and asks God to be forever Israel's deliverer. If desired, various popular songs and counting-out rhymes may be sung ("One kid, one kid/Father bought for two zuzim;/One kid, one kid" or "Who knows one?"). These have for their purpose to hold the attention of the participants and to pass on the abiding values of the Jewish tradition in language that is popular and simple.

b) From Exodus to Promised Land

The entire Passover seder, with its various phases and its inexhaustibly rich symbolic, ritual, narrative, gestural, and mythological elements, celebrates the event by which the Jewish people is established: its birth to freedom through rescue from slavery. But the birth is not of the Jewish people alone but of every people and every individual. Thus toward the end of the narrative section the leader says: "In every generation it is man's ('adam, therefore not just Jews) duty to regard himself as though he personally had come out of Egypt."

This deliverance and freedom is celebrated in the symbolic language of a spring festival which is reread and reinterpreted as applying to historical events and to which new elements have been added. In that spring festival ancient peoples had celebrated the return of life out of the silence and cold of winter into the beauty of spring with its wealth of forms and colors. The transition, which was felt and experienced as a passage from death to life, was expressed by means of various symbols such as unleavened bread and a lamb. The unleavened bread translated into metaphor what the spring was accomplishing in the natural world: putting an end to the old, which was death-dealing, and inaugurating the new period which brings life. The same can be said of the lamb, the first-born of the flock, whose coming marked the reappearance of life that overcomes death.

Onto this nature symbolism, which Israel reinterpreted and deepened, it grafted a more radical insight: as nature passes from winter to spring, so the Jewish people have passed from slavery to freedom; but, unlike the transition in nature, which is automatic, the birth to freedom is a journey of commitment and responsibility. For these former slaves and exiles in Egypt, the spring festival thus becomes a festival of freedom at which they recall and reexperience the end of oppression and the beginning of a new identity. This liberation, this historical springtime that is effectively imaged forth by the springtime of nature, is the content of the haggadah.

At the beginning of the narrative section, the youngest child present asks the head of the family four questions:

Why is this night different from all nights?
1. On all nights we eat hametz [leavened bread] and
    matzah [unleavened bread].
   Why only matzah on this night?
2. On all nights we eat any kind of greens.
   Why the bitter greens on this night?
3. On all nights we do not dip even once.
   Why dip the greens twice on this night?
4. On all nights we eat sitting or leaning.
   Why do we all lean this night?

These questions are answered in the lengthy text of the narrative, first in a general way and then more specifically.

We were once the slaves of Pharaoh in Egypt, but the Lord our God brought us out from there with a mighty hand and outstretched arm. Had not God brought our fathers out of Egypt, our children and grandchildren would still be enslaved to a Pharaoh in Egypt. Even if we all were wise and intelligent, learned and versed in the Torah, it would nevertheless be our duty to tell about the exodus from Egypt. The more anyone discusses the exodus from Egypt, the more praise he deserves.

The thing that is celebrated on Passover night and that makes this night different from all others is the fact that "we were once the slaves of Pharaoh in Egypt, but the Lord our God brought us out from there."

This general answer is then repeated, enlarged, and illustrated by various passages of the Bible that are read, linked together, and interpreted by the midrashic method. Here are the more detailed replies.

Why eat the Passover lamb? "Because God passed over the houses of our fathers in Egypt, as it is written: 'You shall say: It is the Passover offering (pesaḥ) in honor of the Lord, who passed over (pasaḥ) the houses of the children of Israel in Egypt when he smote the Egyptians and spared our houses. The people bowed and worshiped' (Ex 12:27)."

Why eat unleavened bread? "Because the supreme King of kings, the Holy One, blessed be he, revealed himself to our fathers and redeemed them even before their dough had time to ferment, as it is written: 'They baked matzoth of the unleavened dough which they had brought out of Egypt; they were thrust out of Egypt and could not wait, nor had they prepared any food for their journey' (Ex 12:39)."

Why eat bitter herbs? "Because the Egyptians embittered the lives of our fathers in Egypt, as it is written: 'They made life bitter for them with hard labor, with mortar and bricks, and with all kinds of work in the fields; whatever work they imposed on them was rigorous and harsh' (Ex 1:14)."

Why drink while leaning on one's elbow? "It is our duty to thank and praise, laud and glorify, extol and honor, exalt and adore him who performed all these miracles for our fathers and for us. He brought us out of slavery into freedom, out of grief into joy, out of mourning into festivity, out of darkness into great light, out of subjection into redemption. Let us recite a new song before him! Halleluyah, praise the Lord!"

The joy felt at the freedom bestowed by the Passover events is expressed in the course of the supper by four cups of wine: the first accompanying the *qaddesh*, the second the *maggid*, the third the *barek*, and the fourth the *hallel*. A cup of wine is a sign of joy because "wine gladdens the heart of man" (Ps 104:15). The four cups symbolize an unparalleled, supreme fullness of joy (the number four, being the number of the letters in the Tetragram, which no one may utter, is a symbol of totality).

c) The Four Models of the Human Person

In addition to being a memorial of freedom bestowed, the Passover meal is a tool for learning, for what actually exists is not freedom but human beings who seek and defend it. The main purpose of the haggadah, the composition of which shows a great deal of pedagogical insight, is to stir up in the children, year after year, a passionate love for this inalienable value. I pointed out above that the children play a central part in the narrative section, for it is the youngest present who puts a series of questions which the head of the household and the other guests answer in the form of professions of faith ("We were slaves in Egypt"), passages from the Bible (Jos 24:2–4; Gen 15:13–14; Ex 8ff. on the ten plagues, and so on), midrashic parables, symbolical explanations (of *pesah*, *massah*, and *maror*; Rabban Gamaliel, Paul's teacher, used to say: "Whoever has not explained these three things on Passover has not fulfilled his duty"), and the singing of hymns and psalms. The entire set of answers is formulated and, as it were, measured out in such a way that the children will grasp the true meaning of *pesah* and become, ideally, "men and women of freedom."

The narrator tells of four sons who are four figures or archetypes: one is wise (*hakam*), one evil (*rasha'*), one simple, and one unable to ask questions. The positive archetype is the first, the negative the second; every Jew and indeed every human being has the potentiality for becoming the one or the other.

The wise son is the one who knows Passover and experiences freedom and joy; he is a person who asks the right questions and finds the right answers. He asks: "What is the meaning of all the laws and statutes that the Lord our God has commanded us?"[25] There can be only one answer: "Explain to him the laws concerning the Passover"; in other words, let him enter ever more fully into the reality of pesaḥ, which is the foundation and home of freedom and truth.

The evil son is just the opposite: he pays no heed to Passover and has no experience of freedom. He is incapable of "asking" and therefore of learning.

> The evil son asks: "What does this service mean to you?" By the expression "to you" he implies that this service means nothing to him. Since he excludes himself from the community and denies God, tell him bluntly: "This is on account of what the Lord did for me when I came out of Egypt." For me, not for him; had he been there, he would not have been liberated.

Observe the definition given here of wickedness (rasha'): the bad person is not one who acts wickedly but one who lacks freedom ("Had he been there, he would not have been liberated"). (The Italian word for "evil," cattivo, reflects something of this; in keeping with its Latin origin in captivus [one who has been taken, and remains, a prisoner], cattivo means a slave and therefore someone hampered, cut off, handicapped.) Wickedness springs not so much from freedom as from a state of existential deficiency; before being an ethical error it is an anthropological sickness and should therefore spur others to mercy and solidarity rather than ostracization and condemnation.

If the wise son and the wicked son represent two human possibilities, the simple son and the son who is unable to ask questions represent two pedagogical situations in which the one or the other possibility is actualized. The simple son is the superficial person who is incapable of "real questions" and therefore of developing, changing, and following a new path. He is the person who indeed asks: "What does this mean?" but the question is a rhetorical ploy and does not reflect a real sense of need. He is the person who thinks he knows and, victimized by his own self-delusion, is condemned to ignorance.

> No one sins deliberately or deliberately does ugly and evil actions; all who do ugly and evil actions do them out of ignorance. For no one who knows or believes that there are better actions than those he does and that such actions are possible for him, will continue to do the ones he does when he has the possibility of doing better ones. If he allows him-

self to be conquered by himself, the only cause can be ignorance; if he succeeds in overcoming himself, the only cause
can be wisdom.[26]

The simple son is therefore one in danger of becoming "wicked"; it is
the "path missed," an "erroneous pedagogy," that produces the
"evil" son (rasha'), the wicked person, and evil-doing.

The son "who is not able to ask a question" is a son who knows
that he does not know, but is ready to learn. "As for the son who is
not able to ask a question, you must open up the subject to him, as it
is written: 'You shall tell your son on that day: This is on account of
what the Lord did for me when I came out of Egypt' (Ex 13:8)." This
son represents the "right path," the "successful pedagogy," that
leads to experience of the exodus and of freedom. He represents the
right relationship to life and to God himself.

> Rabbi Levi Yishag of Berditchev reached the part of the hag-
> gadah that tells of the four sons; when he read the passage
> on the fourth son, the one who is not able to ask a question,
> he said: "I, Levi Yishag of Berditchev, am the one who is
> unable to ask a question. I do not know how to speak to you,
> Lord of the world, but even if I did, I would be unable to do
> it. How could I dare ask you . . . why we are driven from
> exile to exile, or why our enemies are able to torment us so
> greatly." But the haggadah cites the Torah, "You shall tell
> your son . . ." and thus obliges the father of the son who is
> unable to ask a question to give an answer to the son. There-
> fore Levi Yishaq of Berditchev said: "Lord of the world, am I
> not your son?"[27]

The wise are those who, like Rabbi Levi Yishaq, are so conscious
of the mystery of the world that they do not know "what to ask." At
the same time, however, they are so trusting in these matters that
they allow themselves to be constantly educated and changed. Wisdom dwells in the hearts of those who are sensitive to and receptive
of the mystery; wickedness dwells in the hearts of those who think
themselves self-sufficient but are ignorant.

d) Dayyenu

The "wise" human beings whom the haggadah proposes as the
only valid anthropological model are characterized by a basic realization: that their worth consists not in what they do but in what is done

to them. Before being active subjects, the "wise" understand themselves to be the objects of attentive love; they undergo a radical shift
of center from themselves to another in whom they believe and to
whom they abandon themselves. The haggadah is the enthusiastic
retelling of this surprising and liberating event: "I took your father
Abraham from the other side of the river and led him through all the
land of Canaan"; "This promise has sustained our fathers and us. For
not only one enemy has risen against us; in every generation men
rise against us to destroy us, but the Holy One saves us from their
hand"; "I made you thrive like a plant of the field; you grew up and
became tall and beautiful; your breasts were formed and your hair
grew long; but you were bare and naked"; "The Lord brought us out
of Egypt with a mighty hand and outstretched arm, with great awe,
signal acts and wonders"; "I will pass through the land of Egypt that
night, myself and not an angel; I will strike down all the firstborn in
the land of Egypt, myself and not a seraph; on all the gods of Egypt I
will execute judgments, myself and not a messenger; I am the Lord, I
and none else." The emphasis is evidently on God, whose unmerited
love and mighty deeds are being celebrated.

When the men and women of the Bible discover themselves to
be objects of love, they also discover themselves to be capable of
rejoicing and enjoyment; this indeed is the secret and meaning of
their wisdom. However dark their days may be, however bitter their
enslavement, however powerful "the pharaoh of Egypt," God never
forgets "their affliction, their cries, their sufferings" (see Ex 3:7).
They are therefore able to find meaning in every circumstance,
without mourning for the past or escaping into the future. All this is
suggested in the splendid *Dayyenu* ("That would have been enough
for us"), which is sung before the Allelujah psalms:

> God has bestowed many favors on us.
> Had he brought us out of Egypt
> And not punished the Egyptians,   *Dayyenu.*
>
> Had he punished the Egyptians,
> And not castigated their gods,   *Dayyenu.*
>
> Had he castigated their gods,
> And not put to death their firstborn,   *Dayyenu.*
>
> Had he put to death their firstborn,
> And not given us of their wealth,   *Dayyenu.*
>
> Had he given us of their wealth,
> And not split the Red Sea for us,   *Dayyenu.*

Had he split the Red Sea for us,
And not led us through it dryshod,   *Dayyenu.*

Had he led us through it dryshod,
And not engulfed our foes in it,   *Dayyenu.*

Had he engulfed our foes in it,
And not sustained us in wasteland,   *Dayyenu.*

Had he sustained us in wasteland,
And not fed us with the manna,   *Dayyenu.*

Had he fed us with the manna,
And not given us the Sabbath,   *Dayyenu.*

Had he given us the Sabbath,
And not brought us to Mount Sinai,   *Dayyenu.*

Had he brought us to Mount Sinai,
And not given us the Torah,   *Dayyenu.*

Had he given us the Torah,
And not brought us to Israel,   *Dayyenu.*

Had he brought us to Israel,
And not built the Temple for us,   *Dayyenu.*

Dayyenu: this one word, this simple refrain, sums the whole of biblical anthropology, an anthropology that is based on the unmerited and substitutes "I am given" for "I am owed," and that kills at its root the desire for "more" and the logic of possession. It teaches contentment with the "moment," not in order to renounce the "better" but because the "better" may be found in every moment.

These words might seem a rhetorical exaggeration were it not for the testimony of millions upon millions of Jews down the centuries who never ceased to sing the *Dayyenu*, even in the ghettoes and concentration camps. In their mouths it expressed not the nihilistic illusion that turns everything to absurdity, but the flash of meaning glimpsed beyond all the meaninglessness and giving the courage for continued belief and struggle.

This "flash of meaning" not only inspires journeys of hope and liberation; it also fills the soul with inexpressible joy, peace, and gratitude, as can be seen from the following passage that comes near the end of the seder:

Were our mouth filled with song as the sea [is with water],
and our tongue with ringing praise as the roaring waves;
were our lips full of adoration as the wide expanse of
heaven, and our eyes sparkling like the sun or the moon;
were our hands spread out in prayer as the eagles of the sky
and our feet as swift as the deer—we should still be unable
to thank thee and bless thy name, Lord our God and God of
our fathers, for one thousandth of the countless millions
of favors which thou hast conferred on our fathers and
on us. . . .

Therefore, the limbs which thou hast branched out in
us, the spirit and soul which thou hast breathed into our
nostrils, and the tongue which thou hast placed in our
mouth, shall all thank and bless, praise and glorify, extol
and revere, hallow and do homage to thy name, our King.

III. The Liturgy of the Synagogue

Jews pray not only privately and with the family but also with
the community in the synagogue. "Synagogue" (from Greek syn +
agogē, "a bringing together, an assembly") is a translation of the
Hebrew bet ha-keneset, "house of assembly." Not without reason has
the modern state of Israel chosen for its parliament this ancient name
that arose during the Diaspora.

Unlike the temple, which is defined by its place and its sacral
character, the synagogue refers to the community, which gives it its
meaning and substance. Whenever a group of individuals gather to
pray and to hear and study the Torah, there is a "synagogue," no
matter what the place or its size.

The principal characteristics of the synagogue are reducible to
three. The first is its lay character. In the synagogue, "priests" and
"Levites"—those who by reason of birth and caste were in charge of
public worship—are on the same level as everyone else and enjoy no
special privileges. Everyone, regardless of role or social class, can
lead the prayer, intone a hymn, read the Torah, or address the group,
provided only he have reached a certain age (12/13 years) and have
the ability to do the job.

The second characteristic, which derives from the first, is the
sense of equality. In the synagogue there are no special hierarchies,
and all have the same rights and duties. This is why many people,
such as Salomon Freehof, one of the most influential rabbis in Ameri-

can Reformed Judaism, like to say that the experience of democracy began in the synagogue.[28]

The third characteristic has to do with the indispensable minimum number of participants required for a "synagogue": ten adult males (minyan) who through their confirmation (their bar miṣwah ceremony) have become full-fledged members of the community. The minyan is not only important but it is the only condition required for celebration of synagogal worship.

Worship is conducted in the synagogue daily and on the occasion of special events. Though the structure of the celebration is always fundamentally the same, there are always also slight differences and various kinds of additions.

I. Weekdays

Worship is celebrated in the synagogue in the morning (shaḥrit), afternoon (minḥah) and evening (ma'ariv). In addition to the recitation of the shema' and tefillah and the reading of the Torah (the qeri'at Torah, which for reasons of time is celebrated only in the morning on Tuesday, Thursday, and the Sabbath), there are other prayers, as the following outline shows:

    I. Shaḥrit (Morning Liturgy)
        1. Benedictions and introductory psalms
        2. Qaddish
        3. Shema' (with the benedictions and precede and follow)
        4. Tefillah
        5. Qaddish
        6. 'Alenu
        7. Qaddish for mourners
        8. Final prayers
    II. Minḥah (Afternoon Liturgy)
        1. Psalm
        2. Qaddish
        3. Tefillah
        4. 'Alenu
        5. Qaddish
    III. Ma'ariv (Evening Liturgy)
        1. Short readings from the Psalms
        2. Shema'
        3. Tefillah
        4. Qaddish

5. 'Alenu
6. Qaddish (mourners')

a) The Qaddish

Among the prayers listed the Qaddish and the 'Alenu are especially important.

There are three liturgical prayers that derive their name from the word qadosh, "holy": the qedushah, the qiddush, and the qaddish. The qedushah is built around the threefold "Holy" of Isaiah 6 and is recited several times a day in the tefillah. The qiddush is the prayer sanctifying the sabbath and feast days; it is recited over a cup of wine, which symbolizes the new reality that lies ahead. Finally, the qaddish is the best-known doxology of the Jewish liturgy.

The qaddish, now "a great pillar of Judaism,"[29] has a complex history that is not easy to retrace. It proclaims the holiness of God, praises his greatness, and asks him to bestow on the world the fulness of consolation and peace:

> Reader: Magnified and sanctified be his great Name in the world which he hath created according to his will. May he establish his kingdom during your life and during your days, and during the life of all the house of Israel, even speedily and at a near time, and say ye, Amen.
> Congregation and Reader: Let his great name be blessed for ever and to all eternity.
> Reader: Blessed, praised and glorified, exalted, extolled and honoured, magnified and lauded be the Name of the Holy One, blessed be he; though he be high above all the blessings and hymns, praises and consolations, which are uttered in the world; and say ye, Amen (107).
> Reader: May there be abundant peace from heaven, and life for us and for all Israel; and say ye, Amen.
> Congregation: Amen.
> Reader: He who maketh peace in his high places, may he make peace for us and for all Israel; and say ye, Amen.
> Congregation: Amen (207)
> Reader: Bless ye the Lord, who is to be blessed.
> Congregation: Blessed is the Lord who is to be blessed for ever and ever. (109).[30]

According to scholars, the essential and oldest part of this prayer is the response of the congregation: "Let his great name be blessed for ever and to all eternity," which is a citation from Daniel 2:20.

The remainder of the text (it is said) was added at later periods and for various reasons, around these central words. According to one probable reconstruction, the *qaddish* was formed in three stages. Initially, and in the form it had at that time, it would have been used as a brief closing formula at the end of a biblical reading or a homiletic commentary, as can be seen from the following prayer *'al Yiś-ra'el we-'al rabbenu:*

> For Israel and for our teachers, for their disciples and for all the disciples of their disciples, for those who study, here or elsewhere: may they receive abundant peace, favor, grace, and mercy; may they receive prosperity and deliverance from the Father of heaven and earth. And say ye, Amen.[31]

Later on, the *qaddish* passed from the academic setting to the synagogue, where it became the formula for ending either the entire liturgical service or its principal parts (for example, after the preliminary benedictions and after the *shema'* and *tefillah*).

In a third phase, it became the supreme prayer of mourners, being recited by children after the death of their parents, a spouse after the death of the partner, and a parent after the death of one of the children. It is not easy, indeed, to explain how the *qaddish*, in which there is no mention of death, should have become the prayer par excellence of "orphans" (*qaddish yatom*). It is thought that there were two basic reasons or considerations at work. The first is the obligation of praising God at all times, even in time of trial, as with Job: "The Lord gave, and the Lord has taken away; blessed be the name of the Lord" (Job 1:21). Praise of God at the departure of a loved one represents an act of faith and of abandonment to the divine will; it is even the purest and most disinterested act of faith. But, besides expressing an unconditional abandonment to God's sovereign will, the *qaddish* is also implicitly an act of faith in the resurrection of the dead. For in fact the petition for the "kingdom" ("May he establish his kingdom during your life and the life of all the house of Israel, even speedily and at a near time"), a petition that includes the eschatological victory of God over every evil, is closely connected with the resurrection of the dead and the victory over death: "Death shall be no more" (Rev 21:4). "After praising the Name of God and asking for the coming of the divine reign, mourners allude indirectly to the resurrection and the victory over death, although these terms are not explicitly used in the liturgical text."[32]

Whatever its historical development, the *qaddish* is presently used in five forms: 1) the *qaddish de-rabban* (the *qaddish* of teachers), which is recited after a talmudic reading in the presence of a *minyan* or quorum of ten adult males; 2) the *qaddish shalem* (the full *qaddish*), which is recited by a reader at the end of an important segment of the liturgy, especially the *tefillah*; 3) the *haṣi qaddish* (the half-*qaddish*), which is recited by a reader at the end of short segments of the liturgy; 4) the *qaddish yatom* (the *qaddish* of "orphans"), which is recited at the end of the synagogue service by mourners who have lost a loved one; and 5) the *qaddish de-ithadta* (the *qaddish* for funerals), which is recited at the cemetery when the body is interred.

It is not possible to overestimate the importance of the *qaddish* in the Jewish tradition. "The *Kaddish* prayer, binding the generations together in love and respect, has been described as a sacred thread in Israel. The *Kaddish* makes the hearts of parents and children beat in eternal unison."[33]

b) The 'Alenu

Ever since the sixteenth century, on weekdays and feast days alike, the synagogue service ends with the prayer known as the '*alenu* from its opening word, which means "it is our duty." The prayer proclaims God to be supreme King of the universe and God of the entire reunified human race.

Scholars disagree on the origin of the prayer. While tradition likes to attribute it to Joshua, who (it is said) composed it at the time of the entrance into the land of Canaan, historical research traces it back to Rav Abba Areka (160–247 A.D.), the founder of the Babylonian synagogue in Sura and a disciple of Yuda ha-Nasi, who compiled the Mishnah.[34] Rabbi Hertz regards the '*alenu* as "not only one of the noblest of our prayers, but also one of the oldest."[35] He cites Moses Mendelssohn, the philosopher and father of the Jewish Enlightenment, who says: "A proof of its [the '*alenu*'s] age [is] the fact, that there is no mention in it of the restoration of the Temple and the Jewish State, which would scarcely have been omitted had it been composed after their destruction."[36]

Here is the text of the prayer:

> It is our duty to praise the Lord of all things, to ascribe greatness to him who formed the world in the beginning, since he hath not made us like the nations of other lands, and hath not placed us like other families of the earth, since he hath not assigned unto us a portion as unto them, nor a lot as unto all their multitude. For we bend the knee and offer worship

and thanks before the supreme King of kings, the Holy One, blessed be he, who stretched forth the heavens and laid the foundations of the earth, the seat of whose glory is in the heavens above, and the abode of whose might is in the loftiest heights. He is our God; there is none else: in truth he is our King; there is none besides him; as it is written in his Torah, And thou shalt know this day, and lay it to thine heart, that the Lord he is God in heaven above and upon the earth beneath: there is none else.

We therefore hope in thee, O Lord our God, that we may speedily behold the glory of thy might, when thou wilt remove the abominations from the earth, and heathendom will be utterly destroyed, when the world will be perfected under the kingdom of the Almighty, and all the children of flesh will call upon thy Name, when thou wilt turn unto thyself all the evil-doers upon earth. Let all the inhabitants of the earth perceive and know that unto thee every knee must bow, every tongue must swear allegiance. Before thee, O Lord our God, let them bow and worship; and unto thy glorious name let them give honour; let them all accept the yoke of thy kingdom, and do thou reign over them speedily, and for ever and ever. For the kingdom is thine, and to all eternity thou wilt reign in glory; as it is written in thy Torah, The Lord shall reign for ever and ever. And it is said, And the Lord shall be king over all the earth: in that day shall the Lord be One, and his Name One (209–11).

The prayer has two parts: the first develops the theme of election, the second that of universal messianism. The main statement regarding election is the opening one in which God is praised because "he hath not made us like the nations of other lands, and hath not placed us like other families of the earth, since he hath not assigned unto us a portion as unto them, nor a lot as unto all their multitude."

These words express with almost unparalleled clarity Israel's consciousness of being a chosen people. They have also, however, given rise to numerous misunderstandings in the course of history, especially because of the contempt they seem to inculcate toward pagan peoples. For this reason, the Reformed liturgies have chosen to change the text, substituting phraseology that is more general and shows greater tolerance.

The statement regarding universal messianism is found in the words that are rightly regarded as the center of the entire prayer: "when the world will be perfected under the kingdom of the Almighty (le-taqen 'olam be-malkut shadday)." There are two possible interpretations: the prayer is that the world may be disposed to receive the reign of the Almighty, or that the world may change for the sake of the reign of the Almighty. But both interpretations preserve the essential point: the reign of God comes about when human beings are ready to collaborate with him. God's reign, the kingdom of wholeness and peace, replaces the reign of human beings, a reign of injustice and violence, if God's plan is accepted by human wills and becomes their food and nourishment. According to the gospel story, Jesus liked to speak of himself as one whose "food" was to do the Father's will (see Jn 4:34) and whose will and activity were at one with the Father's plan. When this identification takes place, the new world, the messianic world, is born, as it was for Jesus: "The blind receive their sight and the lame walk, lepers are cleansed and the deaf hear, and the dead are raised up, and the poor have good news preached to them" (Mt 11:5).

The central message of the 'alenu is this proclamation of a radically renewed world, when the "abominations" and "heathendom" will disappear.

The contrast between the people of Israel and the pagans applies first of all to Jews. That is, Jews, like "pagans," must free themselves from false gods. "Paganism" (that is, evil) is found not outside Israel (or the Church) but within its unpurified heart.

2. The Sabbath

The synagogue is attended not only on weekdays but also and above all on the sabbath. On this day the liturgy is enriched by symbolic elements and special texts, the most important of which are the qabbalat shabbat ("welcoming of the sabbath"), the nishmat kol ḥay ("the breath of every living thing"), and the reading of the Torah.

a) The Gabbalat shabbat

As the name indicates (literally "reception or welcoming of the sabbath"), this is a set of psalms and poetic compositions that are recited in the synagogue on Friday evening, as the opening of the feast of the sabbath.

The sabbath is the bride which Israel, the husband, welcomes with joy because she is resplendent with beauty and a source of

delight. The *qabbalat shabbat* has the following as its main elements:
1) six introductory Psalms (95–99 and 29), selected by Moses of Cordoba, a Cabalist of the Luria school; 2) the mystical song *Leka dodi* ("Come, my beloved"), composed by Rabbi Solomon Halevy Alkabetz, a disciple of Luria; 3) Psalms 92 and 93 as concluding psalms; and 4) in some communities, the reading of the Song of Songs.

The six introductory psalms each represent a workday. They praise God as creator of the universe and look forward to the happiness of the messianic age, of which the sabbath is a reflection and a pledge.

Next comes the singing of the *Leka dodi liqra'at kalah* ("Come, my beloved . . . welcome Bride Sabbath"), which hymns the praises of the sabbath as bride and queen of Israel:

> Come my beloved, with chorus of praise,
> Welcome Bride Sabbath, the Queen of the days.
>
> "Keep and remember"!—in One divine Word
> He that is One, made His will heard;
> One is the name of Him, One is the Lord!
>   His are the fame and the glory and praise!
>
> Sabbath, to welcome thee, joyous we haste;
> Fountain of blessing from ever thou wast—
> First in God's planning, thou fashioned the last,
>   Crown of His handiwork, chiefest of days.
>
> City of holiness, filled are the years;
> Up from thine overthrow! Forth from thy fears!
> Long hast thou dwelt in the valley of tears,
>   Now shall God's tenderness shepherd thy ways.
>
> Rise, O my folk, from the dust of the earth;
> Garb thee in raiment beseeming thy worth;
> Nigh draws the hour of the Bethlehemite's birth,
>   Freedom who bringeth, and glorious days.
>
> Wake and bestir thee, for come is thy light!
> Up! With thy shining, the world shall be bright;
> Sing! For thy Lord is revealed in His might—
>   Thine is the splendour His glory displays!

"Be not ashamed," saith the Lord, "nor distressed;
Fear not and doubt not. The people oppressed,
Zion, My city, in thee shall find rest—
　　Thee, that anew on thy ruins I raise."

"Those that despoiled thee shall plundered be,
Routed all those who showed no ruth;
God shall exult and rejoice in thee,
　　Joyful as bridegroom with bride of youth."

Stretch out thy borders to left and to right;
Fear but the Lord, Whom to fear is delight—
The man, son of Perez, shall gladden our sight,
　　And we shall rejoice to the fulness of days.

Come in thy joyousness, Crown of thy lord,
Come, bringing peace to the folk of the Word;
Come where the faithful in gladsome accord,
　　Hail thee as Sabbath-bride, Queen of the days.

Come where the faithful are hymning thy praise;
Come as a bride cometh, Queen of the days! (357–59).[37]

　　The poem consists of a refrain ("Come, my beloved, with chorus of praise,/Welcome Bride Sabbath, the Queen of the days") and nine stanzas, which in Hebrew form an acrostic spelling the author's name. It is inspired by the Song of Songs and a Talmudic parable. According to the latter, on Friday evenings Rabbi Hanina and Rabbi Yannai used to don festive attire and say to their friends: "Come, let us go out to meet the Sabbath, our Queen, our betrothed!" And the friends would reply: "Enter, Sabbath, our Queen, our betrothed."[38]
　　The poem is about two personages: Israel and the Sabbath, who are represented by the two lovers of the Song of Songs, the bridegroom being Israel and the Sabbath the bride. In the opening two verses, the poet addresses the bridegroom ("My beloved") and urges him to go out to meet the bride: "Welcome the Sabbath." ("Welcome" is in the plural because the poet, as a member of the people and its spokesman, feels himself to be the bridegroom of the Sabbath.) In the next-to-last stanza he addresses the Sabbath: "Come in thy joyousness. . . ." Like the Song of Songs, the poem is an invitation to bridegroom and bride to come together and engage in dialogue, for from their meeting comes shalom, "peace."

Between the opening invitation to the bridegroom and the closing one to the bride lies the body of the poem, which speaks of the
beauty of the "bride," that is, the riches of the Sabbath ("fountain of
blessing. . . . First in God's planning, thou fashioned the last") and of
the welcome the bridegroom should give her ("Wake and bestir
thee! . . . Up! . . . Sing! . . . Be not ashamed . . ."). In addition to calling
upon the bridegroom to welcome the bride/Sabbath, the poet offers
reasons: the bride/Sabbath, which is God's image, brings salvation
("Now shall God's tenderness shepherd thy ways"), redemption
("Freedom who bringeth"), glory ("With thy shining, the world shall
be bright"), victory ("Those that despoiled thee shall plundered be"),
joy ("God shall exult and rejoice in thee, Joyful as bridegroom with
bride of youth"), expansion ("Stretch out thy borders to right and to
left"), and so on. As in fairy tale, the Sabbath has power to transform
her bridegroom Israel by bringing him the fullness of peace.

This text, which Heinrich Heine called a "nuptial hymn,"[39] "is
perhaps one of the finest pieces of religious poetry in existence,"[40]
and despite its late origin and the opposition of circles not open to
mysticism, became part of most Jewish rituals throughout the world.

The rite of the *qabbalat shabbat* ends with the recitation of
Psalm 92, the sabbath psalm par excellence (*mizmor shir le-yom
shabbat*) and Psalm 93. The former is a hymn of praise to the Lord ("It
is good to give thanks to the Lord, to sing praises to thy name, O Most
High"), the latter a profession of faith in the lordship or kingship of
God ("The Lord reigns; he is robed in majesty"). With these two
psalms the entrance of the sabbath is regarded as accomplished: of
that divine time which is the ground of human time and gives it its
meaning.

b) Nishmat kol ḥay

The sabbath liturgy begins on Friday evening with the *qabbalat
shabbat*; this is immediately followed by the evening service
(*ma'ariv le-shabbat*), which is the same as on other days except for
some brief omissions and special additions (for example, the explicit
reference to the sabbath in the *tefillah*, and the *qiddush*, which is
said in the synagogue for the sake of those who could not say it
at home).

The next day's prayer also follows the pattern of weekday
prayer, except for some important variants in the morning (*shaharit
le-shabbat*), afternoon (*minhah le-shabbat*), and evening (when the
prayer is called *mosse shabbat*, "departure of the sabbath").

In the morning service there is a new element: the prayer *nish-*

mat kol ḥay ("the breath of every living being"), which is an invitation to all creatures to praise and thank the Lord for his wonderful works of creative love:

> The breath of every living being shall bless thy Name, O Lord our God, and the spirit of all flesh shall ever extol and exalt thy fame, O our King. From everlasting to everlasting thou art God; and beside thee we have no King, O thou who redeemest and savest, settest free and deliverest, who supportest and pitiest in all times of distress; yea, we have no King but thee.
>
> Thou art God of the first and of the last ages, God of all creatures, Lord of all generations, adored in innumerable praises, guiding thy world with lovingkindness and thy creatures with tender mercies. The Lord slumbereth not nor sleepeth; he arouseth the sleepers and awakeneth the slumberers; he maketh the dumb to speak, setteth free the prisoners, supporteth the falling, and raiseth up those who are bowed down.
>
> To thee alone we give thanks . . . (417).[41]

This is a very ancient hymn, which a strange legend traces back to the Apostle Peter, who, it is said, composed it as a sign of his repentance after having denied the Messiah (Mt 26:72–74). Although the legend lacks any historical basis, it bears witness to the antiquity of the prayer, which is attested in the Talmud (*Pesaḥim* 118a and *Berakot* 59b) and must have been known as early as the first century of the Christian era.[42]

The morning liturgy of the sabbath is characterized not only by the poem *nishmat kol ḥay* but by an expansion of the first of the two benedictions that precede the *shema'*. This benediction is a hymn of praise to God for his creation of light, which in turn symbolizes the universe as a whole; on the sabbath this theme is enriched by an explicit reference to the institution of the sabbath:

> [All the hosts on high render praise . . .] to the God who rested from all his works, and on the seventh day exalted himself and sat upon the throne of his glory. With beauty did he robe the day of rest, and called the Sabbath day a delight. This is the great distinction of the Sabbath day, that God rested thereon from all his work, when the Sabbath day itself offered praise and said "A Psalm, a song of the Sabbath

day, It is good to give thanks unto the Lord." Therefore let
all creatures glorify and bless God; let them render praise,
honour and greatness to the God and King who is Creator of
all things, and who, in his holiness, giveth an inheritance of
rest to his people Israel on the holy Sabbath day. Thy Name,
O Lord our God, shall be hallowed, and thy fame, O our
King, shall be proclaimed in heaven above and on the earth
beneath. Be thou blessed, O our Saviour, for the excellency
of thy handiwork, and for the bright luminaries which thou
hast made (431).

God is here blessed for the gift of the sabbath, which is the
crown, memorial, and image of creation's splendor.

c) The Reading of the Torah

The sabbath is devoted in a special way to the reading of the
Torah; on this day the reading is longer and more solemn, both in the
passages selected and in the prayers that accompany it.

The Torah is read from handwritten parchment scrolls that are
kept wrapped, usually in velvet, and decorated with ornamentations
and little bells of silver or some other precious material. The scrolls
are kept in a suitable place known as the 'aron ha-qodesh ("sacred
ark"), a kind of tabernacle that is almost always artistically decorated and constitutes the ideal center of the synagogue and of the
congregation's attention. When the ark is opened, the reader and the
congregation join in singing some verses from Numbers and Isaiah;[43]
as the scroll of the Torah is being carried from the ark to the podium
where it is to be read aloud, those present continue to sing God's
praises:

> Thine, O Lord, is the greatness, and the power, and the
> glory, and the victory, and the majesty: for all that is in the
> heaven and in the earth is thine; thine, O Lord, is the king-
> dom, and the supremacy as head over all. Exalt ye the Lord
> our God, and worship in his temple: holy is he. Exalt ye the
> Lord our God, and worship at his holy mount; for the Lord
> our God is holy (481–83).

When the scroll has reached the podium, the reading is proclaimed by a duly prepared lector (ba'al qore' or ba'al qeri'ah). In

antiquity, almost any one could be invited to read the Torah, as we see from *Megillah* 23a, but as time passed, only an expert was capable of giving a correct textual and thematic reading of a biblical text that is unvocalized and unpunctuated.

The reading of the Torah is followed by the reading of the *haftarah* (a passage from the prophetic books), which nowadays is taken not from a handwritten scroll but from an ordinary printed text. The difference here between *parashah* and *haftarah* is meant to highlight the different levels of importance between the various parts of the Bible: first the Pentateuch (Torah), then the prophets, and third the so-called Hagiographa.

On the Sabbath the Torah is read not only in the morning service but in the afternoon service as well. The usual practice is to repeat the morning passages in the afternoon and to go into them more deeply by means of discussion and comparison with the rabbinical writings.

In some months, especially the summer months, the deeper understanding of the Bible is obtained with the help of the *Pirke 'Avot*, one of the important tractates of the Mishnah; it consists of series of religious and moral sayings attributed to the great teachers or fathers of pre-Christian Judaism and Judaism in the period immediately following on the coming of Christianity. Here, by way of example, are some sayings of Hillel, who died in 10 B.C. and was thus almost a contemporary of Christ:

> Hillel said, Separate not thyself from the congregation; trust not in thyself until the day of thy death; judge not thy fellow-man until thou art come into his place; and say not anything which cannot be understood at once, in the hope that it will be understood in the end; neither say, When I have leisure I will study; perchance thou wilt have no leisure.
>
> He used to say, An empty-headed man cannot be a sin-fearing man, nor can an ignorant person be truly pious, nor can the diffident learn, nor the passionate teach, nor is everyone who excels in business wise. In a place where there are no men, strive to be a man.[44]

By means of such simple and immediately comprehensible sayings as these, Jews seek to remain faithful to their spiritual identity as people open to the voice of God and to tradition.

d) *The* Musaf

In addition to some variations and special additions that are inserted into the normal structure of daily prayer, the sabbath service in the synagogue is enriched with a special and entirely new section, known as the *musaf*, which is located after the reading of the Torah in the morning service. *Musaf* means "added"; this "complementary" prayer consists of a *tefillah* of seven benedictions, a *qedushah* that is fuller and more developed than the usual one (it is therefore called *qedushah rabbah*), and some songs and hymns on the subject of the divine oneness and glory.

The *musaf* was added in the course of history as a memorial of the supplementary sacrifice that had been offered in the temple on the sabbath (see Num 28:9–10), and is already attested in the Mishnah (*Berakot* 4, 7, and *Ta'anit* 4, 1). It has been removed from the Reformed liturgies as being redundant (a variant of the preceding *tefillah*) and because its reference to the temple sacrifices is regarded as now dated and outmoded. Other liturgies, however, have preferred to retain and modify it, keeping its historical character but actualizing it in reference to present conditions: "May your will, O Lord our God, be that we may return in joy to our country and find a dwelling within its borders, where our fathers offered ritual sacrifice to you."[45]

The feast of the sabbath ends in the evening with the *havdalah* prayer. While this (like the *qiddush*) is recited in the synagogue for the sake of those not able to recite it at home, its proper and original setting is the home and family. The family, with its concrete, daily reality, is the ideal place for Jews to encounter the sabbath, to contemplate its beauty, and to let themselves be transformed by its meaning as the week goes on.

3. Special Events

In Judaism as in all religions, birth, the attainment of adulthood, marriage, and death are important moments to be marked by communal and synagogal prayer.

On such occasions the family and the synagogue become the basic locations for the celebration.

These events are distinguished less by special rites (most of which were taken over from the Semitic setting in which Judaism was born and reached its maturity) than by a special interpretation that Israel makes of them in the light of its own experience. From a literary point of view, this interpretation takes the form of a *berakah*, a category we have discussed at length in this book. Jews pronounce a *berakah* over persons at birth or when they become adults, marry, or die. They thus link the event to the divine will, interpreting and accepting it in accordance with God's intention, which gives the event its value and meaning. When thus interpreted, birth and life, growth and death transcend the level of simple "happening" and become projects to be carried out in a responsible way.

a) *The* Berit-mila

The liturgy that accompanies the birth of a male child is known as *berit-mila* ("covenant of circumcision"); by means of it the new-born boy becomes a "son of Abraham," that is, beneficiary and heir of the blessings of the covenant. The rite is seen as originating directly in God (Gen 17:9–12) and is performed eight days after birth. The male child is carried to the synagogue, where he is given a festive welcome with the words of Ps 118:26: "Blessed is he who enters in the name of the Lord!" The circumcision proper is then performed immediately by two qualified persons: the *mohel* ("circumciser"), who performs the little operation, and the *sandaq* ("sponsor"), who holds the child. Two chairs are placed for the ceremony: one for the *sandaq*, the other for the prophet Elijah, who, according to popular tradition, is present at every circumcision to protect the child from possible dangers or mishaps.

The rite of circumcision is accompanied by several benedictions that explain and interpret it. When the *sandaq* takes the child, the *mohel* prays: "Blessed art thou, O Lord our God, King of the universe, who hast hallowed us by thy commandments, and hast given us command concerning the circumcision" (1027). At the end of the circumcision another benediction is said, this time by the child's father: "Blessed art thou, O Lord our God, King of the universe, who hast hallowed us by thy commandments, and hast commanded us to make our sons enter into the covenant of Abraham our Father." Those present respond: "Even as this child has entered into the covenant, so may he enter into the Torah, the nuptial canopy, and into good deeds" (1097).

The rite ends with a special *qiddush* that is recited by the *mohel*:

O our God and God of our fathers, preserve this child. . . .
May his father and mother find joy in him. May they lovingly and wisely reveal to him the meaning of the covenant into which he has entered today, so that he may practice uprightness by seeking truth and walking in the ways of

peace. May this child grow as a human being and be a blessing to his family, the family of Israel, and the human family.

The prayers bring out the meaning of circumcision. It is a bodily,
and therefore irreversible, sign of membership in a people who are
called to live according to the logic of the covenant. It is not a magical
gesture but an "introduction" into a world that is both gift and task,
enjoyment and collaboration; it opens the person to a way of life
inspired by a "heart" that is not turned in upon itself but is in harmony with the heart of God himself: "Circumcise therefore the fore-
skin of your heart, and be no longer stubborn. For the Lord your
God . . . executes justice for the fatherless and the widow, and loves
the sojourner, giving him food and clothing" (Deut 10:16–18). Circumcision brings the person into the covenant and inspires him to
make his heart like God's by "executing justice for the fatherless,"
and so on.

In addition to the rite of circumcision, the Jewish tradition has
developed a supplementary rite known as "The Redemption of the
First-Born." If the boy is a first-born child he is brought to the synagogue thirty-one days after birth to be "redeemed," that is, in order
to acknowledge that he belongs to the Lord and to be dedicated
to him.

Circumcision, which is explicitly attested in the gospels (Lk
2:21) and fully documented in the Talmud (Shab. 137b),

> can be said to be the rite which Jews of every tendency have
> most faithfully preserved; despite persecutions, it has be-
> come the test of membership in the Jewish people and the
> sign of fidelity of those who know that, no matter what their
> circumstances, "the Jewish people live and will live
> eternally."[46]

b) The Bar miṣwah

Bar miṣwah is the name given in the Talmud to the adult male
Jew, who, as such, is obliged to every miṣwah (commandment) of the
Torah. In time, the expression was applied to the ceremony at which,
from the first centuries of the Christian era on, a Jewish boy became
an adult and accepted the duties required by the Torah. The rite
usually takes place in the synagogue on the first Saturday after the
boy's thirteenth birthday. On this occasion, the father recites a benediction in which he acknowledges his son's full autonomy and declares his own role as educator to be now ended: "Blessed be he who
hath freed me from the responsibility for this child" (491). The child

whose adulthood has been acknowledged leads the Friday evening and Saturday morning liturgy in whole or in part, and is called upon, for the first time in his life, to read a passage from the Torah. He blesses God "who hast chosen us from all peoples, and hast given us thy Torah" (487).

In some communities the boy is also obliged to give a commentary on the text which he has read, or a more general and personal explanation in which he shows that he is aware of his new responsibilities. Among the Sephardic Jews, access to the adult state is signified less by the reading of the Torah than by the wearing of the tefillin in the synagogue during morning prayer on weekdays.

In recent times, especially among Liberal Jews, there has been celebrated, in addition to the bar miṣwah, a bat miṣwah (bat in Aramaic is the feminine form of bar and means "daughter") for girls who have reached their twelfth year.[47]

c) The Rite of Marriage

The biblical sources show no trace of a marriage liturgy. On the other hand, such a liturgy is extensively attested in the Talmud, which determines its essential elements: the qiddush; the formula in which the spouses consecrate themselves to each other; the ketubah, or marriage "contract"; the birkot ḥatanim, or "benedictions of the spouses"; and the breaking of a glass filled with wine.

The first part of the qiddush is the usual blessing pronounced over a cup of wine. Bridegroom and bride both drink from this cup as a sign of the shared joy and commitment that lie ahead of them. To marry is to share in "the cup of life": in life's happiness and responsibilities. After the qiddush, the groom puts a ring on the bride's finger while saying these words that are already found in the Talmud: "Behold, thou art consecrated unto me by this ring, according to the Law of Moses and of Israel" (1011; see b. Kid. 5b). In many Liberal synagogues the formula is repeated by the bride to the bridegroom.

The formula of consecration is followed by the reading and signing of the ketubah, a legal document setting forth the rights and duties of the spouses and especially of the wife (in case she is divorced or widowed). This ceremony is immediately followed by the seven benedictions, which are a hymn of praise to God for his wonderful acts, the greatest of which is the invention of the couple, that is, the creation of man and woman for one another:

> Blessed art thou, O Lord our God, King of the universe,
> who createst the fruit of the vine.

Blessed art thou, O Lord our God, King of the universe, who hast created all things to thy glory.

Blessed art thou, O Lord our God, King of the universe, Creator of man.

Blessed art thou, O Lord our God, King of the universe, who hast made man in thine image, after thy likeness, and hast prepared unto him, out of his very self, a perpetual fabric. Blessed art thou, O Lord, Creator of man.

May she who was barren [Zion] be exceeding glad and exult, when her children are gathered within her in joy. Blessed art thou, O Lord, who makest Zion joyful through her children.

O make these beloved companions greatly to rejoice, even as of old thou didst gladden thy creature in the garden of Eden. Blessed art thou, O Lord, who makest bridegroom and bride to rejoice.

Blessed art thou, O Lord our God, King of the universe, who has created joy and gladness, bridegroom and bride, mirth and exultation, pleasure and delight, love, brotherhood, peace and fellowship. Soon may there be heard in the cities of Judah, and in the streets of Jerusalem, the voice of the bridegroom and the voice of the bride, the jubilant voices of bridegrooms from their canopies, and of youths from their feasts of song. Blessed art thou, O Lord our God, who makest the bridegroom to rejoice with the bride (1013).

The marriage rite ends with the breaking of a glass of wine, either as a reminder that for no one, not even for these newlyweds, can there be a definitive and total joy in this life, or so that they will not forget that there will be no fullness of joy until the "temple in Jerusalem" (symbol of the divine presence) has been rebuilt.

During the marriage ceremony the couple stand under a huppah, a nuptial canopy that symbolizes the bridal chamber, the place of fruitfulness.

d) Funerals

When faced with death, Jews reaffirm their submission to the divine will. They see death not as an unjust imposition but as an act of meaningful love on God's part.

When someone dies, the announcement of the fact is accompanied by a benediction: "Blessed art thou, O Lord our God, King of the universe, the true Judge" (995). A series of prayers is then recited,

some in the room where the person died, some during the procession
to the cemetery, and some, finally, at the cemetery before the interment of the body. The body is usually taken not to the synagogue but
directly to the cemetery, where the funeral liturgy takes place.

On the way from the place of death to the cemetery Psalm 91 is
recited; when the cemetery is reached, the funeral rite proper is
celebrated, which is known as ṣidduq ha-din ("justification of the
divine judgment"). The name was inspired by the great words of
Rabbi Hanina ben Teradion and his family, which are reported in the
Talmud:

> The Romans led R. Hanina ben Teradion ... out to be
> burned, his wife to be killed, and his daughter to be
> raped. . . . As they left the tribunal, the three declared their
> submission to the just judgment of God. The first said: "The
> Rock, his work is perfect; for all his ways are justice" (Deut
> 32:4). The wife continued her husband's citation of the
> scriptures: "A God of faithfulness and without iniquity, just
> and right is he" (Deut 32:4). And the daughter said: "Thou
> art great in counsel and mighty in deed; whose eyes are
> open to all the ways of men, rewarding every man according
> to his ways and according to the fruit of his doings"
> (Jer 32:19).[48]

Finally, just before the closing of the grave, a qaddish is recited
that is a hymn of purest praise of God's sovereignty and an explicit
confession of faith in the resurrection of the dead: "May his great
Name be magnified and sanctified in the world that is to be created
anew, where he will revive the dead, and raise them up unto life
eternal . . ." (1085).

In reciting these words, Jews learn to reread death and give it a
new meaning in a setting of trust in God, in keeping with this impressive story from the Talmud:

> Rabbi Meir, the Talmud records, lost both his sons on one
> day. It was on a Sabbath afternoon, when he was in the
> House of Learning. His wife, the brilliant Beruria, did not on
> his return break the news to him, in order not to sadden his
> Sabbath-joy. She waited till the evening, and then timidly
> approaching her husband, she said: "I have a question to ask
> of thee. Some time ago, a friend gave me some jewels to keep
> for him. To-day he demands them back. What shall I do?" "I
> cannot understand thee asking such a question. Unhesitat-

ingly thou shalt return the jewels." Thereupon she led him
to the room where their children lay dead. "These are the
jewels I must return." Rabbi Meir could but sob forth the
words of Job: . . . "The Lord hath given, and the Lord hath
taken; blessed be the Name of the Lord."[49]

e) The Admission of Proselytes

In ancient times Jews proselytized, and those who accepted conversion were introduced into the Jewish religion by a period of preparation and a rite of initiation. In fact, according to the rabbinical
tractate Gerim ("Proselytes"):

> One who is about to become a proselyte is not received at
> once. But he is asked: What has induced you to join us? Do
> you not know that this nation is downtrodden and afflicted
> more than all the other nations, that they are subjected to
> many ills and sufferings? . . . If the candidate replies: "I am
> unworthy to take upon myself the obligations of Him who
> created the world by the mere uttering of words, blessed be
> He," he is received at once; if not, he takes leave and
> departs.[50]

Once the convert's intentions have been probed, and after a
suitable period of formation and study, a twofold rite, of circumcision and immersion, is celebrated in the presence of at least three
witnesses. In the case of a woman only the rite of immersion is celebrated. During the immersions the proselyte recites two berakot:

> Praised art Thou, O Lord our God, King of the universe, who
> sanctified us by His commandments, and commanded us
> concerning the rite of immersion.
>   Praised art Thou, O Lord our God, King of the universe,
> who kept us in life, and preserved us, and enabled us to
> reach this season.[51]

By the immersion the proselyte becomes "a newborn child,"[52]
and a new name is added to the name the person had before: for men,
Abraham ("son of Abraham"), and for women, Ruth ("daughter
of Ruth").

This rite of immersion is important for an understanding of
Christian baptism, which, according to the theology of Paul of Tarsus, is the death of the "old self" (palaios anthrōpos) and the emergence of "newness of life" (kainotēti zoēs).[53]

Chapter 4

The Celebration of Feasts

Like all peoples and all religions, Israel introduces rhythms into the cycle of time by means of recurring feasts. These include: feasts in the full and proper sense, the "pilgrimage feasts" (*pesaḥ, shavu'ot,* and *sukkot*); the solemn, that is, sober or austere feasts (*rosh ha-shanah* and *yom kippur*); and the lesser feasts (*hanukkah* and *purim*).

The difference between the three kinds of feasts resides in their degree of theological density or weight. The pilgrimage feasts (the only ones that merit the appellation *hag*, "feast") celebrate and actualize the greatest saving event in Israel's history: the event comprising the exodus, the covenant, and the entrance into the promised land. They are therefore the most important of all the feasts; they are called "pilgrimage" (*regalim*) feasts because in biblical times they were marked by a great influx of visitors to the temple in Jerusalem, the holy city.

The "austere" feasts celebrate not the divine event but the human event of freedom's failure: they recall the infidelity of human beings in response to God's fidelity, and they are days of great repentance and profound conversion. They are "austere" because the prevailing mood is not joy but a critical facing up to self and to God.

The lesser feasts are so called because they are not commanded by the Torah and are concerned with secondary events of Jewish history. Though enriched with a variety of elements, chiefly folkloristic and popular, they cannot be put on the same level as the first two types, which provide the real structure of the Jewish liturgical year.

These feasts are celebrated, for the most part, in the synagogue through the addition of special texts, both biblical and euchological, to the daily three times of worship: the *shaḥarit* (morning liturgy), the *minḥah* (afternoon liturgy) and the *ma'ariv* (the evening liturgy).

I. The Pilgrimage Feasts

A feast is a sign of the divine in history; it is a "word" that rescues history from its failures and allows us to glimpse luminous

189

meaning through, and beyond, the absurdity and monotony of historical time. Some authors make a richly meaningful suggestion regarding the origin of the word "feast": they say it derives from *phainomai*, a Greek verb meaning "to show oneself," "to appear"; for a feast allows a new horizon of values and meanings to manifest itself, without which life and hope would become impossible. Like all other peoples, the Jewish religion has feasts and celebrates them; on the one hand, these feasts have the same function as feasts everywhere, but on the other they take on a new, more explicit and radical meaning in light of the religious experience this people has had of the God of the exodus and the covenant. For this reason, before discussing the three pilgrimage feasts, I shall say something about feasts generally and about the rereading of "feast" that occurs in the Jewish biblical tradition.

I. The Meaning of "Feast"

A feast is a statement that the world is a good place because human beings can enjoy it and because it is God who made it. Unwittingly, and prior to any reflection on the point, the celebrants of a feast relate their activity to three independent but interrelated poles: human beings, the world, and God—human beings as subjects who are good, the world as an object that is good, and the divinity as the foundation of the two goodnesses. It is chiefly the third that a feast states and brings out: the world is good and human beings can dwell in it as their native place *because* it is willed by and founded on the sacred. Here is the heart and secret of every feast; in the celebration of a feast we reappropriate, beyond and despite appearances, the positive character of existence as a space filled with fruition and meaning.

As an interpretation of meaning, a feast can be seen as having three moments or phases. First of all, it is a rejection of negativity and death. The lives of individuals and groups are marked by pain and privation, poverty and injustices, violence and absurdity. Instead of displaying the original harmony, life seems under a constant threat that frustrates all efforts and undertakings. Instead of being drawn by a beneficent *telos*, it seems driven by a maleficent demon that has donned the hands and eyes of *thanatos*. A feast represents a suspension of this entire order of things, a profession of faith that this world, in its present form, is not the true world (*kosmos*) but its negation (*chaos*) or counterfeit: not a home for human beings but an unrewarding wilderness. A feast challenges the primacy of evil and its claim to be ultimate reality; it is a rebellion against evil's perverse power and its claim to have the final say; it is a sign—which turns into a certainty—that evil can be dethroned and overcome. Therefore feasts are the greatest wealth of a people, especially the poorest among them, for feasts with their myths and rites preserve in concentrated form the most fruitful seeds of hope and struggle that human history contains. As long as people are able to celebrate feasts, they will also be capable of life and commitment.

Secondly, a feast asserts the quality of life and defines its positive side spoken about. But what is this "quality" that a feast expresses, not conceptually but in a concrete, corporeal way? Many terms are used to describe this quality, but one seems especially important: joy. "You shall rejoice in your feast" (Deut 16:14). But the rejoicing here is something other than what is usually understood by the term in our affluent societies. The passage in Deuteronomy continues: ". . . you and your son and your daughter, your manservant and your maidservant, the Levite, the sojourner, the fatherless, and the widow who are within your towns." Rabbi E. Munk comments on this passage as follows:

> People should eat meat and drink wine, because it is these things especially that contribute to their gladness. But when we eat and drink, it is our duty to provide the necessities for the foreigner, the widow, and the orphan, that is, for all who are in need. Those who double-lock their doors and eat only with their own families, without helping the unfortunate, will not experience the joy of the *mişwah* but "only the satisfaction given by their meal." This is why the prophet Hosea says: "They shall not please him with their sacrifices. Their bread shall be like mourners' bread; all who eat of it shall be defiled; for their bread shall be for their hunger only" (9:4).[1]

This passage summarizes nicely the two basic aspects of the joy which a feast proclaims and bestows: the enjoyment of things ("eating and drinking") and fraternal sharing ("providing the necessities for the foreigner . . ."). Instead of understanding joy in a purely psychological or pseudo-spiritual way, a feast emphasizes its corporeal element and its necessary connection with the fruits of the earth; instead of making this joy something self-centered, a feast asserts its comprehensive and non-exclusive character. True joy is born of two encounters: with the fruits of the earth and with our brothers and sisters. Where one of these two is missing, a feast changes from an end to a means; it ceases to be an expression of life and becomes a means of obtaining satisfaction. The joy proper to a feast is in reality the plenitude of being that is in harmony with the things of this world and with this world's inhabitants; it is the fruit produced by a recovered Eden in which the original Adam and Eve, symbols of the men and women of every age, live reconciled with each other, with the garden, and with God.

The third and most important aspect of a feast is that it is an assertion of that which is the ontological foundation of the goodness and meaning of the human person. Are the rebellion against the power of evil and the proclamation of the victory of the positive over the negative simply an expression of impotent and deceptive desire, or are they an echo of the truth that conquers falsehood and triumphs over self-deception? A feast reveals its full depth when understood as the assertion of the second alternative: human life has meaning, beyond all its historical failures and despite all its privations, not because it is subjectively given meaning by each individual but because it is objectively founded by and on the sacred.

A feast thus not only asserts the existence of meaning but at the same time sets the conditions for the attainment of this meaning: meaning grows and flourishes if and because it is located within a different horizon that transcends that of the profane: the horizon of the divine, the sacred. By means of its mythical narratives and reactualizing rites, a feast calls to mind and makes present again this foundational root; by returning to this root, human behavior overcomes fragmentation, conquering chaos and recovering kosmos, that is, order, strength, motivation, the ideal. A feast indeed abolishes the established order (we need think only of the violations of standard norms that are to be seen in every feast), but it does so not for the sake of libertinage and chaos but in obedience to a higher order that is closer and more faithful to the divine order. A feast overturns the world and recreates it according to the divine model.

2. The Agricultural Feasts and Their Historicization

According to the unanimous view of scholars, the three principal Jewish feasts (Passover, Pentecost, and Booths) had an agricultural origin, and their meaning as such did not differ greatly from the meaning of "feast" as just described. The three were connected with the most important harvests in the three productive seasons of the year and expressed the deep joy of a people that was led and nourished by its God: Passover celebrated the barley harvest in the spring,

Pentecost the wheat harvest in the summer, and Booths the fruit harvest in the fall. In keeping with an almost universally known and attested religious custom, the heart of each feast consisted in the offering of part of the harvest to the divinity. The Book of Deuteronomy makes explicit reference to this practice in the case of Pentecost and Booths, two feasts that, unlike Passover, which has been reread and historicized to a greater degree, allow us to glimpse their original agricultural basis:

> You shall keep the feast of weeks [Pentecost] to the Lord your God with the tribute of a freewill offering from your hand, which you shall give as the Lord your God blesses you. . . . You shall keep the feast of booths seven days, when you make your ingathering from your threshing floor and your wine press. . . . They shall not appear before the Lord empty-handed; every man shall give as he is able, according to the blessing of the Lord your God which he has given unto you (16:10, 13, 16–17).

What is the meaning of such an offering, which is both the expression and the basis of feasts and their joy? To offer God the produce of the earth is not an act of self-deprivation (to renounce something in order to give it to God) but an act of self-definition and acknowledgment that the fruits of the earth belong to the Lord and that human beings may use them only as his beneficiaries. This simple action sums up in a symbolic way three basic concepts and attitudes: 1) the produce gathered belongs to God, who is its master and owner; 2) the produce is given to human beings as a gift to meet their needs and to comfort them; 3) since this is their true character, the fruits of the earth are to be enjoyed not according to the logic of possession and hoarding but according to the divine intention that brings them into existence.

When Israel offered the Lord part of its harvests in the three important seasons of the year, it was reaffirming this pattern of conviction and choice. It professed its belief that the "bread" and "wine" of the promised land were not the result of its own efforts or of magical practices but were due to the creative good will of God; and it renewed its commitment to share these things with others as brothers and sisters. This accounts for the biblical insistence that on these festival days no one should be in want but all should have and fully enjoy: "You shall rejoice in your feast, you and your son and your daughter, your manservant and your maidservant, the Levite, the sojourner, the fatherless, and the widow who are within your towns" (Deut 16:14). This emphasis on feeding the poor reflects a theological rather than a sociological concern: God intends the fruits of the earth for the enjoyment of all; if the poor as well as the rich enjoy them, God's reign is being brought to pass and his will is being fulfilled in a concrete way.

Sharing the fruits of the earth is not simply an imperative of social ethics, but is the very heart of the theological directive that "you shall love the Lord your God with all your heart, and with all your soul, and with all your might" (Deut 6:5); here, to "love the Lord" means to obey his will by accepting and doing it within history.

The sacrifice of animals, which had a privileged place in the worship offered in the Jerusalem temple, had at bottom the same twofold meaning as the offering of firstfruits: it was an acknowledgment of God's lordship over the animal world, and a readiness to take nourishment from that world in a spirit of sharing and not of hoarding, that is, as gifts intended for all and not a privilege of a few.[2]

Israel derived the three agricultural feasts from the surrounding Semitic world. On the other hand, it evidently did not make them its own in a purely passive way; it turned them into original creations by enriching them with its own specific spiritual outlook. The name usually given to this process of reinterpretation is "historicization." By this is meant that focus of the feast was shifted from events of the natural world to special historical events: the deliverance from Egypt in the feast of Passover, the gift of the Torah in the feast of Pentecost, and the enjoyment of the Torah's fruits in the feast of Booths.

It is certainly true that Israel "historicized" the agricultural feasts. It is necessary, however, to understand this process correctly: the process took the form not of contrasting the new with the old or ignoring the old, but of further explaining the original meaning and reaching down to its root.

The central event of Jewish history is the exodus from slavery in Egypt, a single action with three stages: departure from Egypt, gift of the Torah (or covenant), and entrance into the promised land. Israel was liberated from slavery and brought into the "good and broad land" of Canaan, but the entrance was neither automatic nor taken for granted, for between departure and entrance came Mount Sinai, the place of covenant where the Torah was offered and accepted. Here is the epicenter and secret of all Jewish history and Jewish originality: the discovery that the land, their own land, would produce "milk and honey" in abundance (see Ex 3:8, 17; Num 13:27;

Deut 6:3; 11:9; and so on), not, however, spontaneously but only if, and to the extent that, Israel would be faithful to the covenant. This connection between the fertility of the soil and obedience to the Torah is clearly expressed in a passage like Lev 26:3–6, which we find bewildering because the fruits of which it speaks are not the fruits of some special world but the normal produce of the trees of any part of our world. Yet if these fruits are truly to bring joy to all and become a sign of communion instead of destruction, a precise divine condition must be met: they must be cultivated and eaten according to the logic of the covenant, that is, Jews must acknowledge them to be gifts and must consent to their universal destination.

This "historicity" is peculiar to the Jewish situation, but clearly it does not contradict the meaning of "feast," as explained above, but rather further clarifies that meaning by getting to the root of one of its fundamental aspects. When early human beings offered God part of their seasonal produce, they were recognizing his fatherhood and accepting the produce as his gift. Israel accepted this logic, but had a better grasp of its dynamic and its requirements. It realized that if the fruits of the earth are to be truly a gift and a blessing, it is not enough simply to accept them; rather they must be shared in a way of life based on justice and responsibility. Justice and the fruitfulness of the land are partners in an "indissoluble marriage" in which the two shed light on each other. Israel's originality lies in its having transcended a purely "natural" view of nature and having connected the abundance of the land's fruits with its own free choices, as M. Buber has seen and well described.[3]

3. The Feast of Pesaḥ: The Splendor of the Beginnings

Pesaḥ is the greatest of all the Jewish feasts, not only in post-biblical Judaism, which dedicated a special tractate (Pesaḥim) of the Mishnah to it, but also in the Old and New Testaments. Originally an agricultural feast, it became in Israel the great commemoration of the deliverance from Egypt.

There is an abundance of data on Passover in the Old Testament, but it does not permit us to determine exactly how and when this passage took place. In a study of Israel's early feasts, R. de Vaux sums up as follows his researches on pesaḥ:

> There was a feast called the Passover, probably even before Israel became a people; there was also a feast of Unleavened Bread, adopted perhaps from the Canaanites, but adopted in the fullest sense by the Israelites; and these two feasts were

celebrated in the spring-time. One spring-time there had been a startling intervention of God: he had brought Israel out of Egypt, and this divine intervention marked the beginning of Israel's history as a people, as God's Chosen People: this period of liberation reached its consummation when they settled in the Promised Land. The feasts of the Passover and of Unleavened Bread commemorated this event, which dominated the history of salvation. Both feasts took on this meaning, but in the older traditions there are two separate feasts which commemorate the event independently; their common feature, however, made it almost inevitable that they should one day be combined.[4]

It is not easy historically to reconstruct the connection between the two springtime feasts and the deliverance from Egypt. In any case, the basic theological point, which I recalled above, remains valid: The celebration of the event does not cancel out the earlier meaning of the feast but incorporates it and gives it a new basis.

When commenting on the seder, which is the heart of the domestic liturgy of Passover, I spoke of the meaning of Passover and the dynamics of freedom that are at work in it.[5] Whereas the domestic celebration of *pesaḥ* is rich, imaginative, and impressive, the celebration in the synagogue is concise and reduced to essentials.

The liturgy of morning, afternoon, and evening has the same structure as on other days, with some exceptions: an expanded central benediction in the *tefillah*; the *hallel*; and special readings connected with the event being celebrated.

A well known benediction gives the theological meaning of Passover in the following terms:

> Blessed art thou, Lord our God and King of the universe, who hast chosen us from among all peoples and hast set us apart among all tongues and hast sanctified us with thy commandments, and who in thy love hast given feasts for our joy—this feastday of unleavened bread, the day of our freedom and happiness, devoted to a holy assembly and the remembrance of the departure from Egypt. Thou art the one who hast chosen us and sanctified us beyond other nations and given us joy and gladness for an inheritance. Blessed art thou, Lord, who sanctifiest Israel and the feasts.[6]

The prayer combines in an intelligent way the natural aspect of Passover ("this feastday of unleavened bread"), its historical aspect ("devoted to a holy assembly and the remembrance of the departure from Egypt"), and the interpretative aspect ("day of our freedom and happiness"). All these are placed in the setting of divine election and sanctification: "Blessed art thou, O Lord, who sanctifiest Israel and the feasts." Note that in this pair, "Israel" and "the feasts" are placed on the same level. The reason is that sanctification, which is a return of things to their truth, is obtained by two agencies: a subjective ("Israel") and an objective ("the feasts"). In other words, sanctification is an event that has not only an individual, spiritual aspect but also an historical, temporal aspect. Therefore God does not sanctify Israel alone nor time alone, but both together, since neither can do without the other: as Israel needs time, so time needs Israel.

A second distinctive element in the synagogal liturgy of Passover is the recitation of the *hallel* (Pss 113–18) after the morning *tefillah*. These psalms are sometimes called "the Egyptian Hallel," after the first verse of Ps 114, which speaks of the departure from Egypt.

A third element characteristic of Passover is the reading of one of the five *megillot* (scrolls), namely, the Song of Songs. The connection between this love poem and Passover is perhaps suggested by a verse of the poem in which the bridegroom compares his beloved to "a mare of Pharaoh's chariots" (1:9). But there is a better reason than this tenuous textual connection for the reading of the Song of Songs at Passover: that the freedom given by God is at the root of the beauty and love of which the poem sings and which are universal expressions of the human. God alone, by delivering human beings from slavery, makes them capable of the luminous love that is represented by the lovers in the Song of Songs. God alone, through the "miracle" of the exodus and covenant, bestows the subjectivity depicted in the two lovers.

Other distinctive elements of the Passover celebration are: the priestly blessing, which is reserved to *kohanim*; the prayer for dew (*tefillat tal*), which replaces the prayer for rain, since rain at this period is more abundant than at other times); the counting of the *'omer*, which in Hebrew means "measure," and the meaning of which is connected with the feast of Pentecost; and the so-called *piyyutim*, liturgical poems of a popular kind that underscore certain aspects of the Passover celebration.

4. The Feast of Shavu'ot: *The Gift of the Firstfruits*

Pentecost is par excellence the feast of the firstfruits; the feast of unleavened bread (Passover) is simply a preparation for it, the two

marking the beginning and end of the grain harvests.[7] The connection between Passover and Pentecost is stated in the very name of the
latter, since the Greek word *pentekostē* means "fiftieth" (i.e. day) in
relation to Passover, which is the "first" day. The same connection
merges in the Hebrew name *shavu'ot*, which means "weeks": this
feast is celebrated seven weeks after Passover. But the connection of
the two feasts is brought out most clearly by the counting of the
'*omer*, a practice attested in Leviticus: "And you shall count from the
morrow after the sabbath, from the day that you brought the sheaf of
the wave offering; seven full weeks shall they be, counting fifty days
to the morrow after the seventh sabbath; then you shall present a
cereal offering of new grain to the Lord" (23:15–16).

The connection between the two feasts is important because it
helps us understand how they obey the same theological logic,
namely, the acknowledgment of God as giver of the land and Lord of
history, as magnificently expressed in Deut 26:1–11. Few passages
express with such depth and simplicity the meaning of the agricultural feasts and their historicizing reinterpretation by the people of
the Bible. Like any feast centering on firstfruits, Pentecost expresses
Israel's awareness and conviction that the fruits of the earth are
God's gift: "Behold, now I bring the first of the fruit of the ground,
which thou, O Lord, hast given me" (Deut 26:10).[8]

Until the destruction of the temple in 70 A.D., this was the pre-
dominant stress in the celebration of Pentecost, which was carried
out with a rich and impressive ritual that is described as follows in
the Mishnah:

> How do they take up the first-fruits [to Jerusalem]? [The
> men of] all the smaller towns that belonged to the *Maamad*
> [group of representatives of a district] gathered together in
> the town of the *Maamad* and spent the night in the open
> place of the town and came not into the houses; and early in
> the morning the officer [of the *Maamad*] said, Arise ye and
> *let us go up to Zion unto the house of the Lord our God.*
>
> They that were near [to Jerusalem] brought fresh figs
> and grapes, and they that were far off brought dried figs and
> raisins. Before them went the ox, having its horns overlaid
> with gold and a wreath of olive-leaves on its head. The flute
> was played before them until they drew nigh to Jerusa-
> lem. . . . The rulers and the prefects and the treasurers of the
> Temple went forth to meet them. . . .
>
> The flute was played before them until they reached

the Temple Mount. When they reached the Temple Mount even Agrippa the king would take his basket on his shoulder, and enter in as far as the Temple Court. When they had reached the Temple Court, the levites sang the song, *I will exalt thee, O Lord, for thou hast set me up and not made mine enemies to triumph over me.*[9]

Once the temple had been destroyed, Pentecost lost its agricultural character, and the emphasis was put on Pentecost as the feast of the giving of the Torah, *zeman natan toratenu* ("the season of the giving of our Torah"), as is said in the central benediction of the *tefillah* on this feast. But in acquiring this new dimension there is no denial of the feast of firstfruits but rather an explicitation of the chief condition for such a feast: active responsibility for justice and solidarity, without which the fruits of the earth become a curse instead of a blessing. In Deut 26:1–11 the feast of firstfruits is accompanied by a profession of faith: "A wandering Aramean was my father. . . . And the Egyptians treated us harshly. . . . Then we cried to the Lord . . . and he . . . gave us this land, a land flowing with milk and honey." The land flowing with milk and honey is not the geographical but the theological land of Canaan, that is, the land in which the people live in accordance with the Torah and the covenant. It is this way of life, and not the natural fertility of the soil, that makes it flow with milk and honey and, in a more than metaphorical way, produces abundant fruits for the enjoyment of all and not merely for the satisfaction of a few.

By a natural process of incorporation and penetration Pentecost thus changes from feast of firstfruits to feast of the Torah, especially for rabbis and students of the holy book. The synagogues are therefore adorned with green branches that recall both the firstfruits and, above all, the revelation on Sinai,[10] as well as the tree of life in paradise (Gen 2:8) and in the Book of Proverbs (3:18). At home special foods are eaten, especially milk and honey, which recall both the promised land ("a land flowing with milk and honey") and the Torah (Ps 19:11: "more to be desired than gold, even much fine gold; sweeter also than honey and the drippings of the honeycomb"). A great deal of time is spent reading passages from the Bible, such as Ex 19, Num 28, and Deut 14.

On this occasion the *megillah* ("scroll") of Ruth is also read; it is one of the most beautiful of the biblical stories, being filled with poetry and enchantment. There are perhaps two reasons why this book was chosen: the fact that it speaks of reaping and harvests and especially the fact that its chief figure was descended from the Moabites, one of Israel's traditional enemies. The reason for reading this story was to emphasize the universalism of the Jewish Pentecost: the Torah, though given to Israel, is meant for all; its promises extend to the pagans; those who, like Ruth, are motivated by goodness already belong to the chosen people.

But there is still another reason for selecting the Book of Ruth: "to teach us that the Torah is given only through poverty and suffering. . . . For this reason the Book begins with the words, 'In the days when the judges ruled there was a famine in the land.' "[11] The Torah is the real answer to the "famine," the only one that can overcome it. In fact, where the land is experienced in the light of the Torah, that is, in the light of the covenant code, as it was by Ruth, all will "eat until they are satisfied" (see Ru 2:14). Might we not adopt the same perspective in looking at the gospel stories of the multiplication of loaves (Mt 14:13–21; Mk 8:1–9; and parallels)?

In addition to being the feast of firstfruits and of the Torah, Pentecost is also known as 'aseret, meaning "conclusion." There are two reasons for the name: at the agricultural level the feast of shavu'ot ends the cycle of firstfruit offerings that began with the barley harvest and the feast of massot; secondly, and more importantly, at the level of historicization it fills out the meaning of Passover, since this is completed by the gift of the Torah. Maimonides expresses this second point in a very effective way:

> We count the days that pass since the preceding Festival, just as one who expects his most intimate friend on a certain day, counts the days and even the hours. This is the reason why we count the days that pass since the offering of the omer, between the anniversary of our departure from Egypt and the anniversary of the Law-giving, for this was the aim and object of the exodus from Egypt.[12]

The giving of the Torah is not simply a phase following upon the deliverance from Egypt (as though God first brought Israel forth and then offered it the Torah); rather it is the inherent, motivating reason for the deliverance: God brought Israel forth in order to give it the gift of the Torah. The exodus from Egypt was not an end in itself but was ordered to Sinai; Israel passed from dependence on the Pharaoh to obedience in God's presence; from living for itself, which is slavery, to living according to God, which is freedom; in short, from slavery to service.

Thus as a feast of the firstfruits and feast of the Torah, Pentecost celebrates a double event: the fruitfulness of the earth and the obedience of human beings. It celebrates these as interdependent and correlated, not separate, events, for the earth is fruitful if human beings live on it and work with it according to justice, that is, according to the covenant. Upright heart and abundant fruits are two necessary and irreplaceable poles. Only when the two join does the feast yield its joy; only from their marriage does the song of paradise arise.

> Could we with ink the ocean fill,
> Were every blade of grass a quill,
> Were the whole world of parchment made,
> And every man a scribe by trade,
>   To write the love
>   Of God above
> Would drain that ocean dry;
>   Nor would the scroll
>   Contain the whole,
> Though stretched from sky to sky.[13]

This hymn, which is sung before the reading of the Torah and is attributed to a medieval writer of the eleventh century, is a splendid summary of the riches and beauty of the feast of shavu'ot: feast of firstfruits and of the giving of the Torah.

5. The Feast of Sukkot: *The Joy of the Harvest*

Sukkot (usually translated as Booths or Tents) is the greatest of the annual pilgrimage and harvest feasts (see Lev 23:39; Num 29:12; Ez 45:25; 1 Kgs 8:2, 65). Flavius Josephus describes it as "the holiest and the greatest of Hebrew feasts,"[14] and Plutarch uses almost identical language.[15] The feast is marked by great popular joy that goes on for seven days and ends on an octave which bears the significant name, śimḥat Torah, "joy in and through the Torah." While the key words of pesaḥ are exodus and freedom, and those of shavu'ot are gift of the Torah, the key words of sukkot are joy in the Torah, as is expressly said in the main benediction of the tefillah. On this feast, in ancient times, the young girls of Jerusalem went out in white garments to dance in the vineyards and sing: "Young man, raise your eyes and see whom you are going to choose."[16] And in New Testament times the devout and important men of the city would dance in the courtyard, singing and carrying lighted torches.[17]

This feast of the year's final harvest, and especially the grape and oil harvest, was celebrated with a very rich and original rite. Of particular importance were the rite of the *lulav* and the libation of water.

The rite of the *lulav* was connected with the ordinance in Leviticus prescribing how the feast of Booths was to be celebrated: "You shall take on the first day the fruits of the cedar, branches of palm trees, leafy boughs of myrtle and river willow, and you shall rejoice before the Lord your God seven days."[18] In obedience to this ordinance the faithful went to the Jerusalem temple carrying a cedar branch (Hebrew: *'etrog*) in their left hand and, in their right, a palm branch (Hebrew: *lulav*) intertwined with myrtle and willow; as they went they sang the Hallel (Pss 113–18), and waved the branches aloft toward the four cardinal points.

This rite passed from the temple to the synagogue, where it is still practiced as one of the most joyous and popular of all rituals and where it has been given symbolic interpretations that display profound wisdom. According to one of these interpretations, the cedar, palm, myrtle, and willow represent four different human types. The cedar which has a tang and a sweet odor represents those who are intelligent and good; the palm, which has a taste but no odor, those who have intelligence but not goodness; the myrtle, which has an odor but no taste, those who have goodness but not intelligence; finally, the willow, which has neither odor nor taste, those who have neither intelligence nor goodness.

According to another interpretation, the *lulav* and the *'etrog* represent various categories in both Israel and the human race generally; however much these categories differ among themselves, they make up a single, unified reality.

The libation of water is attested in the gospel of John (7:37–39). The rejoicing that accompanied it was such it could be said in the Mishnah: "He that never has seen the joy of the Beth ha-sho 'evah [the place of the water-drawing] has never in his life seen joy" (Sukkah 5; Danby 179). The rite was as follows. Throughout the night the priests carried water in golden cruets from the spring of Siloam to the court of the temple; they were accompanied by the celebrating populace with torches and lamps, dancing and singing, the recitation of the pilgrimage psalms (Pss 120–134) and the playing of the musical instruments. The next day, the water was used for libations during the morning service.

The origin of the rite is uncertain and lost in the distant past. Perhaps it was originally intended for use at the beginning of the rainy season, as a way of asking for and winning an abundance of rain. The rite disappeared with the destruction of the temple and has left only a minor trace in the synagogue liturgy, in the *tefillah ge-shem*, the prayer for rain.

Like the other pilgrimage festivals, *sukkot* too was given a theological rereading in Israel and a deeper, sapiential interpretation. This final harvest feast, which would be followed by winter, stimulated more than the other feasts a sense of human dependence on the fruits of the soil. If these had been abundant, the winter could be faced without worry; otherwise the threat of hunger would be on the horizon. Israel, however, had been taught by its experience of divine revelation that the harvest was not the result of fortuitous or natural forces but a gift of God and the fruit of the covenant logic of submission to God and service to his will.

It is this logic that the feast of *sukkot* brings out by means of several symbolic and ritual elements.

The first of these is the erection of little huts, at home, in the fields, or around the synagogues, as a reminder of Israel's journey through the wilderness. Such huts were originally little shelters made of branches, which the peasants built in the vineyards and orchards during the harvest; in time, however, they acquired a symbolic character of a theological kind: "You shall dwell in booths for seven days; all that are native in Israel shall dwell in booths, that your generations may know that I made the people of Israel dwell in booths when I brought them out of the land of Egypt: I am the Lord your God" (Lev 23:42–43). Israel looks upon the harvest with the awareness it had developed in the wilderness: the awareness that it had overcome "hunger and thirst" thanks to the Shekinah and that it had entered a "good and broad land" (Ex 3:8) by God's gift and not as a result of its own cleverness.

This experience of gratuitousness and radical dependence marked the people of the Bible to such an extent that they turned the wilderness into a quasi-archetypal image, the supreme symbol of encounter with God (see especially the prophet Hosea). As a result, Israel saw itself called to live by the divine gratuitousness not only in the wilderness but even when its harvests were abundant and its grain plentiful. To think of the harvest as the fruit of their own efforts would have been as idolatrous in the eyes of Jews as to think that they had survived in the wilderness by their own wits.

The other element in the reinterpretation is to be seen in the reading of Ecclesiastes or Qoheleth: "Vanity of vanities! All is vanity" (1:2). It might seem strange that this particular *megillah* should be read at Pentecost, which is a joyous popular feast. The fact is, however, that, contrary to appearances, Ecclesiastes is a book not of pessimism but of human and spiritual wisdom. It does indeed teach that "all is vanity," but the reason for this is that "all" is separated from God. The author expressly says: "I know that it will be well with those who fear God, because they fear before him; but it will not be well with the wicked, neither will he prolong his days like a shadow, because he does not fear before God" (8:12–13). He teaches the way of "fear of God," that is, abandonment to his will; just as in the theology of the wilderness, he urges faith in the presence of the Shekinah. Repeated on the occasion of even the most abundant harvests, this act of faith prevents Jews from being blinded by the wealth they have accumulated and causes them to trust solely in God, as we read in the hymn that begins the synagogal liturgy for the feast of Booths:

> May it be thy will, O Lord my God and God of my fathers, to let thy divine Presence abide among us. Spread over us the canopy of thy peace in recognition of the precept of the Tabernacle which we are now fulfilling, and whereby we establish in fear and love the unity of thy holy and blessed Name. O surround us with the pure and holy radiance of thy glory, that is spread over our heads as the eagle over the nest he stirreth up (813).

Israel is under the protection of the Shekinah, as the little ones in a nest are protected by their mother's wings. Before being the fruit of toil, the harvests that have been gathered are a sign of the benevolence of this Shekinah; they are to be stored up and used not as a source of security but as gifts to be enjoyed and shared with our brothers and sisters.

The reinterpretation of sukkot with the aid of the wilderness category and the Book of Ecclesiastes does not therefore mean a move away from the joyous and popular character of this feast; it means rather that the joy is established on a new and radical basis: If the joy of the people is great because of the abundant harvest, it becomes even greater when they realize that every harvest is a gift to them. The deepest source of joy is not the harvest as such but the divine love which the Torah proclaims and attests. It is for this reason that the seven festive days of sukkot are followed by an eighth, known as śimḥat Torah, "the joy of the Torah," that is, the joy that is based on the Torah.

Śimḥat Torah, "the most joyous day in the whole year,"[19] has two important ritual elements. The first is the completion and restarting of the proclamation of the *sefer Torah*. The final section of Deuteronomy is read and, immediately after, the first pages of Genesis, in order not to interrupt the cycle of the Torah and in order to make clear that the Torah is not a "burden" but a "crown" which Jews desire to wear with joy throughout their lives. The reader who proclaims the final section of Deuteronomy is called ḥatan Torah, "spouse of the Torah," while the one who is privileged to read the initial section of Genesis is called ḥatan bereshit, "spouse of Genesis." The symbolism is clear: the Torah is a "bride" whose "husband" Israel becomes fully only when it has assimilated the Torah from beginning to end. The reader of the final pericope is therefore called ḥatan Torah, whereas the reader of the passage from Genesis is only ḥatan bereshit.

But the climactic moment of the celebration is the seven processional circuits (hakkafot) around the synagogue. All the scrolls are taken out and carried, while the crowd, and especially the children, dances and waves flags bearing such slogans as "We tremble with joy because of the Torah." In the State of Israel the practice has been growing of carrying the Torah scrolls in the public squares, while the people sing and dance spontaneously.

While the Torah scrolls are being carried in procession around the synagogue, litanic prayers made up of biblical phrases, in more or less verbatim form, are recited. In this way, by singing, praying, and dancing, the people express their intimacy with God, whose loving will is responsible for all the fruits of the soil and whose saving word, revealed in the Torah, is the source of joy and life.

6. Addition of a New Feast Day in the Diaspora

The feast of Passover lasts seven days, from the evening of 15 Nisan to the evening of 21 Nisan; the feast of Pentecost lasts but a single day, 6 Sivan; and the feast of Booths lasts eight days, 15 to 21 Tishri. These dates, however, hold only for the State of Israel and, in ancient times, for the communities residing in 'Ereṣ Yiśr'el.

In the Diaspora, on the other hand, Passover lasts eight days, Pentecost two, and Booths nine. In other words, each feast has been lengthened by a day, which is known as yom ṭov sheni shel galuyot, the "second feast day in the Diaspora."

The reason for the difference in the liturgical practices of the Diaspora and the homeland is to be sought in the complexity of the

Jewish liturgical calendar, which follows both a lunar and a solar cycle. Since the Jewish feasts were originally agricultural and, like all the feasts of antiquity, followed a lunar cycle, their dating required a precise determination of the beginning of the new month. In ancient times this beginning was determined by direct observation of the onset of the new moon. Later on, the task was taken over by the Palestinian patriarch who, once the beginning of the new month was determined, sent word to the other communities by means of signal fires lit on one hilltop after another throughout Jewish territory.

This method was impossible, however, for the communities of the Diaspora, for those of Egypt, for example, or Babylonia. Messengers were sent to these communities, but could not always arrive on time in all areas, especially those far distant. This situation necessitated the addition of an extra day of festival, the *yom tov sheni shel galuyot*.

The practice of the extra day continued even when, in the fourth century A.D., Patriarch Hillel II published a calendar based on astronomical calculations and thus rendered previous methods useless, for now every Jewish community could determine exactly the beginning of all months and therefore of all feasts.

> R. Zera said . . . : We are now familiar with the system for determining the beginning of a new moon, yet we continue to observe two feastdays. . . . But if we are now familiar with the system for establishing the moment when a new moon begins, why do we continue to observe two days? The reason is that such is the teaching we received from Palestine: Be solicitous for the traditions passed on to you (*Bezah*, 4b).

The Talmud thus justifies the continuation of this custom with an appeal to the principle of respect for tradition: "Be solicitous for the traditions passed on to you."

Today the additional feastday is still observed by Orthodox communities, but has been dropped by Reform communities, which regard it as a pointless duplication.

II. THE AUSTERE FEASTS

In addition to the pilgrimage feasts, the Jewish liturgical year has the feasts of *rosh ha-shanah* (New Year's Day) and *yom kippur* (Day of Atonement), two especially solemn and important celebrations that because of their penitential character are called "austere feasts." There are two main differences between these two feasts and the pilgrimage feasts: the former make no reference to natural and historical events, and their prevailing mood is not the spirit of festivity but rather reflection and the confession of one's sins.

The main thought that underlies and is expressed by *rosh ha-shanah* and *yom kippur* is *teshuvah* (literally: return) with its twofold meaning of: consciousness of violation of the covenant and determination to restore it; consciousness of having betrayed the Torah and renewed submission to its authority.

Teshuvah, an indispensable mainstay of both the Jewish and the Christian traditions, says that evil is not part of the plan of creation (as an element that crept in by mistake or inevitably) but is due to human responsibility which introduced it through disobedience and can remove it by renewed fidelity and obedience. As we are told in the incomparable pages of Genesis 3, God expelled *'Adam* from Eden because of his disobedience and closed its gates to prevent his return. *Teshuvah* expresses the hope—indeed the certainty—that these gates are not irrevocably closed; that *'Adam*, who represents every human being of every age, can enter through them again and that creation's beauty can be resplendent once more.

Rosh ha-shanah and *yom kippur*—the former celebrated on 1 Tishri (September–October) and the latter on 10 Tishri—make up, along with the days separating them, the *'aseret yeme teshuvah*, the "ten penitential days." These are called *yamim nora'im*, "awesome days" or "days of awe," because during them individuals decide to take a position for or against God, for the service of his creative word or the service of their own destructive wills:

> On *rosh ha-shanah* all the inhabitants of the world pass before God like a flock before its shepherd. Three books are opened in which may be read the destiny of the good, the wicked, and those who are neither good nor wicked. The names of the upright are written in the Book of Life, while the names of the wicked are erased from it. Those who are neither good nor wicked are given a period of ten days, to the end of *yom kippur*. These ten days, during which the destiny of the majority of humankind is decided, are called *yamim nora'im*, "awesome days."[20]

In view of the importance of these *yamim nora'im*, there is advance preparation for them in the form of special prayers called *selihot*, "penitential invocations," which are recited throughout the

month of 'elul that precedes Tishri. Chapter 6, verse 3 of the Song of
Songs says: 'ani le-dodi u-dodi li, "I am my beloved's and my beloved
is mine." Read anacrostically, the initial letters of the words in this
verse form the word 'elul. The idea was thus poetically instilled that
the feast of rosh ha-shanah is a time of loving encounter between God
and human beings.[21]

l. Rosh ha-shanah

Like other peoples of antiquity and even of modern times, Israel
had several annual cycles. Rosh ha-shanah is only one of the Jewish
New Year's Days but it is the most important one religiously.[22] Rosh
ha-shanah, a term used ever since the Mishnah, signifies not so
much the chronological beginning of the year as it does the year's
foundational content. As in other religions, so here the temporal
beginning is a metaphor for an ontological, metatemporal beginning.
This is why on rosh ha-shanah Jews recall, first of all, the creation of
the world, the bereshit bara' 'Elohim et ha-shamaim we-et ha-'arez
(Gen 1:1) as well as the world's essential goodness, the wayar' 'Elohim . . . we-hinneh ṭob me'od, "and God saw . . . and behold, it was
very good" (Gen 1:31). The years that pass in the rhythm of the
calendar are not empty containers nor threats to human existence
but gifts and words rich in meaning. Every New Year's Day, as on the
first morning of creation, God makes the world anew and entrusts it
to human beings in order that in collaboration with him they may
enjoy it and use it.

But rosh ha-shanah marks not only the beginning of creation but
also the beginning of the events of salvation: it was on rosh ha-
shanah that God remembered Sarah, that Isaac was begotten, that
Hannah bore Samuel, and so on. This day therefore asserts that the
root of time is not within time but in the divine love that wills and
creates it. Seen at this level, time is "salvation" and reveals its density of value and meaning; otherwise, time is "loss," that is, dispersion and emptiness.

New Year's Day is called not only rosh ha-shanah but yom
teru'ah, the day of the blowing of the shofar or ram's horn which in
antiquity was used to call out the inhabitants of a village or town into
the fields for the harvest. In a liturgical setting the shofar becomes
the symbol of the voice of God who, as on Mount Sinai (see Ex 19:16),
reveals himself to his people and obtains their fidelity and obe-

dience: "All that the Lord has ordained we will do and hear" (Ex 19:8).[23] The melancholy, penetrating sound of the shofar calls the Jewish people once again to the holy mountain for the renewal of their covenant. According to Moses Maimonides, the sound of the shofar is like a voice addressing us today and saying:

> Awake, awake, O sleepers, from your sleep!
> O slumberers, arouse ye from your slumbers!
> Examine your deeds; return in repentance; and remember
>   your Creator.
> Those of you who forget the truth in the follies of the
>   times, and go astray the whole year in vanity and
>   emptiness, which neither profit nor save, look to
>   your souls.
> Improve your ways and works.
> Abandon, everyone of you, his evil course and the thought
>   that is not good.[24]

A third name for New Year's Day is *yom zikkaron*, "day of memorial" or "day of remembrance." The name is used in the main benediction of the *tefillah:* "Blessed art thou . . . who hallowest Israel and the Day of Remembrance" (855). *Rosh ha-shanah*, then, is a day for remembering, but who does the remembering and what is it that is remembered? It is not human beings who "remember" God but rather God who "remembers" human beings. This surprising fact is emphasized in all the texts for this feast, especially the biblical pericopes: Gen 21:1–4 and 1 Sam 1:19–20, which are read on the first day, and Gen 22:1 and Jer 31:20, which are read on the second.

But what does it mean to say that God remembers a human being? "The Lord visited Sarah as he had said, and the Lord did to Sarah as he had promised. And Sarah conceived, and bore Abraham a son in his old age at the time of which God had spoken to him" (Gen 21:1–2). God's "remembering" is his creative love that hears and brings aid, replacing the barrenness of the wilderness with a miraculous fertility. True, human beings, too, must "remember," but their remembering is to be a "remembering God." That is, they must not forget that God "remembers" them; that he loves them and protects them by making them lie down in "green pastures" and leading them "beside still waters" (Ps 23:2).

Human "remembering" is an acceptance of God's "remember-

ing," an abandonment to the surprises which this remembering
brings and the demands it makes:

> Is Ephraim my dear son?
>   Is he my darling child?
> For as often as I speak against him,
>   I do remember him still.
> Therefore my heart yearns for him;
>   I will surely have mercy on him (Jer 21:20).

Finally, rosh ha-shanah is also called yom ha-din, "day of judgment," on which all human beings are summoned by the divine
Judge in order to be examined regarding their actions in light of the
covenant code. This "judgment" has for its purpose not condemnation but conversion and forgiveness: "I have no pleasure in the death
of the wicked, but that the wicked turn from his way and live" (Ez
33:11). God "judges" in order that the splendor of creation may not
be obscured by sin, but human beings may enjoy it to the full; in
order that human beings may return from "outside Eden" to
"within" it and dwell there joyously. This unbreakable connection
between the beginning of the world and the proclamation of judgment is emphasized in all the texts of rosh ha-shanah, and especially
in this final text of the benedictions accompanying the blowing of the
shofar:

> This day is the world's assize: this day Thou causest all the
> creatures of the Universe to stand in judgment, as children
> or as servants (875, note). . . . Thou rememberest what was
> wrought from eternity and art mindful of all that hath been
> formed from of old: before thee all secrets are revealed, and
> the multitude of hidden things since the creation; for there
> is no forgetfulness before the throne of thy glory, nor is there
> aught hidden from thine eyes. . . . O Lord our God, [thou]
> lookest and seest to the end of all the ages. For thou wilt
> bring on the appointed time of remembrance for the judg-
> ment of every spirit and soul. . . . This day, on which was
> the beginning of thy work, is a remembrance of the first day,
> for it is a statute for Israel, a decree of the God of Jacob. . . .
> Each separate creature is judged thereon [on this day], and
> recorded for life or for death. . . . Happy is the man who
> forgetteth thee not, and the son of man who strengtheneth

himself in thee; for they that seek thee shall never stumble, neither shall any be put to shame who trust in thee (877–79).

In the liturgy there are three main elements that distinguish *rosh ha-shanah* and bring out its specific meaning: the *tefillah*, the *musaf*, and the blowing of the shofar. The first two are the same in structure as any other *tefillah* and *musaf*, but the added prayers are so numerous and of such a character that this basic structure is not easily discerned.

The first benediction of the *tefillah* is enriched by a prayer for life: "Remember us unto life, O King who delightest in life, and inscribe us in the book of life, O living God" (845). The intermediate benedictions, in their turn, have a lengthy invocation of God's lordship:

> Our God and God of our fathers, reign thou in thy glory over the whole universe, and be exalted above all the earth in thine honour, and shine forth in the splendour and excellence of thy might upon all the inhabitants of thy world, that whatsoever hath been made may know that thou hast made it, and whatsoever hath been created may understand that thou hast created it, and whatsoever hath breath in its nostrils may say, The Lord God of Israel is King, and his dominion ruleth over all. Hallow us by thy commandments, and grant our portion in thy Torah. . . . O purify our hearts to serve thee in truth, for thou art God in truth and thy word is truth, and endureth for ever. Blessed art thou, O Lord, King over all the earth, who hallowest Israel and the Day of Remembrance (853–55).

The tefillah is followed by the *'Avinu malkenu* ("Our Father, our King!"), a litany of forty-four invocations, many of them attributed to R. Aqiba, in each of which God is addressed as "Our Father, our King!":

> Our Father, our King! we have sinned before thee.
> Our Father, our King! we have no King but thee.
> Our Father, our King! deal with us [kindly] for the sake of thy Name.
> Our Father, our King! let a happy year begin for us. . . .
> Our Father, our King! be gracious unto us and answer us,

for we have no good works of our own; deal with us
with charity and kindness, and save us (163–67).

A second peculiarity of *rosh ha-shanah* is a *musaf* in which are
included three prayers known as *malkuyot* ("kingships"), *zikronot*
("remembrances"), and *shofrot* ("shofar-soundings"). The first develops the theme of the divine lordship, the second the theme of
God's remembrance and love of Israel, and the third the theme of
some events in salvation history. The prayers are quite lengthy, especially if we bear in mind that the morning liturgy on *rosh ha-shanah*
usually takes six hours.

A third characteristic of the liturgy for this feast is the blowing of
the shofar. It was originally blown at dawn, before the beginning of
the morning service, as an invitation to the *teshuvah* that lasts until
the Day of Atonement. After the rebellion of Bar Kokhba (135 A.D.),
however, the blowing of the shofar was made part of the synagogal
service, lest the Romans misinterpret it as a call to rebellion. It is at
present blown during the *musaf* service, after each of the three special prayers mentioned above.

There is, finally, still another ceremony that may be regarded as
peculiar to *rosh ha-shanah*: the *tashlik* ("mayest thou cast"), which is
a procession before sundown on the first day of the feast; in this
procession Jews walk to the banks of a river in order to cast their sins
into it, in accordance with the words of Micah: "Thou wilt cast all
our sins into the depths of the sea. Thou wilt show faithfulness to
Jacob and steadfast love to Abraham, as thou hast sworn to our fathers from the days of old" (7:19–20). Once the river bank is reached,
Psalms 33 and 130 are recited, as is the following prayer:

Who is a God like unto thee, that pardoneth iniquity and
passeth by the transgression of the remnant of his heritage?
He retaineth not his anger for ever, because he delighteth in
lovingkindness. He will again have mercy upon us; he will
subdue our iniquities. And thou wilt cast all the sins of thy
people, the house of Israel, into a place where they shall be
no more remembered or ever again come to mind (889).

According to the Zohar, "everything that is cast into the depths
is lost for ever."[25] By symbolically throwing its sins into the flowing
river, the community expresses its desire and intention of renewing
itself in depth and separating itself from its sinful past.

Rosh ha-shanah has many meanings: it is a feast of creation, a feast of saving events, a feast of judgment, and a New Year's feast. These meanings, however, are not opposed among themselves nor simply juxtaposed to one another, but represent emphases on several aspects of a single insight, namely, that time, when lived before God, is not a threat but the house of meaning. For this reason, *rosh ha-shanah* is marked not only by an intense penitential spirit but also by an equally intense, even if diffuse, joy. The joyous side can be seen in: the blessing of apples and honey, which are symbols of happiness and prosperity; the use of white garments, which symbolize purity and beauty; and the exchange of wishes that each person's name may be written "in the book of life (*sefer hayim*)." All these are eloquent images that give positive expression to the meaning, at once theological and anthropological, of this feast and of the *teshuvah* which is its principal category. The images represent the emergence of the positive and edenic dimension of the feast, and of the will to turn around and once more dwell responsibly in the midst of creation.

2. Yom kippur

This is the climactic point of the *'aseret yeme teshuvah*, the "ten penitential days," that began with *rosh ha-shanah*, the Day of Divine Judgment. Those who accept *teshuvah* and are renewed thereby come now to the *yom kippur* or *yom a-kippurim*, the day of the great forgiveness. This feast is also called the Great Sabbath (*Shabbat Shabbatot*, the Sabbath of Sabbaths), or simply *Yoma* in the Mishnah. It is the feast on which the people regard themselves as cleansed (*kipper* = expiate; whence *kippur*) from all their sins, in keeping with the prophetic promise: "Though all your sins are like scarlet, they shall be as white as snow; though they are red like crimson, they shall become like wool" (Is 1:18). This wiping out of sins and purification from them is not the work of human beings but of God, who renews the promise made in creation and covenant by not holding his partners' infidelity against them. Thanks to this forgiveness, the creative plan can never be regarded as a definitive failure, for it is always possible to break the chains of destiny and begin anew.

The forgiveness meant here is not a magical formula that does away with the sinner's responsibility but a demanding gift that awakens the conscience to the meaning of its choices. Commenting on Lev 16:30, the tractate of the Mishnah devoted to *yom kippur* says clearly: "For transgressions that are between man and God the Day of Atonement effects atonement, but for transgressions that are between a man and his fellow the Day of Atonement effects atonement only if he has appeased his fellow" (*Yoma* 8, 9; Danby, 172).

Sometime before, Jesus had voiced or confirmed the same principle:

> If you are offering your gift at the altar, and there remember that your brother has something against you, leave your gift there before the altar and go; first be reconciled to your brother, and then come and offer your gift. Make friends quickly with your accuser, while you are going with him to court, lest your accuser hand you over to the judge, and the judge to the guard, and you be put in prison (Mt 5:23–25).

God's forgiveness is thus linked to our forgiveness of our brothers and sisters; *yom kippur* reconciles with God if on *rosh ha-shanah* and the succeeding penitential days we are reconciled with our brothers and sisters. The connection between God's forgiveness and our forgiveness of others is, however, not causative but revelatory. The meaning is not: "God forgives you *because* you have forgiven others," but "Your forgiveness of others means that you already have God's forgiveness." Forgiveness of others is both a sign and a fruit of the divine forgiveness when this is willingly accepted.

When God created, he entrusted the garden of Eden to human beings in order that they might "till it and keep it" (Gen 2:15). When he forgives, he recreates the garden for them and entrusts it to them once again, even though they have ruined and ravaged it. Forgiveness is God's recreative energy that refuses to allow the failure of human history. It is the Amen to meaning and life, an Amen repeated after every "no" of blind and ungrateful human beings. Consciousness of this situation has made "the Yom Kippur services the ones which are the most widely observed" in Judaism[26] and so rich in liturgical and ritual elements "that they usually last from early morning to sunset."[27]

The principal rites that are distinctive of *yom kippur* are the *kol nidre*, the confession of sins, the biblical readings, the *musaf*, and the concluding rite known *ne'ilah*.

The feast of *yom kippur* begins with a rite whose origin cannot easily be determined and which consists in appearing, before sundown, before the rabbinical tribunal in the synagogue and there rescinding *kol nidre*, that is, "all vows": "All vows, obligations, oaths, and anathemas . . . which we may vow, or swear, or pledge, or whereby we may be bound from this Day of Atonement until the next, we do repent. May they be deemed abolished, forgiven, annulled, and void. . . . The vows shall not be reckoned vows; the obligations shall not be obligatory; nor the oaths be oaths."[28]

This statement, which is sung three times and heard in silence, is followed by the response of the community, which is likewise repeated three times: "And all the congregation of the people of Israel shall be forgiven, and the stranger who sojourns among them, because the whole population was involved in the error" (Num 15:26).

The "vows" here rescinded are not obligations undertaken toward the neighbor but those undertaken toward God, for example, to abstain from certain pleasures or certain rites. It is therefore wrong and unjust to accuse Jews, on the basis of this text, of being treacherous, corrupt, and untrustworthy. The reason for this "loosing of vows" is twofold. It is a way of asserting the sovereign freedom of God's forgiveness, which does not depend on human promises and oaths. Secondly, it springs from a consciousness that the real human "commitment" that is needed is not toward God but toward our fellow human beings. Reform Judaism has dropped the rite of the kol nidre, but this still remains almost universally one of the most impressive and meaningful moments in the Jewish liturgy. Back in 1913, Franz Rosenzweig was so moved by it that he converted back to Judaism and became one of its best masters through his books and teaching.

The heart of yom kippur, however, is the confession of sins (widduy), which is included in the tefillah and is repeated five times during the day. It takes the form of a lengthy penitential formula that has two parts: 'ashamnu ("we have sinned") and 'al het' ("for the sin which we have committed . . ."):

Our God and God of our fathers, let our prayer come before thee; hide not thyself from our supplication, for we are not so arrogant and hardened that we should say before thee, O Lord our God and God of our fathers, we are righteous and are sinless; but verily, we have sinned.

We are guilt-laden ('ashamnu); we have been faithless, we have robbed, and we have spoken basely;

We have committed iniquity, and caused unrighteousness; we have been presumptuous, done violence, framed falsehood;

We have counselled evil, we have failed in promise, we have scoffed, revolted, and blasphemed; we have been rebellious, we have acted perversely, we have transgressed, oppressed, and been stiff-necked;

We have done wickedly, we have corrupted ourselves and committed abomination; we have gone astray, and we have led astray.

We have turned aside from thy commandments and good judgments, and it availed us nought. But thou art righteous in all that has come upon us; for thou hast acted truthfully, but we have wrought unrighteousness.

What shall we say before thee, O thou who dwellest on high, and what shall we recount unto thee, thou who abidest in the heavens? dost thou not know all things, both the hidden and the revealed?

Thou knowest the secrets of eternity and the most hidden mysteries of all living. Thou searchest the innermost recesses, and dost test the feelings and the heart. Nought is concealed from thee, or hidden from thine eyes.

May it then be thy will, O Lord our God and God of our fathers, to forgive us for all our sins, to pardon us for all our iniquities, and to grant us remission for all our transgressions.

For the sin ('al het') which we have committed before thee under compulsion, or of our own will;

And for the sin which we have committed before thee in hardening of the heart;

For the sin which we have committed before thee out of ignorance;

And for the sin which we have committed before thee with utterance of the lips;

For the sin which we have committed before thee by unchastity;

And for the sin which we have committed before thee openly and secretly. . . .

For all these, O God of forgiveness, forgive us, pardon us, grant us remission (907–13).

This list continues on with implacable sternness through forty-four headings of sin, which are confessed in the plural ("we") and while striking the breast.

A third prayer distinctive of yom kippur is found in the tefillah of the musaf service. This calls to mind the solemn priestly rite celebrated in Jerusalem, when the kohen gadol ("high priest") confessed sins in the name of the entire populace, pronounced the Tetragrammaton, and prayed as follows when he entered the Holy of Holies (the one and only time that he entered it during the year):

> May it be Thy will, O Lord our God and God of our fathers, that this year that hath now arrived be unto us and unto all Thy people, the house of Israel, a year of plenteous store; a year of blessings . . . a year in which Thou wilt bless our going out and our coming in . . . a year of peace and tranquillity . . . a year in which Thy people, the house of Israel, may not be in need of support, one from the other, nor from another people, in that Thou wilt set a blessing upon the work of their hands.[29]

In the area of biblical readings, various special passages are chosen for *yom kippur*, among them Lev 16; Is 57:14–58; and the Book of Jonah.

Lev 16:1–34 describes the temple ritual on *yom kippur*, the role of the *kohen gadol*, and especially the rite of the "scapegoat," the goat that was symbolically laden with the sins of the people by means of a laying on of hands and then sent out into the wilderness to a place far from any human presence. Although the account displays elements of magic, it was reread in the synagogal liturgy as an historical narrative and, above all, as an image of a personal moral purification which was the individual's responsibility. This is the point that is forcefully expressed in the *haftarah* from Isaiah, in which the prophet criticizes fasting as an end in itself and then shows its value as a tool for moral progress:

> Behold, you fast only to quarrel and to fight
>   and to hit with wicked fist.
> Fasting like yours this day
>   will not make your voice to be heard on high.
> Is such the fast that I choose,
>   a day for a man to humble himself? . . .
> Is not this the fast that I choose:
>   to loose the bonds of wickedness,
>   to undo the thongs of the yoke,
> to let the oppressed go free,
>   and to break every yoke? (Is 58:4–6).

If we bear in mind that *yom kippur* is the only day of the year on which a strict, indeed total, fast is observed for twenty-four hours (from one evening to the next), we will better appreciate the challenge this *haftarah* contains.

But the most distinctive text read on *yom kippur* is the Book of Jonah, one of the most beautiful and richest of the Bible. It uses the language of poetry and myth to describe the sovereignty of God and his love for all nations, to say how it is possible for every human being, regardless of race or nationality, to repent and be converted, and to show the hardness of heart represented by Jonah who did not believe in God's forgiveness or the Ninevites' change of heart and whom God had to challenge and prove wrong.

The final element that sets *yom kippur* apart is the liturgy of the *ne'ilah*, which is short for *ne'ilat she'arim*, "closing of the doors." It calls to mind the prayer that used to be said in Jerusalem when the temple gates were closed at the end of the day. Once the temple was destroyed, this rite was taken over in the synagogal liturgy as a conclusion for *yom kippur*. In this context the "closing of the doors" becomes symbolic: the doors are an image of the "doors of heaven" which were opened on *rosh ha-shanah* and are closed again, after ten days, on the feast of the Great Forgiveness. This symbolic "closing of the doors" does not mean that the grace of God is accessible to Israel only during the ten penitential days, for this grace is always available to it. The image emphasizes rather the urgency and radical character of the expected human response, which may not be put off with impunity.

The rite takes place in the evening before sunset. Among other prayers Ps 145 is read, and the *tefillah* and some *piyyutim*, or poems, are recited. The *tefillah* shows some important changes when compared to the *tefillah* of the morning service: for example, instead of "O inscribe all the children of thy covenant for a happy life," the prayer here is: "O seal all the children of thy covenant for a happy life"; the *piyyutim* develop the theme of the "door to be closed." The rite ends with the sounding of a long-drawn-out note on the shofar; this symbolizes the forgiveness of God by which Israel is renewed and can live the new years as both "inscribed and sealed in the book of life."

III. THE MINOR FEASTS

In addition to the pilgrimage feasts and the austere feasts, Jewish tradition has others that are called "minor" or "little," because the Torah does not speak of them. The most important of these are the feasts or festivals of *hannukah* and *purim*, which are connected with two historical events: *hannukah* with the recovery of the temple in the war against Syria (165 B.C.), *purim* with the deliverance of the Jewish people from Persian enslavement thanks to the courage and prayers of Esther.

Like *pesah*, which serves as foundation and model, these two feasts celebrate events having to do with freedom. They call to mind all the attempts throughout history to annihilate the Jewish people (the Persians, the Romans . . . the Nazis); at the same time, they bear witness to the strength of the children of Israel who, sustained by God, have managed to survive and triumph. The enemies of Israel may be many and aggressive, but *hannukah* and *purim* remind us that God is always stronger than they and that deliverance from slavery is always possible.

Though the meaning of the two feasts is basically the same, their liturgical celebrations are quite different: the first is more sober and serious, the second more joyous and popular.

I. Hanukkah

In the second century B.C. Antiochus IV, King of Syria, tried to Hellenize Judaism by banning all of its basic religious practices: the temple ritual, the teaching of the Torah, the observance of the sabbath, and the circumcision of male infants. The violence reached its climax in 167 B.C., when the Syrian king forced his way into the temple in Jerusalem and there offered sacrifice to Zeus and desecrated the place. This supreme abomination led to a revolt under the Hasmoneans, led by Judas Maccabaeus, who in 165 B.C. succeeded in conquering the Syrians, winning back the temple, and rededicating it at a great festival. The festival, repeated each year, became the feast of *hannukah*, "dedication," known also as the Festival of Lights and celebrated for eight days beginning on 25 Kislev (December).

Scholars are not in full agreement in their attempts at an historical reconstruction of the liturgical elements of *hannukah*. These, however, certainly focus primarily on the rebuilding of the temple that had been desecrated by Antiochus IV. They remained practically unchanged when, after the destruction of the temple, they were taken over into the synagogal liturgy.

The most important part of the *hannukah* ritual is the lighting of the lamps, a ceremony that originally took place in the temple and that now takes place in the synagogue and the home. The eight-branched candlestick (*hanukiyyah*), when lit and shining out in all

its splendor, is a symbol of God's reconsecrated temple and its restoration to its original brightness (see 2 Chr 29:17). The reconsecration
was God's gift rather than the work of the Maccabees. This is the
point made in the talmudic story of how the little flask of oil that was
found in the temple after its desecration burned miraculously for
eight days until a new one could be obtained.

The lighting of the candles is accompanied by the singing of a
very beautiful and popular hymn, ṣur ma'oz ("rock of my strength"),
which is attributed to Mordecai, a German writer of about 1250 A.D.:

> Rock of my strength, my citadel,
> you whom we delight to honor,
> give your faithful people back
> their temple, wherein to honor you.
> Once our wicked enemies
> have been defeated,
> we shall celebrate
> and sing of
> your reconsecrated altar.[30]

A second important part of the liturgy is the prayer known as 'al
ha-nissim ("for the miracles"), which is included in the tefillah and
the birkat ha-mazon:

> We thank thee also for the miracles, for the redemption, for
> the mighty deeds and saving acts, wrought by thee, as well
> as for the wars which thou didst wage for our fathers in days
> of old, at this season ... when the iniquitous power of
> Greece rose up against thy people Israel to make them for-
> getful of thy Torah. ... Thou didst plead their cause, thou
> didst judge their suit, thou didst avenge their wrong; thou
> deliveredst the strong into the hands of the weak, the many
> into the hands of the few, the impure into the hands of the
> pure, the wicked into the hands of the righteous, and the
> arrogant into the hands of them that occupied themselves
> with thy Torah (151–53).

The reader will observe that the biblical readings for the celebration of Hanukkah do not include passages from the Books of the
Maccabees, because these books are not part of the Jewish canon.
Instead, Num 7 is read which describes the consecration of the altar
in the time of Moses. The haftarah is from Zechariah (2:14–4:7),

which speaks of "a lampstand all of gold, with a bowl on the top of it, and seven lamps on it, with seven lips on each of the lamps which are on the top of it" (4:2). This passage would evidently be a reminder of the candelabrum that was reconsecrated and relit by the Hasmoneans after the desecration of the temple. The *haftarah* ends with these words: "Not by might, nor by power, but by my Spirit, says the Lord of hosts" (4:6). The feast of Hanukkah is a celebration of precisely this certainty: that Israel cannot fail, but that this preservation is due not to its own power but to that of God. It is this that has encouraged it to struggle against injustice and oppression, and spurred the movement of return to 'ereṣ Yiśra'el, and that is an effective bulwark against the temptations and risks of an unconditional and uncritical assimilation.

2. Purim

The festival of *purim* is connected with an historical event that is narrated in one of the five *megillot* ("scrolls"), namely, the Book of Esther. The Jews, who had settled in Persia in about the fifth century before the Christian era, were now threatened with extermination due to the hatred of Haman, minister plenipotentiary of King Ahasuerus (or Xerxes). But the intervention of a young Jewish woman, Esther (whose name means "Star"), a Jewish orphan and niece of Mordecai, whose exceptional beauty caused her to become the king's wife and queen, frustrated this plan of extermination by reversing the situation: Haman was hanged, Mordecai took over Haman's office, and the Jews massacred their enemies.

The feast of *purim* recalls this victory and reversal in which loser becomes victor and victor loser. The name (pur/purim) is explained in the Book of Esther: "Haman . . . the enemy of all the Jews, had plotted against the Jews to destroy them, and had cast Pūr, that is, the lot, to crush and destroy them. . . . Therefore they named these days Pūrim, after the term Pūr" (9:24–26). But because God had changed the "lot" of death into victory and life, "Mordecai . . . sent letters to all the Jews who were in all the provinces of King Ahasuerus . . . enjoining them that they should keep the fourteenth day of the month Adar, and also the fifteenth day of the same [= February–March] . . . as the month that had been turned for them from sorrow into gladness and from mourning into a holiday" (9:20–22).

Although of all the feasts *purim* is the one that has most taken on secular traits, to the point of becoming a kind of carnival, and although the Book of Esther never mentions the divine Name and is therefore not in the Qumran canon, its religious structure is the same as that of the other historical Jewish feasts: God delivered the children of Israel from the power of Haman, just as he had delivered them from the power of the Egyptians and from all other tyrannies.

The most important liturgical elements that distinguish purim are the prayer 'al ha-nissim ("for the miracles"), which is included in the tefillah, and the reading of the megillah of Esther, the megillah par excellence ever since the time of the Mishnah. The prayer 'al ha-nissim is a prayer of thanksgiving to God for having delivered the Jews from the hands of Haman:

> We thank thee also for the miracles, for the redemption, for the mighty deeds and saving acts, wrought by thee . . . in days of old, at this season, in the days of Mordecai and Esther, in Sushan the capital, when the wicked Haman rose up against them, and sought to destroy, to slay and cause to perish all the Jews, both young and old, women and little children . . . then thou didst in thine abundant mercy bring his counsel to nought, didst frustrate his design, and return his recompense upon his own head (151–53).

But the heart of the purim liturgy is the reading of the megillah, which is done twice during the day, once in the morning and once in the afternoon, in an atmosphere of noisy rejoicing. When the name of Haman is uttered, it is greeted with rancorous remarks and various noises expressing scorn and derision; the names of Mordecai and Esther are greeted with applause and shouts of joy and exultation. The teaching of the rabbis emphasizes the positive meaning of these actions and expressions, which "are not intended to commemorate revenge, vindictiveness and the downfall of our enemies, but to keep ever-green in our minds the hope of the ultimate triumph of that which is just";[31] not to arouse negative feelings but to nourish the faith and certainty that "the Glory of Israel will not lie or repent; for he is not a man that he should repent" (1 Sam 15:29).

The reading of the megillah is followed by a benediction that is prescribed in the Talmud (Meg. 21b) and, in the afternoon, by a hymn that ends with these words:

> Accursed be Haman who sought to destroy me;
> Blessed be Mordecai the Jew;
> Accursed be Zeresh, the wife of him that terrified me;

Blessed be Esther my protectress; and may Harbonah also
be remembered for good.[32]

Many writers have pointed out that *purim* is a kind of Jewish
carnival that celebrates violations of law, disorder, and the turning of
the world upside down and topsy-turvy. The description is acceptable, provided we understand the meaning of this "world turned
upside down": it is not a world in which a new disorder reigns, but a
world of true order, the order willed by God. *Purim* challenges our
present world which is based on injustice and on the oppression
practiced by one Haman after another; it proclaims the possibility of
a new world in which the beauty and harmony of "Esther" hold
sway. *Purim* turns the world upside down in order to set it on its feet,
because the world usually regarded as "on its feet" is in reality a
world "turned upside down."

Conclusion

From Ignorance to Understanding and Cooperation

Jules Isaac was a Jewish French historian whose thinking was profoundly marked by the "iniquitous tragedy" of genocide that had claimed the majority of his loved ones, including his wife and children, as its victims. In his book *The Teaching of Contempt*, which appeared a year before his death in 1963, he denounced the wickedness of the Christian Churches in fostering misunderstanding, rejection, hatred, ill treatment, and persecution of Jews. The enormous effort made by this prophet of our times did not fail to bear fruit in Vatican II's Declaration *Nostra Aetate*, which owed its existence in part to his passionate concern and courage.[1]

Today, twenty years after the conciliar document, the "ideology of contempt," as used to discredit Jews and add demonic traits to the picture people have of them, has been overcome for good; in its place there is a growing awareness of the need of a new and different relationship with the Jewish people. But, while "contempt" has been eliminated, the same is not true of the "ignorance" that was both its effect and its cause. There is ignorance not only of the "Old" Testament (which too many theologians still look upon as secondary, propaedeutic, and typological), nor only of history (so that many still think Judaism disappeared with the fall of Jerusalem in 70 A.D.), but also and above all of the Jewish liturgy, from which the Christian liturgy derived elements and models.

Jewish Liturgy and Christian Liturgy

According to David Flusser, "Judaism and Christianity could be likened to two students with similar backgrounds who have been assigned the same tasks."[2] This statement holds not only for the theological and spiritual background or setting of the two religions, but also, and especially, for the liturgical and cultic setting which I have sought to reconstruct in the preceding pages by leading the reader through the complex and fascinating world of Jewish prayer. From that world the Christian liturgy has taken over more elements that can readily be imagined; this is a fact which only stubborn ignorance can hide. It is true that today we do not lack for authoritative scholars who emphasize and seek out the substantive links between the Jewish liturgy and the Christian liturgy.[3] At the same time, however, what Louis Bouyer wrote over two decades ago still holds true:

> The continued persistence of this state of mind [that the Eucharist has no prehistory in Judaism], even with scholars who are deeply intuitive as they are well-informed, is somewhat disconcerting.
>
> When we see Dom Odo Casel's immense effort to find the antecedents of Christian worship in the most incongruous pagan rites, and the small concern he brought to the least contestable Jewish antecedents, we wonder how such an open mind could have remained so little open to certain obvious matters of fact.[4]

A little further on, the same author writes: "The question which then arises is unavoidable. Why have people wished with all their might to search so far and wide, and with such unlikely detours, in order to avoid finding the true source of the Christian liturgy close at hand?"[5]

The author supplies various answers to these questions,[6] but surely one of the most important is ignorance of the Jewish liturgical texts; I mean not so much ignorance of their historical existence as ignorance of their spiritual and theological structure and substance. As a result of long-inherited anti-Jewish prejudice, Jewish liturgical texts are unconsciously regarded as "Pharisaic" (with all the negative connotations attached to this word); people forget that Jesus prayed these texts, and so did the Virgin Mary, the apostles, and the early Church for many decades. Use of the category of "Phariseeism," a handy but harmful weapon used by the Christian Churches as well, has not only distorted the picture of intertestamental and rabbinical Judaism; it has also distorted our vision of the Jewish liturgy and prevented Christians from drawing upon it as "living water," in the same way that the New Testament draws upon the Old. This "Phariseeization" of the Jewish liturgy is perhaps most truly to blame for feelings of alienation and distance which Christians have toward the texts of Jewish prayer.

By "alienation" I mean a sense of bewilderment and remoteness, so that we feel more at home with the texts of "pagan" prayers than with Jewish texts. Speaking still of Odo Casel, Louis Bouyer says:

(He) was in no way ignorant of the Jewish texts whose comparison with Christian texts is indispensable before any other comparison can be made. He cites them. He observed their most striking parallels. But for him they are just noteworthy parallels. It seems he cannot see that the origin and also the explanation of what is most *sui generis* in the Christian Eucharist is to be found here. He looks for neither origin, nor explanation anywhere except in the pagan mysteries.[7]

If, however, we allow the Jewish liturgical texts to speak and if we yield to their poetic beauty and, more importantly, their interior spiritual movement, we see how surprisingly relevant and close to us they are. What Christian can fail to hear his or her own voice in the *berakot*, the *tefillah*, the reading and commentary on the Torah, the sabbath *qiddush*, the *havdalah*, the *dayyenu*, the *nishmat kol hay* ("the breath of every living thing"), and in the spirituality of *pesaḥ*, *shavu'ot*, *sukkot*, *rosh ha-shanah*, *kippur*, and so on? What Christian . can fail to find therein expressions of the trust and abandonment of Jesus to his Father?

The result and ultimate fruit of this alienation has been the breakaway of the Christian liturgy from its natural historical roots.

Here again is Louis Bouyer:

To imagine that the Christian liturgy sprang up from a sort of spontaneous generation, motherless and fatherless like Melchizedek, or trustingly to give it a sort of putative paternity which would definitively erase any perception of its authentic genealogy, is from the start to reduce all reconstructions to a more or less scholarly, more or less ingenious mass of misconceptions.[8]

But how can the *ekklesia* be understood apart from the synagogue, the liturgy of the word apart from the *qeri'at Torah*, the Eucharistic Prayer apart from the *berakah*, the cycle of readings apart from the *parashot* and *haftarot*, baptism apart from the *miqweh*, the supper apart from the *birkat ha-mazon*, Easter apart from *pesaḥ*, Pentecost apart from *shavu'ot*, Sunday apart from *shabbat*, the divine office apart from the *tehillim* (hymns and psalms), conversion apart from *teshuvah*, Lent apart from *yom kippur*, liturgical translations apart from the *targumim*, the homily apart from the *midrashim*, and so on?

To point out these connections is not to deny the originality of the Christian liturgy by reducing it to a product or prolongation of the Jewish liturgy. It is rather to identify the soil from which the Christian liturgy sprang and the source with which it must be compared. The new element in the Christian liturgy is due not to a creation out of nothing but to a Christological reinterpretation of what Judaism provided; not to a doing away with it but to a differentiation from it.

This point is especially important for an understanding of Christian feasts. It is usually said that as Judaism historicized the agricultural festivals, so the Church christologized them, with the result that Christmas, Easter, and Pentecost now commemorate the birth, death, and resurrection of Jesus and his presence among us through the gift of his Spirit. The statement is true, provided it does not imply an emptying out of the content of the Jewish feasts but rather their reassertion and fulfillment. Just as the Jewish feasts did not eliminate the material, earthly content of the agricultural festivals (and can any festival fail to be "agricultural"?), so the Christian feasts do not eliminate but take over and radicalize the meaning of the Jewish feasts: the Garden of Eden (that is, our present world in the divine plan) flourishes and produces its fruits only where human beings live their lives with Jesus and like Jesus, the Messiah and Son of God.

Jews and Christians Pray to the Same God and for the Same Kingdom

A second level of ignorance shows itself in the notion that the Jewish liturgy is an historical document telling us of a people that has disappeared and not, as it in fact is, the prayer of a living, believing community. Schalom Ben Chorin recently said something that should make many Christians reflect on their own conduct:

> I can say from personal experience that I have often been utterly bewildered by the questions which Christians ask me in all good faith. At the end of a week spent on an introduction to Judaism, one participant asked me: "Do Jews pray to God?" A highranking churchman, the abbot of a German monastery, asked: "Has Judaism experienced any theological development since the establishment of the Old Testament canon?"[9]

Christians must change their mental outlook in two ways by realizing that the Jewish liturgy is not something purely of the past and that in the Jewish liturgy the worshipers pray to the same God as we do and in behalf of the same cause. So influential a book as *Non di solo pane*, a catechism for youth (1979), has this to say when dealing with the institution of the Eucharist:

> When the father of a Jewish family *celebrated* the Passover supper with wife and children . . . the Law *required* him to explain what he was doing. . . . The meal with its unleavened bread *was* interpreted as a present sharing of the Jews in the salvation wrought by God for Moses and his people. It *was* the "memorial" of those ancient saving events. The rite *appeared*, however, to be a symbolic representation of that salvation rather than a real participation in it.[10]

A catechism for adults, *Signore da chi andremo?* (1981), uses the same past tense. "The [Jewish] rite *ordered* the father of the family to explain to his children the deeper meaning of the foods which they *were eating*. Why the bitter herbs, why the unleavened bread and the roast lamb? The herbs *recalled* the oppression of enslavement; the unleavened bread, the haste with which the Jews had had to leave Egypt."[11]

These books constantly speak of the Jewish rite as something belonging to the past. This enables them to show that from a general historical viewpoint and from a Christian viewpoint in particular, there has been a development from a "before" to an "after." The danger, however, is that the reader will end up assuming that the rite has now disappeared and failing to realize that it is a matter of daily spiritual experience for millions of believing Jews in our time.

If, on the other hand, we bear in mind that the Jewish faith is still being lived by multitudes today, the Church will be helped not to "forget that she received the revelation of the Old Testament by way of that people with whom God in his inexpressible mercy established the ancient covenant" (Vatican II, *Nostra Aetate*, no. 4), and that, in the words of Paul the Apostle, "the gifts and the call of God are irrevocable" (Rom 11:29). To be familiar with the Jewish liturgy is not only to add to one's store of historical and cultural lore; it is, above all, to enter into the praying soul of the Jewish people as down the centuries it raises its voice in praise and invocation of the God who is also the God of Jesus and of Christians, the one God of all humankind and all religions.

It is certainly at this level that these "sisters," the Jewish liturgy and the Christian liturgy, find themselves in closest contact and harmony: both proclaim the reign of God, both proclaim and sanctify his

Name, both praise and thank him and appeal for his coming. The
qedushat ha-shem, or sanctification of the Name, is the very heart of
both the Jewish and the Christian liturgy; it is the point at which the
two covenanted peoples meet and may be seen to be alike.

Jews in the tefillah and Christians in the Mass cry: "Holy, holy,
holy is the Lord of hosts; the whole earth is full of his glory" (Is 6:3).
To unite oneself with the choir of angels in professing that God is
qadosh is to acknowledge his sovereign and absolute lordship: not
because he is "the boss" but because he is the fountain of life. The
qedushat ha-shem is indeed an assertion of the holiness of God, not
however simply as an objective fact but insofar as it is the foundation
and pledge of human happiness. In Isaiah's hymn the triple "holy" is
followed by a statement of fact: "The whole earth is full of his glory."
The earth is beautiful and inhabitable, and productive of life and not
of death, not in virtue of human effort but because it is "the glory of
God," that is, a concrete expression of his love. Apart from this
"glory" the earth is an empty wilderness, like the land of Adam the
sinner; with this "glory" it is, like Eden, rich in "every tree that is
pleasant to the sight and good for food" (Gen 2:9). The qedushat ha-
shem is therefore not an exercise in irrelevant rhetoric. Its function is
to restore a world marred by sin to its original beauty; to put the
"glory of God" back at the center of the world and have it remain
there; to burst the bonds of injustice and violence that cause the
Shekinah to withdraw from the earth.[12]

No special energies or abilities are needed in order to accom-
plish this "miracle":

> Each time we are about to drink a glass of water, we remind
> ourselves of the eternal mystery of creation, "Blessed be
> Thou . . . by Whose word all things come into being". . . .
> Wishing to eat bread or fruit, to enjoy a pleasant fragrance or
> a cup of wine; on tasting fruit in season for the first time; on
> seeing a rainbow, or the ocean; on noticing trees when they
> blossom; on meeting a sage in Torah or in secular learning;
> on hearing good or bad tidings—we are taught to invoke His
> great name and our awareness of Him. Even on performing a
> physiological function we say "Blessed be Thou . . . who
> healest all flesh and doest wonders."

This is one of the goals of the Jewish way of living: to

experience commonplace deeds as spiritual adventures, to feel the hidden love and wisdom in all things.[13]

If it is true—as is being emphatically claimed in many quarters —that the world is being threatened today as never before with triviality and a crisis of meaninglessness, then the Christian liturgy and, even more, the Jewish liturgy with its focus on berakah offer the most satisfactory answer to the emergency, for they help us to rediscover "the hidden love and wisdom in all things."

Jews and Christians are called upon to affirm this "love" and "wisdom" that are summarized in our liturgical texts. Different though these texts may be, they call for and influence one another as notes in a single song: the song of love for God, which is the foundation and pledge of love for our fellow human beings.

Notes

Preface

1. *Presenting Judaism in Catechesis.* Notes released by the Vatican Commission for Religious Relations with the Jews on the proper way to present the Jewish faith in Roman Catholic Preaching and Teaching (June 24, 1985), in *The Pope Speaks* 30 (1985) 365.
2. The Mishnah, Tractate 'Avot 11, 17, in H. Danby, *The Mishnah* (Oxford: Oxford University Press, 1933), 449. Henceforth: Danby, with page number.
3. *Berakot* IV, 4 (Danby, 5).
4. J. Leibovich, *Ebraismo, popolo ebraico e stato d'Israele* (Rome, 1980), 127.

Introduction

1. *Guidelines for Catholic-Jewish Relations (Orientations and Suggestions for the Application of the Conciliar Declaration on the Relationship of the Church to the Non-Christian Religions, No. 4)*, issued by the Commission for Religious Relations with Judaism (December 1, 1974); trans. in *The Pope Speaks* 19 (1974–75) 352–57 at 352.
2. L. Swidler in *Sefer* 15 (1981) 5–6.
3. See P. Ricoeur, *Freud and Philosophy. An Essay on Interpretation*, trans. D. Savage (New Haven: Yale University Press, 1970).
4. Translated in A. Flannery (ed.), *Vatican II: Conciliar and Postconciliar Documents* (Collegeville: Liturgical Press, 1975), 740 (italics added). Further quotations from the documents of Vatican II are from the Flannery edition.
5. M. Righetti, *Manuale di storia liturgica* (4 vols.; Milan: Ancora, 1964–69³); A.-G. Martimort (ed.), *L'Eglise en prière* (Paris: Desclée, 19 [but see now the new edition in 4 vols.: *The Church at Prayer*, trans. M.J. O'Connell (Collegeville: Liturgical Press, 1986–88)]); S. Marsili (ed.), *Anàmnesis 2. La liturgia. Panorama storico generale* (Casale: Marietti, 1978); D. Sartore and A.M. Triacca (eds.), *Nuovo Dizionario di liturgia* (Rome: Edizioni Paoline, 1983).

6. As was the case a few decades ago; see, e.g., R. Reitzenstein, *Die Vorgeschichte der christlichen Taufe* (Leipzig–Berlin, 1920); L. Loisy, *Les mystères païens et le mystère chrétien* (Paris, 1930).
7. B. Neunheuser, "Storia della liturgia," in *Nuovo Dizionario di liturgia* (n. 5), 1453.
8. S. Marsili, in *Anàmnesis* (n. 5) 2:11.
9. For example, S. Marsili in *Anàmnesis*, in a section entitled "Cristo e la liturgia ebraica" (14–15), refers to synagogue worship and the sabbath (barely four lines) but without telling us, or reconstructing, what these cultic forms meant in light of the Jewish tradition.
10. Again see S. Marsili, whose next section is entitled "Annuncio della fine del cultu ebraico" (15–18).
11. Cited by M. Rimaud, *Chrétiens devant Israël serviteur de Dieu* (Paris: Cerf, 1983), 28.

Chapter I

1. R. Aron, *The Jewish Jesus*, trans. A.H. Forsyth and A.M. de Commaille, in collaboration with H.T. Allen, Jr. (Maryknoll, N.Y.: Orbis, 1971).
2. [Wherever possible, the text of Jewish prayers is taken from Joseph H. Hertz, *The Authorized Daily Prayer Book. Hebrew Text, English Translation with Commentary and Notes* (New York: Bloch, 1948; rev. ed., 1975). The page number(s) in Hertz is (are) given in parentheses after the cited text.—Tr.]
3. J. Jeremias, *The Prayers of Jesus*, trans. J. Bowden et al. (Philadelphia: Fortress, 1967), 29–65.
4. G. Ravasi, *Gesù una buona notizia* (Turin: SEL, 1982), 45.
5. *Il Regno di Dio è fra noi* (Milan: Jaca Book, 1982⁵).
6. From the Midrash *Tanhuma Genesi*, cited in *The Prayers of Jesus in Their Contemporary Setting*, published by the Study Centre for Christian-Jewish Relations (London, 1977), 13. [I do not have access to this volume and have translated the Midrash passage from di Sante's Italian version.—Tr.]
7. A. Cronbach, "Worship in NT Times, Jewish," in *Interpreter's Dictionary of the Bible* (Nashville, 1962), IV, 895.
8. J.J. Petuchowski, in J.J. Petuchowski and M. Brocke (eds.), *The Lord's Prayer and the Jewish Liturgy* (London: Burns and Oates; New York: Seabury, 1978), 47.
9. *Ibid.*, 48.
10. Cited in E. Garfiel, *The Service of the Heart. A Guide to the Jewish*

Prayer Book (New York–London: Thomas Yoseloof, 1958; reprinted: North Hollywood, CA: Wilshire Book Company, n.d.), 35.

11. *Ibid.*, 36.
12. *Ibid.*, 32.
13. *Ibid.*, 33.
14. *Ibid.*, 40.
15. See note 2.
16. The words are those of G.E. Biddle, cited in A.E. Millgram, *Jewish Worship* (Philadelphia: Jewish Publication Society of America, 1971), 89.

Chapter 2

1. Cited in A.E. Millgram, *Jewish Prayer* (Philadelphia: Jewish Publication Society of America, 1971), 69.
2. See A.E. Millgram (n. 1), who describes the *berakah* as "a foundation stone of Jewish prayer" (92). I prefer the description "generative nucleus" as being a more dynamic and structuring image.
3. E. Garfiel, *The Service of the Heart. A Guide to the Jewish Prayer Book* (New York–London: Thomas Yoseloof, 1958; reprinted: North Hollywood, CA: Wilshire Book Company, n.d.), 49.
4. *b.* (= Babylonian Talmud) *Ber.* 35a; see E. Munk, *Le monde des prières* (Paris, 1970), 30.
5. The use and meaning of this sign is connected with Ez 9:4–7, where the prophet speaks of a "man dressed in linen" whom God orders to "mark a cross [literally a *taw*] on the foreheads of all who grieve and lament" (New Jerusalem Bible).
6. Translation in L. Ginzberg, *The Legends of the Jews* I (Philadelphia: Jewish Publication Society of America, 1968), 5–8.
7. *b. Ber.* 54a.
8. *b. Ber.* 58b.
9. Cited by A.J. Heschel, *God in Search of Man* (New York: Meridian Books, 1966), 85.
10. *Ibid.*, 75.
11. *Ibid.*
12. *Midrash Rabba Gen.* 49, 4.
13. Ginzberg (n. 6), I, 14–15.
14. See W.G. Braude, *The Midrash on Psalms* I (New Haven: Yale University Press, 1959), 498. *b. Ber.* 32a says: "Before petitioning, you must always praise first."

15. See W.O.E. Oesterley, *The Jewish Background of the Christian Liturgy* (Oxford: Oxford University Press, 1925), 44.
16. Mishnah, *Tamid* 5, 1 (Danby 586–87).
17. For this historical development of the *shema'*, with the pertinent documentation, see L. Jacobs, in *Encyclopedia Judaica* (Jerusalem: Keter Publishing House, 1971), under "*Shema'*, Reading of," 1370.
18. The text plays on the two meanings of the Hebrew word *derek*, which can signify "way" = course traveled from place to place, and "way" = manner. See also *b. Ber.* 11a.
19. According to Flavius Josephus the *Shema'* was already being recited twice a day in the time of Moses; see D. Lattes, *Commento al Torah* (Assisi—Rome: Carucci Editore, 1976), 576.
20. See B. Gerhardsson, "Du Judéo-Christianisme à Jésus par le *Shema'*," in *Judéo-Christianisme (Mélanges Cardinal Jean Daniélou)* (Paris, 1972), 21–36.
21. E. Munk, *La voix de la Torah. Commentaire du Pentateuque. Deutéronome* (Paris: Fondation Samuel et Odette Levy, 1981³), 60.
22. For this terminology and typology see A. Rizzi, *Differenza e responsabilità* (Casale Monferrato: Marietti, 1981), 22–23.
23. The letter *h* is part of the word *'eḥad* but was often omitted in popular speech.
24. *b. Ber.* 13b.
25. See E. Munk, *La voix de la Torah* (n. 21), 60.
26. On the rabbinical use of the expression see H.L. Strack and P. Billerbeck, *Kommentar zum Neuen Testament aus Talmud und Midrasch* 1 (Munich: C.H. Beck, 1974), 172ff. Note that "kingdom" here refers not so much to the "place" where God reigns as to the fact that he reigns. A better translation would be "reign" or "lordship."
27. *b. Ber.* 5a.
28. *Ibid.*
29. Text in M. Lehmann, *Rabbi Akiba* (Paris: Merkos L'Inyonei Chinuch, 1979), 299.
30. E. Garfiel (n. 3), 82–83.
31. *b. Ber.* 11b; *Tam.* 5, 1.
32. See Mishnah, *Oholoth* 1, 8.
33. Here is the text of the Midrash (given in E. Munk, *Le monde des prières* [n. 4], 138): "Do not take the words of the *shema'* lightly, for they number 248, the same as the number of our bodily members. It is as if God were, in a way, saying to us: 'If you keep

what is mine, I shall keep what is yours. (I shall be for you) what I was for David. He petitioned the Eternal: Guard me as the apple of your eye, and God answered him: Keep my commandments, and you shall live.' "

34. See E. Munk, *Le monde des prières*, 234.
35. *Ibid.*, 239.
36. *b. Ber.* 16b.
37. In A.E. Millgram (n. 1), 106.
39. E. Gugenheim, *Le judaïsme dans la vie quotidienne* (Paris: Albin Michel, 1978), 25.
39. Hertz, 130–31.
40. E. Munk, *Le monde des prières* (n. 4), 152.
41. *Ibid.*, 154.
42. See Sch. Ben Chorin, *Le judaïsme en prière. La liturgie de la synagogue* (Paris: Cerf, 1984), 81.
43. *Pesikta de-Rab Kahana. R. Kahana's Compilation of Discourses for Sabbaths and Festal Days*, trans. William G. (Gershon Zev) Braude and Israel J. Kapstein (Philadelphia: Jewish Publication Society of America, 1975), 4–6.
44. Palestinian Talmud, *Ber.* 2, 4; see E. Munk, *Le monde des prières* (n. 4), 174.
45. Targum on 2 Sam 16:14; see E. Munk, *Le monde des prières*, 180.
46. For example, *qaddish shalem* is the *qaddish* recited in its entirety, no parts omitted.
47. E. Munk, *Le monde des prières* (n. 4), 165.
48. Sch. Ben Chorin (n. 42), 73.
49. Translated in C. Thomas, *A Christian Theology of Judaism*, trans. H. Croner (New York: Paulist Press, 1980), 147.
50. Cited in E. Munk, *Le monde des prières* (n. 4), 165.
51. Sch. Ben Chorin (n. 42), 74.
52. C. Thoma (n. 49), 147–48.
53. *Ibid.*, 150.
54. Sch. Ben Chorin, for example, does not accept Thoma's hypothesis and thinks that the *Birkat ha-minim* points to a real split between Church and synagogue; see his *Le judaisme en prière*, 78ff.
55. Cited in Thoma (n. 49), 148.
56. *Ibid.*
57. In Sch. Ben Chorin (n. 42), 73.
58. In Thomas (n. 49), 149.
59. Sch. Ben Chorin (n. 42), 84–85.
60. See L. Ginzburg (n. 6), 81.

61. *Sayings of the Fathers* 1, 2, in Hertz, 615.
62. Cited in E. Munk, *Le monde des prières* (n. 4), 204.
63. See M. Jastrow, *Dictionary of Talmud Babli, Yerushalmi, Midrashic Literature and Targumim* (New York, 1950), *s. v. yrh.*
64. C. Perrot, *La lecture de la Bible. Les anciennes lectures palestiniennes du shabbat et des fêtes* (Hildesheim: H.A. Gerstenberg, 1973), 15.
65. *b. Bava Meṣiʿa* 59b.
66. *Sayings of the Fathers* 6, 2 [but I do not find this in Hertz's translation, and have translated it from the author's Italian version.—Tr.].
67. In A.E. Millgram (n. 1), 113.
68. In J. Zegdun, *Il mondo del midrash* (Rome: Carucci, 1980), 19.
69. *Ibid.*
70. C. Perrot (n. 64), 21.
71. See J. Mann, *The Bible As Read and Preached in the Old Synagogue. A Study in the Cycles of the Readings from Torah and Prophets, as well as from Psalms, and in the Structure of the Midrashic Homilies* I (New York: Ktav Publishing House, 1971), xiv.
72. See above.
73. See J. Mann (n. 71), xvii.
74. See R. Le Déaut, *Introduction à la littérature targumique* (Rome: Institut biblique, 1966; *ad usum privatum*), 50.
75. See C. Perrot (n. 64), 22–23.
76. *Ibid.*, 32; R. Le Déaut (n. 74), 48–51.
77. *Pesikta de-Rab Kahana* (n. 43).
78. *Ibid.*, 4–6.
79. Reflected here is not so much the biblical text as Targum Jonathan on Gen 3:24.
80. On the significance and range of such a method see J. Smeets, "Alcune somiglianze fra tecniche letterarie e tecniche haggadiche," *Quaderni di Vita Monastica* 36 (1983), 87–112.
81. See Braude and Kapstein's introduction to *Pesikta de-Rab Kahana* (n. 43), XXX.
82. *Ibid.*, XXXIII.

Chapter 3

1. *b. Ber.* 60b.
2. Hertz 7–9. The translation is by Israel Zangwill (1864–1926).
3. *b. Ber.* 4b–5a.
4. Hertz 977. The first and last sentences in the Talmud text (as translated into Italian) are in the third person.

5. This benediction is also in b. Ber. 60b.
6. b. Ber. 60b.
7. Hertz 1065.
8. From Forms of Prayer for Jewish Worship I, edited by the Assembly of Rabbis of the Reform Synagogues of Great Britain (London, 1977), 292–93. [I did not have access to this book and have had to back-translate from the Italian.—Tr.]
9. A.E. Millgram, Jewish Worship (Philadelphia: Jewish Publication Society of America, 1971), 290.
10. Sch. Ben Chorin, Le judaïsme en prière. La liturgie de la synagogue (Paris: Cerf, 1984), 102.
11. Cited in E. Munk, Le monde des prières (Paris, 1970), 245–46.
12. b. Ber. 48b.
13. E. Munk (n. 11), 253. For a different explanation see A. Epstein, A. Neher, and E. Serban, Etincelles. Textes rabbiniques traduits et commentés (Paris: Albin Michel, 1970), 16–17.
14. While at least ten persons, all of them men (a minyan), are required for other prayers, three suffice for the birkat ha-mazon, and all three may be women. This shows the special importance of this prayer and its "superiority" over others; see E. Garfiel, The Service of the Heart. A Guide to the Jewish Prayer Book (New York–London: Thomas Yoseloof, 1958; reprinted: North Hollywood, CA: Wilshire Book Company, n.d.), 205.
15. Midrash Rabba Gen 9:9.
16. Cited in J. Zegdun, Il mondo del midrash (Rome: Carucci, 1980), 121.
17. See Hertz 344.
18. B. Jacob, cited in Hertz 343.
19. See A.E. Millgram (n. 9), 297.
20. For the two citations see Hertz 341.
21. Cited in Garfiel (n. 14), 145.
22. b. Ber. 33a.
23. A.E. Millgram (n. 9), 313.
24. Texts from the Passover seder are taken from The Passover Haggadah, edited and translated by P. Birnbaum (New York: Hebrew Publishing Company, 1976).
25. The Jerusalem Talmud reads Deut 6:20 as follows: "What is the meaning of the testimonies and the statutes and the ordinances which the Lord our God has commanded you?" For a commentary on this verse and for the question of why "has given to us" has been substituted for "has given to you," see R. Nerson, La Haggadah commentée. Traduction et commentaire du texte

intégral de la Haggadah de Pâque, with Preface by A. Neher (Paris: Librairie Colbo, 1978), 18.

26. This passage of Plato is cited in E. Di Segni (ed.), *Haggadah di Pesah. Ricordare per essere liberi* (Rome: Carucci, 1979²), 23.
27. *Ibid.,* 22.
28. See Sch. Ben Chorin (n. 10), 35; A.E. Millgram (n. 9), 558–60.
29. P. Birnbaum, *A Book of Jewish Concepts* (New York: Hebrew Publishing Company, 1964), 538.
30. [The Italian translation used by the author combines the Half-Kaddish" (Hertz 107–9) with elements from the "Full Kaddish" (Hertz 207).—Tr.]
31. Cited in Sch. Ben Chorin (n. 10), 94.
32. *Ibid.,* 96.
33. P. Birnbaum (n. 29), 539.
34. See Sch. Ben Chorin (n. 10), 87.
35. Hertz 208.
36. *Ibid.*
37. The *Leka dodi* was composed by Rabbi Solomon Halevy Alka-betz in about 1540; the translation is by Solomon Solis-Cohen.
38. The parable is in *b. Shab.* and *Baba gamma* 32a and b.
39. See Sch. Ben Chorin (n. 10), 117.
40. A. Schechter, cited in Hertz 356.
41. This hymn is the same as that which ends the Passover Hagga-dah; another part of it was cited above (p. 169).
42. On the significance of the legend see Sch. Ben Chorin (n. 10), 121.
43. Num 10:35–36; Is 23:3.
44. *Sayings of the Fathers* 2, 506 (Hertz 633).
45. Cited in Sch. Ben Chorin (n. 10), 128.
46. *A l'écoute du Judaïsme,* 57.
47. See *Forms of Prayer for Jewish Worship* (n. 8), 291.
48. *b. 'Abodah Zarah* 17b–18a.
49. In Hertz 270.
50. In A.E. Millgram (n. 9), 325–26.
51. *Ibid.,* 326.
52. *b. Yevamoth* 48b.
53. See especially Rom 6:1–11, where the most satisfying of all the New Testament theologies of baptism is to be found.

Chapter 4

1. See E. Munk, *Le monde des prières* (Paris, 1970), 295.
2. This conception of sacrifice is evidently opposed to reductive interpretations, such as that of Renan, who wrote: "That state of

madness through which humanity passed in the first ages of its existence has bequeathed us many errors, but of them all, sacrifice is the oldest, the worst, and the most difficult to uproot. Primitive man, whatever his race, thought that the way to quieten the unknown forces around him was to win their favour as one wins the favour of men, by offering them something. This was logical enough, for the gods whose favour he sought were malevolent and selfish. This appalling absurdity (which the first appearance of religious common sense ought to have swept away) had become an act of subjection, with man, as it were, the liege of the Deity" (*Histoire d'Israél*, cited in R. de Vaux, *Ancient Israel: Its Life and Institutions*, trans. J. McHugh [New York: McGraw-Hill, 1961], 447).

3. M. Buber, *Israele. Un populo e un paese* (Milan, 1964), 10f.
4. R. de Vaux (n. 2), 493.
5. See above, Chapter 3, Section I, 3, especially b.
6. Trans. in E. Munk (n. 1), III, 309.
7. See R. de Vaux (n. 2), 490–91.
8. Note the emphasis on the verb "give" (*ntn*), on the object given, namely, "land/soil" (*'ereṣ*), and on the complementary persons "thou" (*li*) and "us" (*lanu*), namely, God and human beings, the former being the giver of the land, the latter its user and enjoyer.
9. *Bikkurim* 3, 2–4 (Danby, 96–97).
10. See Sch. Ben Chorin, *Le judaisme en prière. La liturgie de la synagogue* (Paris: Cerf, 1984), 139.
11. E. Munk (n. 1), III, 327–28.
12. Cited in W.W. Simpson, *Light and Rejoicing. A Christian's Understanding of Jewish Worship* (Belfast: Christian Journals Ltd., n.d.), 83.
13. *Ibid.*, 87.
14. Cited in R. de Vaux (n. 2), 495.
15. *Ibid.*
16. *Ibid.*, 496. De Vaux interprets Jgs 21:19–21 as referring to the feast of Booths.
17. *Ibid.*
18. Lev 23:40, translated by the author from the Hebrew text.
19. W.W. Simpson (n. 12), 89.
20. Cited in *Tishri. Textes pour servir à la préparation des fêtes de Rosh Hashanah, Kippour et Sukkoth* (Paris: Editions des E.I.F., 1945), 14.
21. See E. Wiesenberg, s.v. *'Elul* in *Encyclopedia Judaica* (Jerusalem, 1971), 690.

22. For the other New Year's Days see *Tishri* (n. 20), 13.
23. For the translation and a commentary on this verse, which is translated differently in Christian Bibles, see E. Monk, *La voix de la Torah. Commentaire du Pentateuque. L'Exode* (Paris: Fondation Samuel et Odette Levy, 1980³), 294–95.
24. Cited in A.E. Millgram, *Jewish Worship* (Philadelphia: Jewish Publication Society of America, 1971), 239.
25. Cited in P. Birnbaum, *A Book of Jewish Concepts* (New York: Hebrew Publishing Company, 1964), 561.
26. A.E. Millgram (n. 24), 244.
27. *Ibid.*
28. *Ibid.*, 246.
29. *Ibid.*, 254.
30. Translated in Sch. Ben Chorin (n. 10), 160–61.
31. W.W. Simpson (n. 12), 91.
32. In A.E. Millgram (n. 24), 274.

Conclusion

1. On this great Jew and his pioneering work in behalf of Jewish-Christian dialogue see M. Vingiani, "Jules Isaac," in the collective work, *Ecumenismo Anni '80* (Verona: Il Segno, 1984), 323–38.
2. D. Flusser, "Foreword: Reflections of a Jew on a Christian Theology of Judaism," in C. Thoma, *A Christian Theology of Judaism*, trans. H. Croner (New York: Paulist Press, 1980), 11.
3. See W.O.E. Oesterley, *The Jewish Background of the Christian Liturgy* (Oxford, 1925); F. Gavin, *The Jewish Antecedents of the Christian Sacraments* (London, 1928); G. Dix, *The Shape of the Liturgy* (London, 1945); L. Ligier, "Les Origines de la prière eucharistique. De la cène du Seigneur à l'Eucharistie," *Questions Liturgiques* 53 (1972) 181–201; S. Cavalletti, *Ebraismo e spiritualità cristiana* (Rome: Studium, 1965); C. Giraudo, *La struttura letteraria della Preghiera Eucaristica. Saggio sulla genesi letteraria di una forma. Toda veterotestamentaria, Berakah ebraica, Anafora cristiana* (Rome: Pontifical Biblical Institute, 1981).
4. L. Bouyer, *Eucharist. Theology and Spirituality of the Eucharistic Prayer*, trans. C.U. Quinn (Notre Dame: University of Notre Dame Press, 1968), 16.
5. *Ibid.*, 17.
6. *Ibid.*, 17–18.
7. *Ibid.*, 16–17.

8. *Ibid.*, 15.
9. Sch. Ben Chorin, *Le judaisme en prière. La liturgie de la synagogue* (Paris: Cerf, 1984), 173.
10. *Non di solo pane. Il catechismo dei giovani*, ed. Commissione episcopale per la Dottrina della fede, la catechesi a la cultura (Rome: CEI, 1979), 127–28.
11. *Signore da chi andremo? Il catechismo degli adulti* (Rome: CEI, 1981), 88–89.
12. See above, Chapter 2, Section IV g.
13. A.J. Heschel, *God in Search of Man* (New York: Meridian Books, 1966), 49.

Author Index

Subject Index

Principal Hebrew and Aramaic Terms

'adon 'olam ("Lord of the world": a liturgical hymn of the synagogue), 136

'afiqoman (hidden piece of unleavened bread), 161

'ahavah rabbah ("with abounding love": second benediction of the morning shema'), 50, 63, 66, 74

'ahavat 'olam ("with everlasting love": second benediction of the evening shema'), 72, 74

'alenu ("It is our duty": a synagogal prayer), 173–75

'al ha-nissim ("for the miracles": thanksgiving prayer on the feast of hannukah), 220, 222

'al het' ("for the sin": penitential prayer on yom kippur), 215–16

'al Yiśra'el wē 'al rabbenu ("for Israel and our teachers": formula at the end of a biblical reading), 172

'amidah ("standing": one name for the tefillah), 19, 20, 79, 92

'aron ha-qodesh ("sacred ark"), 180

'aseret ("conclusion": a name for Pentecost), 200

aseret yeme teshuvah ("the ten penitential days": the penitential period between rosh ha-shanah and yom kippur), 207, 213

'ashamnu ("we have sinned": penitential prayer on yom kippur), 215–16

'avinu malkenu ("Our Father, our King": a litany of forty-four invocations on rosh ha-shanah), 211–12

'avot ("fathers": a tractate on the Mishnah and the thematic name of the first benediction of the tefillah), 21, 89

ba'al qeri'ah (reader who proclaims the Torah in the synagogue), 180–81

ba'al qore (reader who proclaims the Torah in the synagogue), 180–81

bar miṣwah ("son of the commandment": ceremony at which a boy becomes a responsible adult), 170, 184–85

berakah (prayer of benediction): description of, viii–ix, 16–18, 32–35, 38–39, 182–83, 227, 231; in the Mishnah, 25–26; and the Parable of the Alphabet, 35–38; for the Torah, 39–40; and miracle, 40–41; and awe, 41–42; and gift, 42–44, 142–43, 146; and sharing, 44–45; and

247

haggadah (to recount, relate), 4, 159, 166–67

hakkafot ("circuits": the seven circuits of the synagogue on *sukkot*), 205

halakah ("reflection on God"), viii, 4

hallel (recitation of the psalms of praise: one phase of the *seder*), 161, 164, 196, 197

hannukah ("Dedication": reconsecration of the Jerusalem temple after its destruction by Antiochus IV), 15–16, 31, 85, 126, 128, 130, 189, 218–21

hanukiyyah (eight-branched candelabrum used on *hannukah*), 219–20

ha-rahamon ("the merciful One": beginning of one of the prayers added to the *birkat ha-mazon*), 149–50

haskivenu ("cause us. . .to lie down": the fourth benediction of the evening *shema'*), 72, 76–77

hatan bereshit ("spouse of Genesis": the reader who reads the opening section of Genesis on the last day of *sukkot* and thus begins the cycle anew), 205

hatan Torah ("spouse of Torah": reader who reads the final pericope of the Torah on *sukkot* and thus ends the cycle), 205

ha-tefillah ("the prayer": the principal name of the Eighteen Benedictions), 78

ha-tov wēha-metiv ("who are kindly and dealest kindly": the fourth benediction of the *birkat ha-mazon*), 148

havdalah ("separation": the closing ceremony of the sabbath celebration), 31, 150, 157–59, 182, 227

hitlahavaut ("fervor"), viii

hodayah ("thanksgiving": from the root *ydh*: the eighteenth benediction of the *tefillah*), 104

huppah (nuptial canopy), 186

ketubah ("legal document for spouses"), 185–86

kol nidre ("all vows": formula for rescinding certain commitments on the feast of *yom kippur*), 214–15

leka dodi ("come, my beloved": hymn greeting the sabbath as a bride), 176

ma 'ariv (evening prayer), 170–71, 189

ma 'ariv 'aravim ("thou who bringest on. . .the evening twilight": the first benediction before the evening *shema'*), 72

ma 'ariv le-shabbat (liturgical service on sabbath evening), 178

maggid (narrator; homilist: one phase of the seder), 160

qedushah ("supreme proclamation of the divine glory"), 73–74, 85, 93–94, 171

qedushah rabbah ("the great sanctification": that is, the one in the musaf; this is more developed and detailed than the usual qedushah), 182

qedushat ha-shem ("sanctification of the name": the third benediction of the tefillah), 21, 89, 230

qedushat ha-yom ("sanctification of the day": the central benediction of the tefillah, which on feast days replaces the petitions), 84

qeri'at Torah ("reading of the Torah"), 112–31, 170, 180–81

qiddush ha-yom ("sanctification of the day": benediction recited by the head of the household over a cup of wine on the sabbath or other feast), 154–57

qodashim ("holy things"), 24

rabbotai nevarek ("Sirs, let us say grace": formula inviting those at table to recite the birkat hamazon), 149

regalim (the pilgrimage feasts), 189

rosh ha-shanah ("head of the year": New Year's Day), 24, 31, 84, 122, 189, 206–13, 227

seder (order of prayer or book of prayers), 28

sefer Torah ('Book of the Torah": the Torah scroll), 205

shabbat shabbatot ("sabbath of sabbaths": another name for yom kippur), 24, 217

shahrit (morning liturgical service), 170, 189

shaharit le-shabbat (sabbath morning service), 178

shalom 'alekem ("peace to you": the hymn to the angels that is sung during the sabbath qiddush), 77, 156

shavu 'ot ("Weeks": the feast of Pentecost, which is celebrated seven weeks or fifty days after Passover), 2, 31, 34, 119, 189, 197–201, 227

shema' Yiśra'el ("hear, O Israel": the supreme confession of faith in the liturgy), 18–19, 25, 31, 33, 49–78, 112, 133

shemoneh-'eśreh ("Eighteen benedictions": another name for the tefillah), 19, 78–79, 108

shofrot ("shofar-surroundings": prayer said during the musaf of rosh ha-shanah, 212

sidduq ha-din ("justification of the divine judgment": the rite of burial, celebrated in the cemetery before the actual interment), 187

siddur (order of prayers; prayer book), 27–31

sidrah ("sections": name used by the Ashkenazy Jews for the parashot), 119

Scripture Index